THE CONCEPT
OF G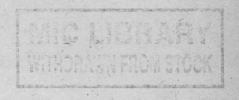

KEIT

COLLINS
FOUNT PAPERBACKS

First published by Basil Blackwell, Oxford 1974
First issued in Fount Paperbacks 1977

Copyright © Basil Blackwell 1974

Made and printed in Great Britain by
William Collins Sons & Co. Ltd, Glasgow

CONTENTS

INTRODUCTION

The concept of God with which I will be concerned is that which has developed within the Christian tradition. It is not possible to deal with some abstract concept of God which derives from no particular religious tradition, and so the analysis of the Christian concept necessarily involves some treatment of themes, such as the incarnation, atonement and the Trinity, which may be considered to belong primarily to theology. However, I would think that a philosophical treatment of God which involved no theological material would most probably treat of something in which no theist would have any interest; and it would certainly give a very incomplete account of any concept of God in actual use by believers. On the other hand, those who are primarily theologians may find the philosophical approach adopted here an unfamiliar and confusing one. I hope that the purpose and strength of this approach may become obvious as the argument proceeds; and in any case I think that any theological working-out of belief must have a particular philosophical basis, whether it is acknowledged or not.

What I have attempted is an explicitly philosophical analysis of a concept of God which is in actual use by communities of Christian believers. I have done this against the background of a general analysis of the structure of religious belief and practice, with reference to a fairly wide range of religious traditions and to the historical development of the Christian concept. Chapters one to six set out a view of the nature of the religious context within which belief in God finds its proper place. Chapters seven to twelve elaborate the specifically Christian concept of God which develops out of one particular way of articulating the religious life. Although I have explored the concept of God in a way which is meant to be comprehensible to believer and unbeliever alike, the general conviction with which I have written is that religion is an area of human activity and experience which is both distinctive and important for human fulfilment. I have certainly wished to show this distinctiveness and argue for its importance; and I have written as one who is a Christian priest as well as a philosopher, and so obviously as one who takes the Christian concept to be of central and enduring—though not exclusive—importance in the rich and complex life of religion.

I wish to thank the editor of *Religious Studies* for permission to use material from *Explanation and Mystery in Religion* (*Religious Studies*, March, 1973).

CHAPTER ONE

THE SOCIAL CONTEXT OF BELIEF IN GOD

I

What does it mean to believe in God? To some, it may seem that the answer to this question is reasonably obvious; to believe in God is to assent to the proposition that there exists an omnipotent, omniscient, perfectly good creator of the universe. One will presumably assent to this proposition if there are sufficiently good reasons for supposing it to be true. So the first important question for the theologian or philosopher of religion is to ask whether sufficiently good reasons can be found, or whether the arguments against the existence of such a being are not more telling. When one begins to investigate the problem of belief in God, one begins by marshalling the arguments for and against the existence of such a being. And there, if one really tries to be thorough and impartial and pursue all possible lines of argument as far as possible, one is likely to stay. For such delicate intellectual investigations inevitably bring in, sooner or later, every philosophical problem known to men. Thus one can continue the intellectual pursuit for a lifetime, and still leave many fascinating avenues of research unexplored.

This may seem, and does seem to many philosophers, obviously true. And yet there is a nagging suspicion that all this process of argument and counter-argument, of weighing evidence and balancing reasons, leaves entirely untouched the question of what it really means to believe in God. The believer can hardly say that the business of rational criticism is useless or unnecessary; and yet it somehow seems to miss his central concerns, and to leave unexplored the difference it makes to be a believer. It is true that some religious believers do seem to have a very intellectual faith, and would explicitly claim to base their faith on a reasoned and systematic view of the world. But that is only one type of religious faith, and is more prominent in some religions than others. It is also true that it is part of the Catholic Christian tradition that the existence of God is rationally demonstrable.[1] But the exact form of that demonstrability is a matter of debate; and one must bear in mind that the rational demonstration of God's existence is more a preamble to faith than part of faith itself. Even if it should turn out to be a necessary condition of believing in God, it does not go very far towards showing what it means to believe in God.

Many Protestants have vehemently rejected the whole idea of rationally demonstrating the existence of God.[2] One must start, they have said, not with human reason, which is devious and fallible, but with the self-revelation of God, as it is found in the Bible or in the person of Jesus Christ. Accordingly, some of them have rejected the whole programme of natural theology; yet they have often retained the view that belief is a matter of assent to the existence of an omnipotent being. That is, it is primarily a matter of asserting the existence of a fairly clearly definable reality, though the ground for such an assertion is non-rational.

However, there has been a reaction against this view of the nature of theistic belief, especially in Protestant circles. Schleiermacher tried to equate belief in God with the occurrence of specific feeling-states, rather than with intellectual assent; and he held that to believe in God is to have the 'sense of absolute dependence'.[3] More recently, Braithwaite has argued that to believe in God is to commit oneself to a specific way of life,[4] so that it is a matter of commitment of the will, rather than of either intellectual assent or the occurrence of feelings. Post-Wittgensteinian philosophers of religion have often stressed that to believe that God exists is not at all like believing that elephants exist. It is, rather,

[1] Denzinger, H. *Enchiridion Symbolorum* (29th. rev. ed.; Herder; 1953), para. 1806: 'that the one and true God our Creator and Lord can be known through the creation by the natural light of human reason'.

[2] Karl Barth is the best known proponent of such a position—cf. *Church Dogmatics* (T. and T. Clark, 1957), vol. 2, 1, para. 26. See p. 172: 'The church . . . must not withhold from the world . . . the fact that God is knowable to us . . . only in His grace . . . it can make no use of natural theology with its doctrine of another kind of knowability of God.'

[3] Schleiermacher, F., *The Christian Faith* (T. and T. Clark, 1928), p. 12.

[4] Braithwaite, R. B. *An Empiricist's View of the Nature of Religious Belief* (Cambridge University Press, 1955).

commitment to using a certain sort of religious language, which must be taken on its own terms, and not assimilated to other sorts of language, such as the language used to state matters of fact about the world.[5] It may be that theists use the language of 'existence' about God; but that use, in religious contexts, may be completely different from its use in contexts of physics or shopping; and one must not therefore assume that one knows what the religious affirmation of God's existence means, without a very careful study of religious language, in its appropriate contexts of use.

It does seem, therefore, that it is not entirely clear what it means to believe in God. Some take it to be the assent to the existence of a supreme being; some take it to be the adoption of certain affective states or dispositional attitudes; others understand it as the entrance into a specific form of life, with its own unique type of language and styles of ritual activity, which is not comprehensible in non-religious terms, or outside that form of life. Even those who take one important element of theistic belief to be that of assent, do not agree on the object of their assent. There are those who conceive God as a supreme person; those who conceive God as an impersonal absolute; those who conceive God as eternal and immutable, and those who conceive God as temporal and in constant change.

This is indeed a bewildering variety of views. But the remarkable thing is that proponents of all these views do often feel able to come together in liturgical gatherings and share in the 'worship of God'. One may sometimes wonder whether they can all be doing the same thing, in worshipping with such different theories in mind. But it is nevertheless a highly important fact that talk about God does not usually take place in a cultural vacuum. It is bound up with the cultic practices of a particular religious community, and it finds there a constant reference-point.

Of course, there exist different religions, and different sects within each religion; and these sects often begin because of just the sort of theoretical divergencies I have mentioned. So one can never say that theoretical or doctrinal issues are unimportant in religion; that would be blatantly false. It may well be, however, that the feeling of unreality and irrelevance which is apt to overtake the believer when he listens to philosophical discussions

[5] Cf. Phillips, D. Z. 'Religious Belief and Philosophical Enquiry', in *Faith and Philosophical Enquiry* (Routledge and Kegan Paul, 1970).

about the existence of God is largely due to the fact that these discussions usually take place in abstraction from, and without reference to, the living context of practices which forms the frame-work for the actual use of theistic language. And it may be that one can only begin to understand what it means to believe in God when one sees such belief within its general religious context.

By studying the practices of theistic religion, one may discover the part which the concept of God plays in the lives of those who use it, and the way in which distinctive patterns of life are re-inforced and maintained by the use of the concept. Language cannot be divorced from the behavioural, cultural and experiential aspects of life in which it finds its use; so to study the concept of God properly is to study the form of understanding of life which the theist has, and to attempt to unravel the part which concepts of God play in enhancing—and, sometimes, in restricting or impeding—that understanding. To see what it means to believe in God is to see how the concept plays an essential part in shaping the life and understanding of the believer. This will most naturally be done by seeing how both the life and language of the believer are shaped by his membership of a specific religious society.

There are degenerate forms of belief in God; that is, forms which have split off from any religious practice or community of faith. These forms are logically (not morally) degenerate, in that they have taken the concept of God out of its primary contexts of use in worship and ritual practice. My interest, however, is in belief in God as a religious phenomenon; and so I wish to locate it within the general context of religious practice. By thus begin-ning with a study of religions as an important human phenomenon I think that new light may be shed on the question of what it is to believe in God. For the nature of that belief may become clearer when it is set in its natural cultural context, instead of being dis-cussed from the first as an isolated matter for academic disputation.

2

What, however, is the natural cultural context of religious belief and practice? When one looks at the wide variety of beliefs and practices which would be covered by normal uses of the word 'religion', it may seem that there is really nothing in common between them. Some people turn to religion for good luck or prosperity; some out of a sense of dependence on a higher power; some want defence against ghosts, demons or malevolent ancestors; some seek a backing and sanction for their moral beliefs; some develop impressive speculative philosophies; some seek mental peace or freedom from guilt; some need an object deemed to be worthy of their devotion and affection. One could go on, listing the sorts of things men seek for or find in religion; and there seems to be very little one could pick on as the essential core of religion. Perhaps it is misleading to look for an essential core. In the much-quoted example of Wittgenstein, there is no essential element which is common to all the things we call games; but there is 'a complicated network of similarities overlapping and criss-crossing'.[6] Similarly, there may be various family-resemblances between the phenomena we call religions, but no essential core, common to them all.

Bearing this warning in mind, it is still proper to try to establish central characteristics which the vast majority of religions have, even though the acceptance of any definition, however vague, will involve drawing clearer boundary-lines than exist in ordinary language, with the corollary that the exact boundary may seem slightly arbitrary. But it is still useful to attempt to draw such boundaries, for purposes of clarity, as long as one is careful to remember that theoretical clarity is not always what ordinary speech requires (for it relies heavily on metaphor, boundary-blurring and ambiguity for many of its effects). No harm can come of drawing such boundaries, so long as one knows that one is legislating, albeit reasonably. And it may be held to be a condition of any advance in philosophical theorising, to get one's own terminology clear and precise, however obscure and blurred ordinary usage is. The hard work comes in arguing that one's definitional stipulations are reasonable and illuminating, rather than arbitrary and misleading.

It seems to me, then, that a central concern of religions (not a necessary or sufficient condition) is with the pursuit of personal well-being and the avoidance of harm. Magical rituals are clearly concerned with obtaining good fortune; and even the most speculative metaphysical theorising aims, in the end, at showing one

[6] Wittgenstein, L. *Philosophical Investigations* (Basil Blackwell, 1963), para. 66.

how to live well—i.e. in accordance with the world as it really is. Conceptions of well-being and harm differ widely; and there is a great difference between ensuring a good crop of wheat next season and aiming at a difficult ideal of personal existence. But the concern with good and harm is there, in both cases.

Religious practices differ from moral practices—which are also centrally concerned with human good or harm—in that they do not limit themselves to dealing with normal human activities for bringing about good or harm. They typically presuppose, or assert, that man's true good can be brought about by a non-human source. How this is to be done varies very much from case to case. But religions typically offer special techniques for putting one into the requisite relationship with the source, or for utilizing its powers for human good. These techniques may range from the wearing of a magic charm, appeasement of the ancestral spirits or obedience to special rules and ceremonies to devotion to a saviour-god, union with the Absolute or the achievement of complete non-attachment to the sensual world. Plainly, the concepts of good and harm utilised by religions differ, and so do concepts of the source of good and the way to right relationship with it (the Way). Religious doctrines develop the world-view within which these concepts are defined, and human life given a meaning by reference to them.

In pointing to this central characteristic of religion, I shall use the concept of the sacred to refer to the non-human source or sources of that human fulfilment which the religious believer seeks by the way his religion offers him. This is partly because the concept has a use in religious contexts, and has been used by Durkheim to characterize the religious concern as opposed to the secular.[7] I do not wish to be committed to an absolute categorical disjunction between the sacred and the secular, as Durkheim was; but I would assent to the view that there is a distinctive object, or objects, of religious apprehension, the source of true well-being. How this is to be characterised is a further question; and one of the advantages of the term 'sacred' is that it is neither masculine nor feminine, neither singular nor plural, neither personal nor impersonal; so it does not tend to prejudge the issue as the masculine, singular, personal term 'God' might.

[7] Durkheim, E. *The Elementary Forms of the Religious Life*, trans. J. W. Swain (Allen and Unwin, 1915).

A religion may be characterized as a social organized way of relating men to the sacred; and a person becomes a religious believer when he commits himself to such a society, accepting its disciplines and goals. Two notions are thus central to the life of religions, the notions of community and of revelation. The community of believers, the church, is a group of men set apart from others by its commitment to a specific tradition of revelation—by its memory of specific events or writings which are taken to define a tradition of relationship to the sacred, now authoritative for the church. Each religion is distinctive both in its membership—those who respond to the proclaimed revelation—and in the content of its revelation.

It may be objected that neither church nor revelation is essential to religion. In fact, Whitehead notoriously defined religion as what man does with his solitariness,[8] and one may find religions without revelations, like some forms of Hinduism, perhaps. I will simply grant these objections. I have no intention of saying what is essential to religion; far from it. But these notions are central to religion, in that almost all phenomena we call religions have some social organization, with attendant rituals of group membership or exclusion, even if membership is by birth. And almost all religions acknowledge an authoritative standard, whether it is a sacred writing, an oral tradition or a historical event. There may be a constant striving for new interpretations, which can make the faith 'come alive' again in each generation. But each religion owes a basic loyalty to a particular authoritative standard—the Vedas, the Vedanta, the teachings of the Buddha or the Bible—which forms the basis of the unity of that religion.

These central elements of community and revelation can be further sub-divided in various ways; and Ninian Smart has suggested a six-dimensional analysis of religion, into mythic, doctrinal, ethical, ritual, social and experiential elements.[9] Under the heading of myth, he includes legends, stories or historical events which form part of the authoritative data of a religion. These are closely bound up with doctrinal beliefs about the nature of man and the world, and with ethical beliefs about how man ought to act in the world; and myth, doctrine and ethics together comprise

[8] Whitehead, A. N. *Religion in the Making* (C.U.P., 1927), p. 6.
[9] Smart, N. *Secular Education and the Logic of Religion* (Faber, 1968), ch. 1.

the element of what I have termed revelation in religion. The ritual activities and social organization are more closely concerned with the nature of the religious community; and the experiential dimension, though it is naturally concerned with personal experiences, is also best considered within the social and ritual context which structures such individual experiences, and gives them their characteristic form.

I shall adopt a slightly different four-fold analysis, into the elements of: way of life (combining Smart's ethical and social aspects, but being rather wider than either); ritual; spiritual discipline (roughly corresponding to Smart's 'experiential', but stressing the element of disciplined prayer); and creed (combining Smart's myth and doctrine, since myth is a word used in so many different senses by different people that its use obscures much more than it can hope to illuminate).

Though these different elements co-exist in most religions, they are not separate and clearly distinct. All are tied together within a religion in a complex way; thus in Christianity, Jesus' resurrection is an empirical event which reveals God's plan, presupposes certain metaphysical truths about the existence of God (creed), is re-enacted in the church (ritual) and gives rise both to ethical demands to trust and follow him by joining the fellowship of the church (way of life); and to following specific disciplines of prayer (spirituality). Each religion consists of a whole set of such interwoven assertions; and so forms a sort of organic unity from which it is impossible to tear doctrines and analyse or compare them in isolation. To understand one part of religious faith adequately, it is necessary to see it in its place within the complex phenomenon of religion, with all its inter-related dimensions. So when one examines what it means to believe in God, one must pay careful attention to the rites and structures of the community within which such belief takes its place, and to the way of life and the authoritative tradition of which it is part. In this way one may be delivered from a one-sided intellectualism of approach, while not being thrown to the blunt alternative of an entirely non-rational or non-cognitive form of belief.

3

One important aspect of religion for the believer is the way of life into which he enters when he adopts his belief. Smart characterizes this as the ethical dimension; but it is rather broader than what would normally be called ethical in modern usage. It is the tradition, or Law, setting out the observances and prohibitions which regulate the community's inter-relations and its special relationship to the sacred. Tradition forms the basis of tribal religious life, but is rarely absent from the most developed religions. Many of the regulations may seem trivial or absurd in themselves (not to eat certain foods, for example), but they serve to mark off the group and give it a sense of identity. And this is not a purely secular matter; what is marked off (made taboo) as dangerous or unclean, is the sacred; and the sacred marks those points at which men feel they have come into contact with a dangerous and mysterious power, which evokes both reverence and fear from them, and may bring fulfilment or destruction to human lives.

The Judaic Torah provides an example of a relatively developed sacred tradition. It contains both ethical and ritual prohibitions, and its observance is held to provide an acceptable qualification for acceptance with Jahweh. The development of such a code of rules shows man's need to define carefully his relations with the sacred, his feeling that it is a dangerous power, hostile in some respects, which needs to be approached by way of purifying ritual, sanctified by long tradition. In many primitive tribes the gods or legendary heroes are said to have delivered the traditions personally; and Judaism and Islam both postulate a supernatural origin for their traditions, the Torah and Koran respectively.

Tradition may degenerate into arid legalism, when the sense of the sacredness of the conforming life is obscured or forgotten, and the rules are elaborated and taken as ends-in-themselves. It may, on the other hand, be moralised, and give rise to a clear notion of the sacred as an absolute moral demand and the source of a power to fulfil that demand. Both paths were taken, in the case of the Torah; and Christians abandoned its non-ethical prescriptions almost entirely. But for a fair appreciation of what the Torah can mean to a believer one must appreciate that it is a way of life which sets all men's actions apart as holy and gives a constant sense of communication with Jahweh, the sacred reality. By obeying the laws of Jahweh, one submits oneself to the power of Jahweh and declares one's trust in the revealed way. It does not intrinsically matter what things are prohibited or enjoined; the origins of such prohibitions, though undoubtedly traceable back to some recognition of a sacred reality, are lost in the past.

An example of how a taboo might arise is found in the Orphic rule to abstain from meat, except for the flesh of the kid or bull which is identified with the god in the communion meal. Here, the meat is taken as sacred by its association with the central mystery of communion, which effects human well-being; so avoidance of meat-eating reinforces the sacredness of the one permitted ritual eating of flesh.

Another illuminating example is to be found in Evans-Pritchard's classic study of the Nuer.[10] A Nuer tribesman may believe that he has some special bond with the lizard-spirit, because of a lizard which seemed to warn him of danger one day. He will make offerings to the spirit and consider himself to be in a special relationship to all lizards, because of that one portentous appearance. That event was very meaningful to the tribesman; it was a sign or portent; and he symbolizes what he believes to be a providential encounter with 'Kwoth', the supreme spirit-force, by imaginatively re-telling the event as an appearance of the lizard-spirit and the establishment of a special bond between it and him. He will then say that this was what *really* happened. But the significance of the experience to him, and his imaginative symbolization of it so as to preserve the distinctiveness of the experience as a providential encounter, will escape the attention of the impartial observer, who will say that what really happened was that the tribesman saw a lizard and, chasing it, avoided the spring of a leopard. Nevertheless, one may hold that there was a providential encounter with some reality (Kwoth or the sacred power) which is undetectable by the senses of another observer, and was imaginatively symbolized in a manner conventional to and comprehensible to the Nuer. The subsequent recital of that imaginative account will sustain and enrich the attitudes which were generated in that first encounter. And this contributes to the formation of a religious tradition, within which subsequent

[10] Evans-Pritchard, *Nuer Religion* (O.U.P., 1956).

individual experiences may be shaped and directed. The encounter becomes a paradigm generative event, whose repetition perpetuates a specific perception of significance for the future descendents of that man.

A more familiar example, for many, is the story of the exodus of the Israelites from Egypt (Exodus 14), in which the escape of the tribes over a reed-sea by a fortuituous combination of winds and tides was interpreted as a providential encounter with the Lord who henceforth chooses this people as his own. This interpretation is a paradigm event both for Judaism, and—when re-interpreted in the light of Jesus' death and resurrection (his 'exodus'—Luke 9, 31)—for Christianity.

These accounts seem to me to offer good examples of the way in which a tradition may grow from some perception of the sacred, and become sanctified by the lives of generations of believers, until it offers an acceptable way of holiness, by sincere obedience to which one can mark oneself off from the world and find union with the sacred for oneself. The way of life, the tradition, of a religious community, originates in revelatory apprehensions of the sacred, often half-forgotten, but preserving a special relationship of the community to the sacred reality. Religious traditions often become legalistic, censorious and rigorist, insisting upon observance of the letter of the rules, in all its minute detail. And they often lead to a sort of narrow exclusivism which looks upon the community upholding a particular tradition as the only true, or 'saved' community, while all outsiders are inferior or even accursed. These traits may be called the pathological forms of tradition.

But it is also possible to see religious traditions as ways of original creative response to the sacred, as articulated within one tradition of revelation, and supported by the fellowship and encouragement of the believing community—the community which takes those revelatory paradigms as its own. In Christianity, this takes the form of a repetition of the exemplary life of Christ, in his humility, obedience, detachment and love. His life, as recorded in the Biblical documents, is taken as the paradigm for the way of life of the Christian community.

Part of what it means to believe in God is the participation in the life of a community which preserves an exemplary pattern of life, which may be codified in a set of rules, as in Judaism, or

illustrated in the story of a human life, as in Christianity. And it is
essential to this pattern that it relates man to the sacred, as it was
held to be apprehended in some paradigm generative event or
experience upon which the community is founded. This account
leaves as yet unexplained how one can establish that the sacred
exists; how it can be apprehended; and how one can distinguish
veridical from illusory apprehensions of the sacred. But it does
help to make the point that some, at least, of the important roots
of theistic belief are in alleged cognitive apprehensions, not in
assents to abstract intellectual formulations. And it may also help
one to realise how much broader and vaguer the bases of theistic
belief may be than a concentration on the rather dogmatically
orientated Catholic Christian tradition may lead one to suppose.

4

The account may be significantly extended by taking note of a
second main dimension of religion, namely ritual practice. In
most societies, there are ritual practices connected with important
stages of human life, birth, initiation, marriage, death, fertility and
propitiatory or piacular sacrifice. Rites can have either a personal
or a social reference; or, usually, both in some degree. The initiation ceremony in Aborigine tribes brings a youth to new birth as
an adult, and so has an intensely personal significance. But, by
participating in it, the whole tribe also reaffirms its own death and
regeneration. Fertility sacrifices are made on behalf of the whole
tribe, to signify submission to and union with the powers of
nature; but each individual can find, in the dedicated offering and
shared communion, a new and liberating power for his own life.

There have been many interpretations of religious ritual in
tribal religions. Marett and Pareto saw religious belief as primarily
a matter of ritual acts which express highly charged emotional
states.[11] Durkheim conceived ritual as creating and expressing the
'collective soul' of a group.[12] Such views stress the emotional
aspect of religion, and see ritual as an important medium of

[11] Cf. Marett, R. R. *The Threshold of Religion* (Methuen, 1909).
Pareto, V. Y. *The Mind and Society*, trans. A. Bongiorno and A. Living-
ston (Harcourt, 1935).
[12] Durkheim, *loc. cit.*, p. 424ff.

emotional expression. On the other hand, Tylor and Frazer, assuming that religious belief is based on superstition, arising from the misinterpretation of dream-images as souls of the dead, tended to view ritual acts as forms of primitive technology.[13] Its aim was to dominate nature and to accomplish purely material ends; and its method was the use of sympathetic or imitative magic, by which the performance of some ritual act could bring about a change in nature.

Both these elements seem to be present in many forms of religious ritual. In Brahmanic Hinduism the recital of the Vedic formulae was said to compel the gods to grant favours to men. In Tibetan Buddhism the practice of decorating prayer-wheels with mystic formulae was thought to have compulsive efficacy upon the gods. In ancient Roman religion the sacrificed numen, or sacred power, was believed to increase the numen of the god and so render him more powerful to grant favours. The concern of primitive societies with the fertility of their crops and herds is natural and understandable; and, where scientific knowledge is non-existent, the prevalence of magical modes of influencing nature is not surprising. It is only to be expected that men should be concerned with their own good or harm, and that they should pursue courses of action which are believed to lead to their good, and avoid those believed to bring harm. Much ritual practice expresses this concern with human fortune; but it may be thought that Tylor and Frazer take too restrictive a view when they see such a concern as simply materialistic, as concerned with good crops and herds, and when they see ritual as simply a form of superstitious (i.e. mistaken) technology to control the forces of nature unscientifically. The notion of human good may be a wider one than that of material prosperity; and the function of ritual in procuring this good may not simply be that of changing material conditions. But Tylor and Frazer are probably correct to point out that ritual practices are largely concerned to bring about human good, in some non-scientific sense.

Some insight into what this sense might be is given by the emotionalist interpretations of Marett and Durkheim. Most men are naturally afraid of the unknown and unusual, of suffering and

---

[13] Cf. Tylor, E. B. *Primitive Culture* (John Murray, 1873). Frazer, J. G., *The Golden Bough: A Study in Magic and Religion* (Macmillan, 1911–15).

death. Where suffering is common, it is natural that disease and death should be regarded as being due to the action of hostile, unseen forces; and so the universe becomes populated with demons and hostile spirits, to be bribed or propitiated with sacrifices. Human sacrifice or self-mutilation have been thought to be required to propitiate the malevolent forces of demons or the dead. Frazer's catalogue of blood-sacrifices in 'The Golden Bough' or a study of the fearsome blood-letting which occurs in some Aborigine rituals for procuring fertility or laying the spirits of the dead, can rapidly bring one to feel that religion is a cruel, repressive and primitive phenomenon which is incompatible with enlightened morality. Rituals can clearly express powerful and primitive emotions of fear and conflict; and they exemplify a commonly felt need to make propitiation and seek escape from bondage to the fears and disasters of human life. The forces which are apparent to man in sickness, deformity, death, storm, earth-quake and flood are predominantly cruel and destructive; and these forces are often personalised as gods, which enter into con-stant conflict and compromise with other imaginatively sym-bolized gods and each give rise to their special rites and groups of devotees.

This is very evident in popular Hinduism, in which Kali, the goddess of death, and Shiva the Destroyer have had large popular followings. The attributes of these terrible gods are bewilderingly diverse to Christian-orientated minds. While Shiva is the god of disease and death, he also represents the creative forces of sexual reproduction, which spring from death; he stands for the pure energy of life itself, with its cycles of death and birth; and he is the god of asceticism, destroying the body to free the life of the soul. Kali, his consort, the terrifying black goddess who devours men whole, is also adored as the Great Mother, and is kind to those she favours, having power over demons. As the power of time, she represents the peace of the 'transcendent night' which follows total destruction; and she too, in her auspicious aspect, is the patron of those who break all worldly ties to seek a higher peace.

The destructive gods are clearly capable of an enobling, bene-ficent interpretation. But they also offer possibilities of less fulfilling relationship. The primitive energy of Kali, ruthlessly and unfeelingly creating and destroying all things, is explored in left-hand Shaktism, wherein morality is transcended and identification sought with amoral power. Durga, one variant of Kali, is the patroness of the Thuggees, who practised ritual murder as a way of rising above normal moral feelings. These demonic gods offer a sort of liberation from the confines of human existence through acceptance of and complicity in destructive activity, an alliance with what one cannot defeat (the Freudian motive of identification with the aggressor). The imaginative symbolization of these dark forces controlling human life, and ritual devotion to them as thus symbolized, can enable men to come to terms emotionally with the grimmer facts of human reality.

It can be instructive for those trained in a Christian tradition, wherein a rather intellectual concept of one God is propounded, to try to understand a polytheistic system of the Hindu type. For here one sees men trying to cope with the largely unknown forces which seem to control their lives, with the facts of birth, suffering and death; and one sees how the gods are born in the attempt to grasp those forces and accept them emotionally. The gods express the sacred realities, the powers which men fear and love; and the rituals proper to each god seek to place men in a relationship to the sacred powers which will enable them to accept their lives and arrive at some conception of what it is to be properly human. There are thus numberless gods (one tradition holds that there are three hundred and thirty million gods in Hinduism); and they are by no means distinct and individual entities. Rather, they merge into one another, change names and designations, divide and re-integrate and form various groupings around certain focal gods, such as Vishnu or Indra or Kali. And they are not fully personal; for though many anthropomorphic things are said of them—as that they guide and know and destroy and heal—they are also powers which can flow into things and people and endue them with sacred force; and in rituals, they can flow into their devotees or be carried around like impersonal substances.

It is only when a religion becomes effete and decadent that these mysteriously elusive and intermingling powers come to be crystallised into a pantheon of more or less definitely personalised individual beings, like the gods of the late Greek and Roman mythologies. In the Homeric and Hesiodic pantheons, the gods have become definite individuals with distinctive personalities, who marry, have families, quarrel and engage in drunken orgies. But this highly articulated and systematised family of gods has also been effectively sterilised, robbed of all sacred significance for men, so that the gods become simply superhumans about whom entertaining stories are told. Deprived of their sacred power, belief in the gods quickly became a merely formal observance and finally disappeared altogether. The gods only live as long as their rituals are carried out; and those practices survive only as long as men find themselves able to achieve some sort of integration and fulfilment in the relationship to the sacred which the ritual is meant to establish.

Combining the partial insights of Frazer and Durkheim, one may say that religious rituals exist to bring about some human good; and this is to be accomplished by establishing and sustaining a relationship to some sacred reality which enables men to understand and accept, at the deepest emotional level, the conditions of being fully human. Such an acceptance, at a more than merely intellectual level, is usually held to bring liberation, release or salvation from the feeling of being bound or overpowered by such restricting conditions, and so to bring freedom from what is variously conceived, in the major religions, as suffering, desire, ignorance or sin.

The believer's relationship to the gods can be conceived in a very materialistic and almost commercial way. He may cajole, implore, beat, dress, wash and feed his god, and so attempt to enter into some sort of mutual contract, whereby services are rendered in return for food. Or he may believe that the literal shedding of blood is necessary to propitiate for his wrongs and failings, or to ensure the yearly renewal of vegetation or food-supplies. The Christian rite of the Mass has been construed as the slaying of an innocent victim to propitiate an angry Jahweh and to save men from his anger. And this is basically a contractual view of the function of ritual, seeing it as a sort of transaction by which a specific good is to be obtained, in return for an offering to the god. So rituals may be conceived either as forms of magical technology, automatically efficacious in obtaining material benefits, if performed correctly; or as forms of contract with a personalised god, by which protection is bought in return for the believer's fealty.

But it is by no means necessary to regard ritual in this way. For one may say that the good which ritual seeks for men is liberation from the restricting conditions of human existence and the attainment of human fulfilment. And it seeks this good by applying the power of the sacred, as it is conceived in some community of faith, to the individual, to release him from that bondage to fear, insecurity, pride, envy and malice which characterizes the human condition. The ritual brings renewal, release and fulfilment so long as men continue to find the traditional characterization of the sacred within their community one which communicates a sense of the significance of the reality of which they are part.

Part of what it means to believe in God is the participation in rites which are held to bring liberation and fulfilment, by relating the believer to the sacred powers which are symbolized and commemorated in a particular religious tradition. This makes the important point that religious belief is a practical, and not merely a theoretical, concern. It is concerned with how men can live well or find true well-being; it is not just concerned with how many strange events or additional beings there are in the universe. So it may well be that sophisticated beliefs in one omnipotent God grow in the first place from attempts to come to terms with the limitations of human life and achieve some sort of enduring human good. It would be going too far to say that religion was concerned with nothing but practical commitment to a distinctive way of life. But it would seem to me to miss the point of what it means to believe in God entirely to ignore the fact that such belief begins with a desire to find release or fulfilment, however obscurely or perversely conceived. Such a desire is what the rituals of religions express. Thus religion seeks not only to apprehend the sacred; but also to utilize it or relate to it so as to achieve the true good for man.

Christianity has dispensed with detailed purification rituals and with the apparatus of intricate and technical observances which must be observed before man can approach with equanimity the hidden powers of the sacred, with priest-initiates and blood-sacrifices; yet it preserves its own rituals for giving participation in sacred power, in the sacraments. In the Eucharist, in particular, the re-enactment of the drama of estrangement, death, re-birth and reconciliation enables men to participate in the power which was first apprehended around the life and death of Jesus. The sacrificial offering expresses the believer's self-commitment; the propitiatory immolation expresses the awareness of failure and alienation; and the act of communion expresses the acceptance of an inward power which effects one's reconciliation to the sacred reality disclosed in Jesus. In this central Christian rite the power of the sacred is thus articulated around the remembered story of a particular historical individual; and it is offered to the believer through the re-enactment of the self-giving of that paradigm figure who has become in his own person the full manifestation and vehicle of the sacred.

I would think that, for most Catholic Christians, belief in God begins here, with this sort of practical participation in what is claimed to be a life-giving rite. And I suggest that, if it moves too far from this sort of basis, which has its analogues in other forms of Christian and non-Christian religious belief, belief in God begins to take on that remote and speculative air which believers protest about when they overhear philosophical debates about the existence of God. That is a good reason why the philosophy of religion should start from the life and practice of a particular living religion, and not from the consideration of reasons for and against the truth of intellectual conceptions of God. In this chapter, I have tried to show, from a consideration of the ethical and ritual aspects of religion, how belief in God is closely tied to participation in a community of belief which is founded on specific apprehensions of the sacred and controls the sacred powers in its ritual practices. Before exploring further what is meant by the notion of the sacred, I wish to examine two further aspects of religious life, namely the experiential and credal aspects, in order to bring out the way in which belief in God has its place in the practice of religion.

CHAPTER TWO

THE EXPERIENTIAL CONTEXT OF BELIEF IN GOD

I

No account of the phenomenon of religion could be complete without some reference to what Ninian Smart calls its experiential dimension. Certainly, in exploring what it means to believe in God one will need to take into account the sorts of experiences which are typically associated with such belief. But the term 'experience' is one which is beset with traps for the unwary. If we ask someone to tell us about his experiences, he will normally reply by giving an account of his journeys through Arabia, for instance; he will describe what the country was like, and who he met; and he may well tell us of how he reacted to what he saw, and what it felt like to be very hot and thirsty, and so on. What he will almost certainly not do is to describe a series of purely mental events, which he directly observed going on in his mind, but of which no-one else could have had direct knowledge.

Philosophers like Ryle have generalised from this point about ordinary language to say that talk about 'experiences' is part of a general category-mistake, which treats mental events as though they were additional entities of the same general type as physical events, but of a type which can only be known through intro-spection.[1] The man who makes such a mistake can proceed to describe his experiences, and sort them into groups—religious, aesthetic, moral and so on—and so become a sort of anatomist of experiences. Philosophers like Ryle, however, would say that psychical anatomy is a subject which is misconceived in principle, and that introspection, far from being a mode of privileged access to one's experiences, is really only a form of remembering what a certain person—myself—did or saw or thought, on a certain occasion. This is information which other people could have had,

[1] Ryle, G. *The Concept of Mind* (Hutchinson, 1949), cf. ch. 1.

and may have gathered more accurately than we did; though we are in fact often in positions where no-one else is in a position to observe us. To talk about experiences is thus not to describe occurrences on a ghostly inner stage; it is to recall what a certain intelligent organism did or said, or how it reacted, in specific environments and situations.

Ryle's account reminds us in a salutary way that experiences are not just inner mental states which happen to us, whatever we are thinking about or doing at the time; they do not come upon us unexpectedly, with clear definite outlines, as physical objects often do. In the case of religion, a man who has been brought up as a Protestant will not suddenly have an experience of the Blessed Virgin; or a Catholic will not suddenly attain Nirvana. On the other hand, it seems altogether too severe to say that there are no inner mental states at all. The man who travelled in Arabia will want to tell us what it felt like to be lost in a sand-storm; and he will certainly know the difference between being excited, depressed or anxious about his situation. The religious believer may speak of the sense of the presence of God, or of the feeling of desolation which sometimes afflicts him. And anyone who has helped another in the pursuit of the spiritual life will know how little behaviour may betray of a man's true feelings and attitudes to his life.

It seems reasonable to say that there are inner feelings and attitudes; but they are closely related both to behaviour and to one's thoughts and beliefs. This means that the experiential dimension of religion really cannot be divorced from the ritual and credal dimensions, the practices and beliefs of a religion. The inter-relation is very complex, but the experiences of greatest concern to religion are those which occur in the context of the life of worship, prayer or meditation which most religions enjoin. These are not themselves experiences, in the sense of feelings which occur to a person; they are distinctive activities in which the believer engages. But they certainly carry with them characteristic sorts of experience; and one may even say that they would lose much of their point if desired experiences never occurred as a result of their practice.

This is perhaps clearest in the case of the meditative techniques practised in Yoga and Buddhism, which are directed to the attainment of Samadhi or Nirvana, conceived as a state of supreme insight or understanding. But Christian prayer, also, is not thought of as a one-way process of 'talking at' God; it has its moments of illumination or refreshment by God. Even if it is not explicitly directed at such moments, it would lose most of its point if they never occurred.

2

Worship, prayer and meditation involve ritual practices, just as the ethical aspect of religion often involves the observance of ritual rules of purity; but such practices and rules are considered separately from what was termed the 'ritual' dimension of religion, because they are not so much public cultic performances as personal acts which carry over into the private life of the believer. Thus prayer is ideally an activity which can characterize the whole of a Christian's personal life; whereas the rite of the Eucharist is performed at intervals as a public cult. However, the lines of division are not altogether sharp; and in some forms of Islam, for example, public cult and private practice may almost coincide.

Worship, prayer and meditation also involve beliefs; for one would not worship unless one thought there was an object worthy of worship; one would not meditate unless one thought that something like union with the Absolute (Brahman) could be attained, which presupposes that there is an Absolute with which one is identical at the deepest level. So it may seem that the situation is this: one first forms certain beliefs about the nature of reality (there is a personal God or an impersonal Brahman); then one engages in private ritual acts; and, one hopes, distinctive experiences will occur which corroborate one's fundamental beliefs.

There is something wrong with that account, however clear it may seem. It is as if one said that, before one can experience the love of another person, one must first form the belief that other minds exist, and then try to establish relationship with them through conventional forms of activity. On the contrary, one is loved and cared for long before one comes to form any theoretical beliefs whatsoever. One learns to accept and give love through the practice of loving; and the problem of other minds may never occur to one at all. With religion, too, one learns to pray or meditate through the practices of prayer and meditation, within a specific tradition; and the problem of the nature of reality may never occur. One has religious experiences, as one has experiences of love, before one comes to analyse them and ask questions about their causes or objects. Monotheism may be a theoretical presupposition of the practice of worship,[2] but if so, it is not one that need ever be recognised by those who worship in their daily lives. Worship, like conversation, is an activity that gets going as part of the normal practice of life for the believer. It may find expression in food or drink offerings placed before piles of stones or trees; in the elaborate washing and dressing of idols; in the recital of poems of adoration and devotion to various gods; in invocation of ancestors; or in silent periods of meditation. Some people become almost obsessed with such ritual activities, and are meticulously concerned with holy things and their care; and extreme forms of this concern may be analogous, as Freud claimed, to obsessional neuroses.[3] But all worshippers cannot be established to be obsessional neurotics, on independent grounds; and so it is permissible to look for the explanation of this widely felt desire to honour sacred powers elsewhere.

Rudolf Otto, in his classic study of the idea of the holy,[4] coined the term 'numinous' to express a sense of mystery, at the same time compellingly attractive and yet dangerously terrifying, which men come to feel in certain situations. He regarded the disposition to have such a feeling as an original, innate and distinctive capacity of the human mind; and he argued that men were able to discern the numinous power in specific historical situations, which then became sacred to them. Rituals of worship would express such feelings, and creeds would try to describe them, always inadequately, by finding analogies of feeling with other human situations of more universal and everyday occurrence.

One may be sceptical about many of the details of Otto's analysis; about whether there is just one numinous feeling, specified just as he describes it, which is an innate endowment of all men; and whether it alone represents adequately the essence of

[2] This case is argued in Findlay, J. N. 'Can God's Existence be Disproved?', in Flew and MacIntyre (eds.), *New Essays in Philosophical Theology* (S.C.M., 1955).

[3] Cf. Freud, S., *Collected Papers*, trans. Riviere, J., vol. 2, 25–50 (Hogarth Press, 1956).

[4] Otto, R. *The Idea of the Holy* (O.U.P., 1950).

religious belief. But there can be no doubt that he has brought into view some of the living roots of worship. There are times and situations in which men can feel a sense of awe and dependence upon the vast powers of the universe, and when they feel helpless before some turn of fortune which changes or devastates their lives. And at other times they can be overcome with a sense of the beauty and wonder of nature, and filled with joy at simply being alive. Men can sometimes feel oppressed at the thought of their own failures and weaknesses; yet on other occasions they can feel called to some specific task, and strengthened with a power beyond their control to create artistic masterpieces or undertake heroic tasks. Men can feel sorrow and pity at the pain of the world; and they can feel reverence and admiration for those who exemplify qualities of character and conduct which are far above the human norm. One may come to feel that there is some greater, upholding sustaining presence and power, upon which one can rely. Such a feeling may just occur, in no particular situation; it may or may not have great significance for one; and it may be vague and un-related to the rest of one's experience. One may have the feeling of being in the presence of something uncanny, eerie or awe-inspiring, which is dangerous or powerful, but evokes great reverence (this is near one common sense of the term sacred or holy, though Otto's characterization of it in terms of fear and love is appropriate only when it is conceived as morally demanding and personalised). One may have a feeling of being absolutely depen-dent on a fathomless power; or one may feel oneself absorbed or embraced within a greater unity.

Feelings of these sorts are probably more common than most people admit; and one must either say that they are common human delusions or pointers to a greater power to which one can be related in various ways. They will be recognisable to the believer as encounters with the object of his belief; but their occurrence does not in itself make a man a religious believer, though it may dispose him to take the claims of religion seriously, or keep any religion he has a living force in his life. Moreover, it may be in such experiences, as tested and developed by discipline and further experience, that the religions of the world begin to take shape.

Such feelings do not just occur in a vacuum, whatever a person is doing or thinking. They arise in the mind as one interacts with and reacts to one's environment; they are forms of response to the environment, not entirely distinct and private mental states. As forms of response, they can be appropriate or inappropriate; violent and uncontrolled or calm and rationally ordered; they can be encouraged or eradicated; and they can be expressed and evoked verbally in the language of poetry or liturgy.

The practices of worship may be seen as attempts to express and evoke such attitudinal responses, and thus to encourage men to adopt certain sets of desired attitudes to the reality in which they live out their lives. When one pours out a libation to a god, one acknowledges its pre-eminence and commits oneself to the pursuit of the particular value or range of values it expresses. This value may be one of a great number of things; each of the gods, mysterious and ambiguous in character, clarifies some aspect of man's complex relationship to his world. I think that Otto was probably too restrictive in positing just one complex numinous feeling as the foundation of worship; for there are many values to which an affective response may be made in worship. For example, in early Hinduism, Indra was worshipped as the god of war and storms, a warrior-champion who drinks and fights hard.[5] But Indra is also the champion of the gods of release from bondage; by slaying the dragon Vritra he released life-giving waters and the sun, and thus made it possible to bring order and life into being. With typical ambiguity, his terrible warlike power is also the power which orders the universe for good and slays powers of evil. So the worshipper's attitude to Indra is not just one of fearful propitiation or awe of brute power; it is one of respectful adoration for the irresistible power which works through conflict to establish final order and goodness. The myths or stories about Indra characterize the aspects under which he is to be worshipped; and so men adore the power revealed in storms, which brings order and life into being through destruction and conflict. Other gods all have their peculiar myths; and so they specify characteristic responses to reality. To worship such a god is to adopt a specific set of values as definitive for one's own basic response to reality.

Very often, of course, a man may worship many gods; for there are many aspects of reality which may call forth affective responses which men wish to express and sustain by ritual behaviour. But

[5] Cf. Griffith, R. T. H. *The Hymns of the Rig Veda* (Benares, 1920–6), 4, 16, 3.

there is a tendency in the very nature of polytheism to work towards an underlying unity, whether this is expressly conceived as monotheism or not. For the gods are not really distinguishable individuals; but imaginatively created expressions of significant aspects of reality. So, as men begin to reflect upon their primitive practices of worship, they tend to treat specific gods as manifestations of more basic principles which give some sort of coherent unity to the diverse experiences of reality; and thus they are conceived as aspects of a remoter but greater High God. However, the reverse process can often be seen to occur, when an idea of one unsurpassably powerful or good god splits up into images of a hierarchy of lesser gods, in order to enable men to relate to particular aspects of experienced reality more closely. The idea of the High God tends to remain, however, though it may not be actively worshipped to a great extent, because of its alleged remoteness from daily life.

Worship, then, is a human activity which is rooted in very basic affective responses to the reality men encounter in their daily lives. It may take a number of forms, but a common element is the submission of oneself to some value in reality which the concept of the god expresses, often in a myth or story. And there is an essential tendency for worship always to transcend whatever particular concepts of the gods it is based upon, as the worshipping response discloses new features and aspects of the reality it opens up. These very varied experiences, conditioned by differences in character and environment, mark areas of life where some valuable or significant aspect of reality is unveiled, in a way which demands and also makes possible a response of submission and creative contemplation. Such experiences are revelatory of the sacred.

Though the basic revelatory experiences of religion may be as diverse and unsystematised as this, they do not really become part of a recognisable religion until they are placed within the context of a community with its own traditions, rituals, spirituality and creed. Within such a community, particular revelations are taken as paradigms; and subsequent revelations modify and develop the basic paradigms, so that an inter-related set of revelatory images is formed, and a particular conception of the sacred is formulated. The rites and disciplines of prayer also help to determine the final notion of the sacred which the religion promulgates; and in this way, the many diverse revelatory intuitions are brought into one developing communal tradition, which in turn will shape the occurrence of future revelatory experiences. In the end, in a fully developed monotheism, one finds the concept of an imageless god which is the unique and underived source of all values, and unsurpassably great. But one cannot start a consideration of worship from that sophisticated concept. One must begin with the natural and direct affective responses to what are taken to be values, requiring the submission of the self, with its desires and inclinations, to them.

3

One may say, then, that worship begins in feeling; but feeling, in this sense, is not to be conceived as a mental state which occurs to a passive percipient, in complete isolation from his thoughts and activities. It is, rather, the appropriate adjustment of the whole person to the reality which confronts him in a specific situation. Iris Murdoch[6] speaks of 'a pure delight in the independent existence of what is excellent' as that which art offers. And she speaks of the discipline of art as being to alter consciousness in the direction of unselfishness, objectivity and realism, so that in the end one is able to attend to what is there, with a loving, contemplative regard for its sheer individuality. One subordinates oneself to what is there, and enters into its reality with both intellect and feelings.

That quest for pure contemplative regard for what there is, seems to me to be what is basic to the activity of worship. The language and rituals of worship fundamentally try to express such affective states of reverential contemplation. The discernment of a worship-worthy object and the feeling of reverence occur in one and the same personal act of response to some aspect of reality; and there must be present, too, as Miss Murdoch notes, a moral element, the dispositional preparedness to submit oneself to the value which is perceived, or to act in response to the challenge to action which reality, justly apprehended, conveys. In worship, one attempts to respond with the whole of one's personal being, intellect, emotion and the will, to what discloses itself to one in

[6] Murdoch, I. *The Sovereignty of the Good* (Routledge, Kegan Paul, 1970), p. 85.

experience. Thus one asserts that reality contains values which claim one's attention and action; one reverences those values; and one responds to them by subordinating the pursuit of one's own interests to the cultivation of a life which exemplifies those values.

The logical basis of religious belief is the adoption of an attitude to reality which is prepared to see in it new levels of significance and value and respond accordingly. The occurrence of a revelation depends upon the existence of the appropriate responsive attitude on the part of the subject. This attitude must be at the same time cognitive, affective and dispositional, involving the total personality. It is cognitive, because it brings to knowledge new aspects of reality. It is affective, because it extends the sorts of appreciation and delight of which one is capable. And it is dispositional, because it extends the sorts of creative response in which one expresses one's interaction with the reality one encounters in experience. It is not the case that one of these aspects precedes the others—that, for instance, the cognition comes first, arouses the emotions and then leads to a commitment of will. For it is the disposition—of freedom from self-concern and openness to new values—which makes revelatory cognition possible. And it is affective delight in the apprehension of what one encounters in experience which deepens one's commitment, as a creative response to what one cognises through such delight. In this area of experience, cognition, affection and disposition move indissolubly together. Revelation thus consists in a creative response of the total personality to the elements of significance and value which encounter one in one's experience.

At this basic level, knowledge and evaluation cannot be sharply divorced; for the basic evaluative choice, of self or objective value, is also a choice to limit one's interests and concerns to finite goods or to be ready to respond creatively to the objective value which transforms the world. To be prepared to apprehend the object of religion is itself the ultimate evaluative decision; and one is not thereby discovering another being, alongside others in the world. One is setting out to discover the interior meaning of being, the significance and value of reality as it is manifested in one's own experience of life.

As worship begins in a feeling-response to reality, its specific manifestations will naturally vary a great deal between different cultures, environments, and persons of different temperaments.

But, wherever the practice of worship begins, it can be trained by means of specific disciplines and techniques. And, as this training increases one's powers of awareness and concentrates them in particular ways, the sorts of religious experience one has will develop accordingly. The almost universal preliminary stages of such training involve adherence to a strict observance of moral codes and some form of ascetic practice; so self-renunciation is seen as an essential prerequisite for the religious life. Then there are various techniques of meditation and contemplation, sometimes associated with breathing and postural exercises, as in Yoga, which aim to calm and concentrate the mind. The pattern is outlined clearly in the Noble Eightfold Path of Buddhism.[7] The path the monk must follow is one of cultivating right belief; right intention; right speech; right action; right livelihood; right effort; right mindfulness and right meditation. The first of these parts of the path is concerned with doctrine—the doctrine that all existence is suffering, caused by desire, which can be ended by the cessation of desire. The next five are ethical, in a broad sense. They enjoin renunciation, compassion, abstinence from lying and stealing, from causing harm or pursuing sensual pleasure unduly. The last two are concerned with meditative practices. First, comes the cultivation of a mental state of self-possession and equanimity at all times, with control over one's thoughts and desires. And finally one passes beyond discursive, intellectual thought, beyond even joy, happiness and sorrow, and enters finally into the 'utter purity of mindfulness and equanimity, wherein neither ease is felt nor any ill' which is akin to, if it is not identical with, Nirvana.

It may seem ironic to choose Buddhism as an example, when the Theravada school is so little concerned with worship. Although the Buddha is popularly worshipped by many, the official doctrine is one of disinterest in the gods, and of the practice of meditation leading to release from desire, not of the worship of values contained in reality. Indeed, since the world is essentially evil and to be escaped from, on the Buddhist view, a doctrine of worship as contemplation of the value of existence is precluded in principle. But it is precisely this divergence in ultimate attitudes towards reality which makes the basic similarity of the disciplines of the religious life more noteworthy. Within Christianity there is a

[7] Cf. Rhys Davids, T. W. and C. A. F. (Trans.) *Dialogues of the Buddha*, Pt. 2 (Luzac, 1910), p. 343.

traditional division of the spiritual life into the purgative, illuminative and unitive ways.[8] The first stage of purgation is one in which one seeks to separate oneself from attachment to pleasures of the world, purify oneself morally and mortify the self until one is wholly surrendered to God. The illuminative stage is one in which the soul finds itself in an affectionate union with Christ, as a living personal presence. And the unitive stage, rarely attained, is one in which one passes beyond knowledge and analytical thinking, to a state which cannot be grasped by thought, and yet is believed to unite one with true reality in a way which is somehow even beyond the grasp of the emotions. Clearly, it is impossible to speak of the unspeakable; all one can do is to trace the stages by which one came to such a state, and testify that they did lead to a sort of experience and insight which is inexpressible.

The parallel of Buddhism with Christianity is even more marked if one considers that, especially in Mahayana schools of Buddhism, an emotional union with the Buddhas or Bodhisattvas is accepted as a normal part of religious experience. And these stages, of ascetic renunciation, personal devotion and mystical union, can be found in all the major religions, even where official doctrinal formulations seem antipathetic to them (as is the case with Islamic Sufism, for instance). That is not at all to say that all religions basically believe the same thing; the Christian belief that individuals will be resurrected bodily for eternity is clearly different from the Buddhist belief that the individual is annihilated in Nirvana. But it is to suggest that the activities of prayer and meditation are significantly similar in most religions, and they carry with them distinctive types of experience which may be recognised as similar, even though they are described in different ways.

On a number of occasions Ninian Smart has suggested that worship and meditation are quite distinct; for whereas the former stresses devotion, numinosity and piety, the latter concerns itself simply with the bliss of higher contemplative states.[9] On the other hand, it is possible to regard devotion to a personal god and the pursuit of enlightenment as two out of a number of ways of pursuing a religious life, which converge at their highest stages and

[8] Cf. Underhill, E. *Mysticism* (Methuen, 1930), Pt. 2 expounds and elaborates on this traditional division.

[9] Cf. Smart, N. *The Concept of Worship* (Macmillan, 1972), 1. 32.

merge into one another. Though it sounds very different to love Jesus or Krishna, and to meditate on impermanence and death, the sort of experience the worshipper has when his love touches the infinite plenitude of God is very similar to the experience of the Void of which the adept Buddhist monk speaks. The sorts of experience one starts from differ, as do personal temperaments and environments; but the techniques are similar in many ways; and descriptions of one's experiences converge as one develops in achievement.

It may be helpful to consider one or two examples. Suppose one is a fairly optimistic person, living a happy and untroubled life in a secure and beautiful country. If one begins to practise religion by seeking to turn from self to experience a greater value, one may naturally seek this value in the positive beauties around one. One's worship will express the joy and wonder of being, and one may develop a polytheism which sees the world as full of gods— sacred forces which enrich experience as they present new values for reverential contemplation through nature.

The optimistic polytheism of nature-worship will not appeal in a country rent by constant war or persecution, or subject to natural disasters, especially to persons of a pessimistic frame of mind. Here, the response may be to develop pantheons of harsh, power- ful gods of war or thunder, to be feared and propitiated, or to revere the mythic heroes or ancestors who embody qualities of courage and endurance necessary to survive in a harsh environ- ment. If one continues to seek a source of value in reality, it will tend to be distinguished from nature, and perhaps be conceived as opposed to the natural world, as moralistic and remote from daily life. On the other hand, one may turn from nature into one- self, and seek value by aiming at complete detachment from the world, and a heightening of sheer inner consciousness.

It is thus seen to be quite natural that differences of circumstance and character should determine one's approach to the valued reality one seeks in prayer. In particular, the tensions of optimism and pessimism, of the beauty of nature and the ruthlessness of natural forces, of introversion and extraversion, characterize all religions, and their complex interplay produces very different conceptualisations of the object or objects of prayer. It is not just a matter of either worship or meditation. There are a great many different strands which enter into the religious life, and they interact with each other in various ways, while it is possible that they may merge and redraw their boundaries in any one person's experience, on a number of occasions.

Forms of prayer are, however, built up into particular traditions, which usually derive from the teachings of founding individuals, like Mohammed, Jesus or Gautama. These forms crystallise particular approaches to the discipline of prayer, as a search for a true reality and value with which man can be in some way united. And they lay down as definitive for one tradition a particular mixture of the strands which go to make up men's religious life. These mixtures may look very different from each other; but they are not totally disparate. The Christian form of devotion to the glorified Christ is placed within the context of contemplation of a self-complete and infinitely perfect reality, God. And the Buddhist form of emptying the mind of all thought is placed within the context of union with the Void, the infinite bliss which is Nothing (not-a-thing), Nirvana or PariNivana.[10] Moreover, these specific forms of prayer carry over into all the experience of the believer, so that the Christian aims to cultivate the constant sense of the presence of God, and the Buddhist seeks to cultivate the constant achievment of Nirvana. Prayer is not confined to specific occasions of ritual or overt activity; its aim is to inculcate general attitudes which determine the whole of a believer's life, and thus to shape his experience in specific ways. Worship carries over into a constant awareness of a valued reality which discloses itself in various ways in one's experience, so that one can accept every moment as a sacrament of value. Meditation carries over into the apprehension of the illusoriness of the separateness of finite things, and of their true unity in the light of the Void beyond them. Forms of prayer are thus properly seen as rehearsals for general attitudes towards reality; and as these attitudes spring from primary affective responses to reality, so they develop to reveal new depths of more complex affective response, as the techniques of prayer refine one's sensitivity.

One thing, however, must be borne in mind, and that is that the pursuit of the techniques of prayer does not guarantee the sort of experience of which adepts speak. There are many reasons why not; prayer can become a mechanical and obsessive activity, which

[10] For a brief comparative estimate, cf. Conze, E. *Buddhism, its Essence and Development* (Cassirer, 1951), p. 39 f.

cuts one off from reality and takes one into a fantasy-world of one's own, unchecked by rational considerations. One may treat prayer too much simply as a means to obtaining thrilling experiences or supernormal powers, instead of as itself part of a full response to the valued reality one seeks; and then it will fail in its true role, even though it may produce the sorts of experience one wants. Or it may be that one is not really prepared for the moral renewal which must precede the pursuit of the life of prayer. Thus prayer may fail of its effect in many ways; but it remains true that the sincere pursuit of the life of prayer, if carefully and wisely directed, can both enrich one's apprehension of and response to reality, and extend one's experience towards awareness of a valued reality which demands the submission of the self and yet offers a fulfil-ment and renewal of human consciousness, in the birth of a new liberated self.

4

In the first chapter, I suggested that part of what it means to believe in God is to be found in the membership of a specific community of believers, within which a particular way of life is promulgated and encouraged. Another important aspect of belief in God is the acceptance of certain sacramental means by which the power of the sacred can be used to attain an important human good. In this chapter, I have suggested that belief in God is also closely bound up with prayer, as a distinctive form of human men-tal activity which has its roots in certain basic human experiences, and develops these towards the culminating experiences of mystical vision or union of which the most spiritually advanced people speak, albeit cryptically. I am not suggesting that belief in God can be based upon religious experience, as though one could be sure, from the mere occurrence of an identifiable feeling-state, like Schleiermacher's 'absolute dependence', that there exists an infinite omniscient being. But it does seem altogether too extreme to exclude experience altogether when one asks for grounds for belief in God. It is simply untrue that no experience can precede an already existent linguistic framework, as though we could only experience what our language had already pre-determined for us. On the contrary, our reactions to the situations in which we find ourselves can have an inner richness and emotional complexity which is able to suggest new developments and refinements of our present linguistic resources. And especially in the field of religion, our language often stammers and blunders in trying to express something; and, as believers, we can know that we have never got it quite right, that our description is always inadequate to the reality. Fortunately, however, new combinations of words do sometimes fall into place, and when they do they are often able to clarify our unexpressed feelings and reactions. So the relation of language and experience is a rather complex one; it is neither true that experiences happen, whatever one's conceptual equipment is, nor that experiences are totally restricted by the concepts one has. That is, someone who had never conceived the idea of an omnipotent, omniscient personal deity could not logically have a sudden experience of encountering such a being. But on the other hand, it is possible to have an experience in prayer which convinces one that the object of one's prayers is more adequately spoken of as personal than impersonal (or vice versa). Often, concepts will be suggested by experiences; but it remains true that experiences are interpreted in terms of the previous life and concepts of the experient.

One must therefore see religious experiences as set in a developing tradition of prayer. One's earliest, most natural responses to reality are provided with 'objects', in the figures of the gods and the myths surrounding them, which enable us to preserve and extend those responses throughout our lives. The activity of prayer arises as a training in the submission of self to the values dimly realised in such responses. There are three main elements involved in this account of religious experience. First, there are the revelatory experiences, of many different kinds, in which a person seems to feel himself encountering aspects of reality which are normally unperceived. The occurrence of such experience does not make a person religious, and it is even possible that a particular religious believer may entirely lack it. But this is an important basis of religious belief. Second, there is the basic twofold attitude of renunciation of self and preparedness to encounter objective significance and value in reality. The adoption and cultivation of such an attitude is essential to the development of those modes of experience which we call 'religious'. And third, there are the disciplines of prayer which aim to both deepen one's response and extend it over the whole of one's experience.

These aspects become properly religious when they are set within the context of a tradition which has been built up around some paradigm revelatory event or the teaching of some religious leader; and when they are associated with rites and credal formulae which organize them in a coherent whole, and provide a particular pattern of interpretation for them. The practices of prayer, worship or meditation within a religious tradition develop and enrich one's original attitude and response, and there is a general tendency for the higher stages of prayer to converge around the notion of an imageless Good, which is the unitary source of all value, but cannot itself be expressed. One may say that the term 'God' is, in part, the name for the object of one set of affective attitudes which have developed within the Judeo-Christian tradition of prayer, with its own special emphases on historical calling and moral claim. More specialised or exotic religious experiences—visions, conversions or revelations—are properly seen as falling within some such context as this; and it is clear that they are often perversions or projective fantasies, to which the human mind seems always prone. However, the central path of religious experience remains that which is sought by the discipline of prayer, preferably guided by an experienced counsellor.

An important part of what it means to believe in God is certainly the occurrence of distinctive experiences, which arise within particular traditions of prayer. This is an aspect of religious life which has been rather neglected by philosophers of religion, and that neglect has led them to give misleading representations of religious belief. What I am trying to stress is that belief in God, in any non-degenerate sense, involves participating in the way of life of a particular community, with its own social structure and set of institutions and roles, its own norms and values, its own way of organizing social and cultural activity. It involves participating in rituals, the point of which one may well be quite unable to verbalise, but by the practice of which one seeks to come to some understanding of one's own life and condition as a human being, and seeks the way to achieving some distinctive human good. And it involves accepting the discipline of a life of prayer, by which one submits oneself to some valued reality, conceived variously in various traditions, and seeks a deeper and more constant awareness of the presence of that reality.

Of course, one cannot divorce these features of religious belief from matters of doctrine altogether, as though they could flourish in complete independence; that would not be so. But it is very important to see that doctrinal beliefs do not come first; they develop and grow at the same time as, and alongside, these other important elements of religion; and all these aspects need to be taken together, to obtain a realistic picture of what it means to be a believer in God. I would think it certainly true that for very many believers, the aspects of religious life I have mentioned are more evident and important than any matters of doctrine, which are often left for learned theologians to converse about. And if one is seeking reasons for belief in God, these aspects provide good reasons for theistic commitment, which may give independent support to the more speculative reasons most often treated by philosophers. Nevertheless, the credal aspects of religion are of fundamental importance; and in the next chapter I will try to bring out the way in which they relate to the aspects of tradition, rite and prayer so far distinguished.

CHAPTER THREE

THE CREDAL CONTEXT OF BELIEF IN GOD

I

The believer in God is a person who participates in the life of a specific community which preserves an exemplary pattern of life, relating one to the sacred, as it was discerned in the paradigm generative events upon which the community was founded. In this respect, concepts of God function to preserve a particular tradition of imaginative apprehension, originating in the primary generative experiences of religious visionaries, and continuing in the life of the community.

The believer in God is a person who participates in rites which are held to bring liberation and fulfilment, by re-enacting the primal authoritative event in which a fulfilling relationship to the sacred was attained, and so renewing this relationship in himself. By the enactment of the rite, the power of the sacred to renew and strengthen human life is offered to bring the believer to an acceptance of the conditions of his existence. In this respect, concepts of God function to articulate a particular way of relating oneself to powers which bring fulfilment and renewal of life.

The believer in God is a person who accepts a particular discipline of prayer, worship or meditation, who pursues the spiritual life as a distinctive form of human activity. In this respect, concepts of God function to specify the object of the set of responsive attitudes which are pursued in the life of prayer, as a rehearsal for the general adoption of those attitudes throughout the whole of one's life and experience.

The examination of these aspects of the phenomenon of religion thus brings to light important strands in the concept of God, as it has developed in the Judeo-Christian tradition. It helps to make clear what it means for the believer to speak of God, and what function the concept of God has, what part it plays, in the life of the believer. As so far analysed, language about God has a three-fold structure; it is revelatory, enshrining paradigmatic revelatory experiences; it is charismatic, functioning in ritual contexts to relate one to sacred powers; and it is exemplary, specifying a set of roles or attitudes which are appropriate responses to reality, and which extend to the whole of one's experience.

To miss this structure of theistic language is to misunderstand the use of the concept of God by believers. It is perhaps because philosophical accounts of the notion of God have not referred to these aspects, but have concentrated almost entirely on intellectual arguments about a first cause or a supreme being, that they often seem to believers to be merely academic or irrelevant to the practice of theism. Yet, of course, there must be a place for intellectual arguments in religion. The three elements of religion which I have mentioned all presuppose or imply, in their working out, certain beliefs about the nature of the universe, of human life and destiny, and about the relation of the sacred to the physical universe. So religion must have a credal aspect; and even those religions which sometimes claim to have no creed (and these include some forms of Judaism, Hinduism and Buddhism) are affected in their attitude to tradition, rite and prayer by the beliefs about the nature of the universe which they do imply. For example, some Buddhists would claim to be agnostic about the nature of the universe; and yet Buddhist thought is influenced radically by the underlying acceptance of the doctrine of re-incarnation and the effects of Karma. And, in a similar way, various doctrines about the nature of reality affect in a fairly basic manner the traditions, rites and techniques of prayer which specific communities uphold.

Ninian Smart divides what I have called the credal aspect into the elements of myth and doctrine,[1] where by myth he means any story, whether true or false, about the activities of the gods or heroes who are of special concern to the religion; and by doctrine he means some statement about the general nature of human existence or the universe. Christianity has, as its central myth, the story of the people of Israel, called by God to a specific destiny, and culminating in the life of Jesus of Nazareth, who is said to have fulfilled in himself the demands of God and entered into the

[1] Smart, N. *Secular Education and the Logic of Religion* (Faber, 1968), p. 15 f.

promise of eternal life. And its doctrines involve beliefs about the immortality of the human person, the necessity for redemption through Jesus Christ and the existence of a purpose in the historical outworking of human existence. Although no-one would claim that these matters are perfectly straightforward, clear and easy to understand, it is true that Christian belief in God does involve distinctive beliefs about the course of human history and the destiny of men. Without this credal element, the Christian practices of prayer and ritual would have to change out of all recognition.

It is in matters of such general doctrine that the major world religions most obviously differ, and very often show a clear incompatibility. If a Hindu says that the soul re-incarnates many times upon earth, and may eventually be absorbed into the absolute reality, Brahman, what he says is incompatible with the Christian doctrine that men live on earth only once, and are not capable of being absorbed in God, since they always have resurrection bodies. If a Buddhist says that all existence involves suffering (dukkha) and that each man must work out his own release, that is incompatible with the Judaic view that human existence is basically good, and man will eventually be brought into God's Kingdom by the Messiah. If a Muslim says that in Heaven men will have sensual delights, that is incompatible with the Buddhist insistence that the highest end of man is an unconditioned, and certainly disembodied state. So religions differ about historical claims—whether or not Jesus rose from death—about human destiny—whether man will survive death as an individual or not—and about the nature of the world—whether it moves to a culminating moral purpose or is an endless cycle of suffering. In view of the intimate way in which credal elements enter into every area of the life of religion, it is thus impossible to say that all religions are really at one, or that each religion may be true for its own believers. For each makes some general claims about the nature of reality, and these claims are often in direct contradiction.

2

However, it might be said that the issue is not as clear as it seems. There are certainly Christian theologians who would deny that

Jesus' resurrection was a physical event, that people actually
persist after death in a temporally continuous existence, and that
the universe is moving towards some sort of moral culmination,
whether gradually or by some cataclysmic divine intervention.
They would not, I think, deny that the Christian creeds have been
very widely taken to state or imply factual assertions about history,
life after death and the destiny of the universe. But their case
would be that the religious character of the creeds has been mis-
understood, when they have been thus interpreted. Religion has
then been mistakenly assimilated to physics or history; whereas it
has in fact quite a different status.

An example of this approach is to be found in Phillips' account
of immortality.[2] He plainly states that no-one is going to survive
death; but, he says, 'the immortality of the soul refers to the state
an individual is in in relation to the unchanging reality of God'.[3]
Death is overcome, for the believer, not in that he will survive it,
but in that he is already dead to self and alive to God, and this is to
have passed from death to eternal life. In this way one can de-
mythologize all those religious beliefs which seem to speak of
factual predictions, so that they speak of a present condition of the
believer and not of future states of the world. If this can be done,
the historical differences between the religions become much
less pronounced, and may be taken as cultural differences to be
valued, rather as incompatible truths which must oppose each
other.

The editor's preface to Phillips' book says that this view is
'provocative';[4] and it certainly does not reflect the opinions of the
vast majority of theologians and believers. But it could be that
such people have been in some way led astray by irrelevant
philosophical or speculative questions, and that religious belief
does not require commitment to any statements about the nature
of the physical universe. It is true that many people are interested
in answers to questions about whether they survive death, whether
the universe has a purpose and whether miracles happen and
prayers can change the course of events. They will probably
always go on asking such questions. But, it might be said, these
are not properly religious questions, and religion, properly

[2] Phillips, D. Z. *Death and Immortality* (Macmillan, 1970).
[3] *Ibid.*, p. 55.   [4] *Ibid.*, p. 1.

speaking, offers no answer to them. They are speculative questions, to be answered on the basis of probable conclusions from scanty evidence; whereas religion is a matter of total, unshakeable commitment, to which the gathering of evidence is irrelevant. If religion asks questions of the form, 'Why does the universe exist?', this is not a request for a factual explanation of some sort; it is 'more like a cry of bewilderment than a straightforward question'.[5] And what answers such questions is not the provision of secret information about the future, but an absolute commitment to a religious 'picture', which governs all one's acts and attitudes thereafter, and to which facts about the future of the world are quite irrelevant.

This is a rather more sophisticated view than that of philosophers who have held that religious language is quite non-cognitive; that it does not deal in truths at all, but expresses commitment to a way of life or expresses certain emotions.[6] Religious assertions do assert something; but they assert it in their own way. What that way is, must be brought out by examining the use which believers make of such assertions, particularly in contexts of worship and prayer. They are not reducible to expressions of feeling; and neither are they reducible to factual predictions. If we look at such assertions, as they are actually used, we find that 'they form the framework within which those who live by them assess themselves and the events that befall them'.[7] The pictures they embody have an ethical and religious role in the person's life. Evidence and prediction are irrelevant; for the picture is used to control the whole of the believer's understanding of things.

This account of the credal aspects of religion is very attractive, in two main ways. First, it does come to terms with the feelings of mystery, depth and significance which surround religious talk, and which accounts simply in terms of speculative theories about how the world is, miss entirely. And second, it enables one to avoid the great problem, posed in a pointed way by Lessing, of how an unshakeable commitment can be based on historical evidence which can never be more than probable, and can lay down in advance that certain things (e.g. life after death) will

[5] Miles, T. R. *Religious Experience* (Macmillan, 1972), p. 20.

[6] e.g. Braithwaite, R. B. *An Empiricists' View of the Nature of Religious Belief* (C.U.P. 1955).

[7] Phillips, D. Z., *op. cit.*, p. 68.

happen, without, in a properly experimental manner, simply waiting to see.[8]

There are, however, very great difficulties about the account. The greatest difficulty centres on the notion that there is a distinctively religious use of language, which can be separated out from other uses of language—factual, moral, mathematical and so on—and which is presumably much the same throughout all the phenomena which one calls religious. It seems that one would have to construct an *a priori* definition of religion for this to be the case; and one would have to be able to say what a religious believer—as the person who uses religious language—is. But can this be done? Some groups hold that a religious believer is one who assents to the creeds, in a literalistic way. Others may hold that true believers are only those who have had specific experiences of 're-birth' or 'conversion'. And yet others might hold that a believer is anyone who has undergone certain rituals of entry into the cult. In view of this great disparity about what a believer is, can one define religious language as that which is used by believers, or must one not rather define believers as those who use religious language correctly?

There are obviously difficulties about discovering what religious language is by looking at particular groups of people. Indeed, if one takes seriously Wittgenstein's dictum, 'Don't think, but look',[9] one will be unable to lay down an *a priori* definition of religion in advance, to which all religions must conform, and one must simply look at the very various similarities and dis-similarities between the things that human beings say, in diverse contexts. It will be very doubtful whether one can separate out a uniform religious language at all; and one must just list the things people say, and point to analogies and correspondences, as and when they occur. One will not be able to say, 'That is not religious language', whereas some other utterance is. Or, at least, if one does so, one will have to leave the boundaries flexible, and be prepared to include and exclude for a variety of different reasons, depending on the particular range of similarities one is interested in.

If this is the case, one will not be able to claim, by inspection of

[8] Lessing, *Uber den Beweis des Geistes und der Kraft* (1777), in vol. 5 of *Sammtliche Schriften* (Berlin, 1825–8).

[9] Wittgenstein, L. *Philosophical Investigations* (Basil Blackwell, 1963), para. 66.

the linguistic habits of religious people, that religion is concerned
with an absolute commitment which must not be based on evidence
and that it cannot include predictions about the future. For, as a
matter of fact, very many believers do claim that their Christian
commitment is based on the evidence of Jesus' resurrection; and
they do not hesitate to pronounce on the future of the world.
Philosophers of Phillips' persuasion must then fall back on the
claim that these believers are deluded about their own use of
language; for a dispassionate examination of that use will make
clear that it is not what they say it is. Their theories may be
wrong; but they use religious language in the special 'picture-
defining' way which Phillips outlines. One can tell that by asking
if they act as though they really expect the world to end to-
morrow, or if they really seek evidence that prayer works. Negative
replies to these questions will show that religious language really
is not fact-stating, in any ordinary sense.

This argument is, however, not very effective. Though some
liberal believers do sometimes say things—about the possibility of
eternal suffering, for instance—which seem to have no effect on
their actions, many other believers are influenced in major ways
by their belief that Heaven or Hell or some future incarnation
awaits them after death; and they may spend much time acquiring
merit or refraining from delights out of fear of Hell. Phillips may
deplore their seemingly self-interested motivation; but that it
exists is not in doubt. That leaves his assertion as a recommendation that, whatever religious people do in fact believe, the only
rational form of religious belief is one which calls for total commitment and is unconcerned with evidence or facts.

3

In assessing this recommendation, it would seem to me that
Phillips is right to stress that religious language finds its proper
place in prayer and worship, not in intellectual speculation about
the universe. And he is right to point out that believers do not
proportion their belief to the evidence, in the same way that
physicists' do. But there are a number of reasons why it seems
irrational to divorce theistic belief completely from beliefs about
the nature of reality. One is that, as I argued in the previous

chapter, in pursuing the life of prayer, men do seek precisely to relate themselves appropriately to reality. Apprehension of that reality may require a specific sort of self-commitment, and it may be quite inappropriate to view that reality in the detached and dispassionate way in which one can view the physical world. But it is reality one seeks, and not a dream or fantasy.

Moreover, in prayer one seeks to extend one's attitudes from some particular focus of prayer to experience as a whole; and therefore the nature of one's total experience must be relevant to the appropriateness of one's attitudes in prayer. If one is to cultivate the Christian attitudes of thankfulness, adoration, contrition and dedication, one must believe that it is fundamentally appropriate to direct these attitudes as responses to the reality which meets one in and through all one's experience. That is one reason why the existence of natural evil occurs as a problem for theists— because it presents areas of experience to which the attitudes of thankfulness and adoration do not immediately seem to be appropriate. So, if the nature of reality, as experienced in one's own life, seems to make Christian attitudes inappropriate, one may lose one's faith, however sincerely one has pursued it.

If one refuses to accept that anything could show one's religious attitudes to be inappropriate, one retracts any claim to truth or falsity in religion, and is left with an unjustifiable commitment, whatever the facts. If, however, as I have held, religion is primarily concerned with coming to apprehend the sacred and utilizing its power for one's own well-being, then that there exists a sacred reality with certain powers is itself a matter of fact, which renders belief in its existence appropriate. Moreover, because the religious attitude is ideally directed to the whole of one's experience, one cannot isolate religious apprehensions in a distinct area of experience, without real connexions with the rest of the apprehended universe. It is consequently possible that one's experiences of the world may undermine one's religious beliefs, by revealing some inappropriateness or inadequacy in the basic attitudes enjoined by one's religion.

This is a sort of falsification-test for theistic belief. Of course, such a test cannot be precisely or crudely applied. There is not one definite stage at which Christian attitudes become measurably inappropriate; there are no laboratory tests for such appropriateness. Yet each individual, as he moves through life in his own distinctive way, builds up a set of responses to the world. And, though these habitual responses do tend to condition his perception of reality, so that he sees the world in terms of them, nevertheless it is possible to come to see that they are somehow inappropriate. One's responses may, suddenly or gradually, fail to fit the facts and one has to reshape them into new forms. The man of faith may say that one never sees the full picture in this life, and that one must trust in God whatever happens. But he must concede that evil poses a problem for theism, which must be resolved by some wider view.[10] And he must have some basis for his trust— some features of his experience must form the basis of a trust that his basic attitudes are not misplaced. For it is vital to see that the Christian is not just one who says that one must be optimistic, whatever happens; as though it was just a matter of a subjective determination to think positively. The Christian is one who tries to respond to reality as it is, in the light of the reality revealed through the discipline of prayer.

It is certainly true that he must hope for a fulfilment of vision that he does not yet have; and this is a form of trusting commitment. But this trust is not adopted, whatever the testimony of others and one's own experience. It is adopted because of the fulfilment some people claim to have achieved through the just perception of reality which prayer brings, and because of one's own dim apprehensions of such a perception. Basil Mitchell suggests that one trusts in the person of Christ;[11] but this needs to be further analysed, since Jesus is not a living person who can be physically met. Perhaps one can say that one trusts in the witness of those who commit themselves to Christ, and in those experiences of one's own which arise in the context of a self-commitment to the Christ who is preached in the Church. At any rate, trust does have its roots in experience, and not either in a sheer unevidenced commitment or in intellectual assent to doctrines about the nature of reality.

So the position of those who say that religious faith must be unshakeable by any subsequent experience, and must not be based on evidence at all, seems to me mistaken. In fact, I would think it

---

[10] Cf. Crombie, I. M. in 'Theology and Falsification (ii)' in *New Essays in Philosophical Theology*, ed. Flew and MacIntyre (S.C.M. 1955), p. 124.

[11] Mitchell, B. in 'Theology and Falsification, C', in *ibid.*

irrational to commit oneself in such an absolute way that no subsequent events could show one to be mistaken. Kierkegaard held that one must commit oneself absolutely to what is absolute, and relatively to what is relative,[12] but it may be that no absolutes can be found with certainty in this world. Even if one says that God is absolute, human claims to know the nature of God are not absolute; and that is really what one is concerned with in religion. One deals with claims made by fallible human beings in limited and often misleading concepts. So, if one continues to talk about God or religion at all, one is bound to the realm of the relative. One's thinking remains fallible, subject to error and inadequacy; so one must be extremely careful about claims that one's own way of putting things has some sort of privileged, absolute status.

But is it not a virtue to keep faith, whatever befalls? Only in a carefully qualified sense. One of the things such an assertion protects is the truth that belief is not simply a matter of intellectual disputation. The human mind is very easily led into making sharp polarisations of concepts, into pursuing arguments to their 'logical' conclusion; so that Christians are often easily trapped into arguments about, for instance, the real presence of Christ in the Eucharist or the nature of the incarnation. Different ways of putting such doctrines develop into opposed systems of theology, and entirely abstract arguments are propounded which lose all contact with living faith. Similar oppositions and arguments develop about belief and unbelief; and in the ensuing welter of opposing voices, all equally certain and intelligent, faith tends to waver and disappear under the barrage of quibbles and attacks. Especially with a religion as complex as Christianity, one needs constantly to warn against the undermining of faith by intellectual disputation, and to enjoin believers to keep faith, while enduring present sceptical doubts.

One needs often to stress, also, that faith must endure through suffering and times of desolation; for these can be used as occasions of strengthening, and some believers, like John of the Cross, have actually prayed for suffering in order to bring them to a closer union with Christ in his sufferings. Nevertheless, these points presuppose that faith is concerned with experienced reality, far from denying it. For the faith which endures is able to find a

[12] Kierkegaard, S. *Concluding Unscientific Postscript*, trans. Svenson, D. (Princeton University Press, 1941), Pt. 2, ch. 4, sect. 2, A, 1.

closer union with the reality which is sought under the name of God; and what is to be preserved from intellectual attack is the experience of wider aspects of reality, however hesitant, which is too valuable to be undermined by merely conceptual attacks.

However, there is a point where faith might become irrational—although naturally the believer will not think that such a point will ever arise. That point is where closer investigation does show one's primary experience to be delusory, in some way; where an alternative interpretation of one's experience fits in better with a set of wider beliefs about the world; where the generalisations one made from that experience seem too wide or sweeping to withstand criticism; or where continuing experience discloses an overwhelmingly greater number of features pointing away from the interpretation which faith placed on experience.

There is no universal calculus for saying where such a point might arise, in the life of a believer; but, in the exercise of personal judgement, and on the basis of personal experience, such a point may well arise, in theory. And in this way religious claims are subject to the verification principle, in the amended form in which Ayer cites it;[13] namely, that there are certain sense-experiences relevant to determining their truth or falsity. For, though the apprehension of evil is not itself a sense-experience, the sense-experiences of seeing men writhing and groaning are relevant to claims to such apprehension; and such claims in turn are relevant to deciding whether one will assent to religious characterizations of reality as true or false.

4

It may seem a rather alarming step to subject religious claims to the verification principle—in however weak a form—just when some philosophers are joyously proclaiming the freeing of religion from such chains. It may be thought, and it has been said, that the unbelievers are victorious on verification grounds.[14] For to introduce the verification principle seems to make religion a

[13] Ayer, A. J. *Language, Truth and Logic* (2nd ed.; Gollancz, 1946), p. 11.

[14] Cf. Hare, R. M. 'Theology and Falsification, B', in *New Essays in Philosophical Theology*, ed. Flew and MacIntyre (S.C.M. 1955), p. 99.

matter of finding evidence. But if one takes this step, one finds that the evidence is very bad, considered simply as evidence. Perhaps God could provide sufficient evidence to convince all but the most hardened sceptic. He could drop thunderbolts, create strange apparitions and foretell future events or provide humanly unattainable knowledge in great quantities, in broad daylight before hundreds of reliable witnesses, at regular intervals, or even unceasingly. This would be the best possible evidence for the existence of a superhuman, personal, being, having power over nature and being concerned to help mankind. Some believers have spoken of God's revelation in Jesus as if it was the provision of evidence of this sort. Acts 2, 22 reports Peter as speaking of the 'miracles, portents and signs' which marked Jesus off as the Messiah. And many commentators have taken the Gospel miracles as evidence of Jesus' divinity, and of the action of God in him.

However, it must be admitted that strong evidence for the existence of a superhuman person does not exist. In particular, the miracles recorded in the Biblical tradition have an extremely low evidential value. That is not to say that they did not happen. But it is to say that, taken as evidence for the action of God, they have negligible value. There are, naturally, no living eye-witnesses; the recorded events occurred two thousand years ago, and were not recorded in written form until several decades after their occurrence. They are rarely, if at all, recorded at first hand, but rely on information gathered from other sources. They were testified to only by a handful of people, while many others who met and heard Jesus have left no record, and were apparently often hostile to him. The events recorded—of virgin births, transfigurations and resurrections—are of very great rarity, and are thus antecedently improbable. The original witnesses are all propagandists on behalf of the Christian faith, and there is no extant impartial account of Jesus' life and death. Moreover, they lived in a primitive, superstitious culture, and many of their beliefs about the supernatural would be quite unacceptable to us. The evidence conflicts on many points of detail (even about the resurrection appearances), and no scientific tests were ever made of the events in question. Finally, the record is further vitiated, as evidence, by the writers' obviously cavalier attitude to historical accuracy. The apocryphal gospels contain a wealth of material, such as the miracles of the infant Jesus, which are pure legend; and

writers of canonical material do not, it seems, hesitate to appropriate the names of apostles to give their accounts authority, to
cite Jesus' private prayers, or to construct convenient genealogies.
In sum, if the Bible is taken as a source of evidence for the existence and activity of a supernatural person, it fails miserably to
live up to any of the usual norms of inductive evidence.

There is very little evidence from any other quarter that is not
both weak and disputable. One might think of dreams or visions,
extra-sensory phenomena or experiences of being providentially
saved from disaster. But, though there is a very great amount of
such evidence, it is all weak and questionable, and it does seem
that the sort of strong evidence one might expect a personal God
to provide simply does not exist. On the contrary, almost all
available evidence points to the hypothesis that the universe is a
vast material system, the fundamental particles of which interact
according to general laws, and within which life and consciousness
have evolved as a natural result of such interactions; no activity
of an intervening superhuman being is required or allowed. So
it may well seem that, once the appeal to verification is allowed in
religion, its claims are at once radically weakened by the lack of
sufficient evidence for its main assertions.

Furthermore, to make religious belief depend on verification
might seem to make it essentially a matter of hypothesis, revisable
in the light of further discoveries and thus never attaining the full
certainty of unshakeable commitment. So it seems that, either
Christianity consists in a total commitment which has nothing to
do with historical fact or the nature of the universe, or it is belief
which is disproportionate to the evidence, and is at best speculative and probabilistic. Between this Scylla and Charybdis, however, a way may be found which allows an approach to reality
which, though cognitive, yet depends essentially upon imaginative
symbolisation and creative personal response to what is apprehended. The very nature of such an approach would rule out the
possibility of a detached experimental concern, which would be
necessarily manipulative rather than responsive and interactive.
One may then say that the basic starting-point of religious belief
is a type of revelatory experience, in which a seeker seems to
discern a non-material reality—it may be in events in his life, in
the forces of nature, or in the silence of inner contemplation—
which brings him to fulfilment, by disclosing a greater value and

significance, by putting things in a new perspective. Such experiences may give a clue to the overall pattern of life, the meaning of life, and so be the centre-points for a new vision and life.

In this way, for example, Jesus' death and resurrection conveys meaning, a pattern of sorrow and new life which is a clue to the meaning and point of all human life. That event changed the apostles' lives, founded the Church and gave rise to a new interpretation of the Judaic notions of salvation. It was symbolized in conceptual images, largely drawn from Old Testament contexts, which help to evoke that sense of the new understanding of the meaning and significance of human life which the image of the cross focuses around the event wherein such meaning became clear. Similar examples can be taken from other religions, in which a key-event or experience provides the clue to a new understanding of the meaning and value of existence in its relation to the sacred, which is apprehended in a unique, untranslatable way in that moment.

So, as one holds oneself prepared to discern a non-material source of values, one may find that certain events or experiences do convey to one an apprehension of such a source, which may give a clue to the significance of one's life. One may express this by saying that there one finds a depth of meaning or significance; for there one finds the beginnings of an insight around which one may centre one's entire life. It is not at all that one comes to know some further finite being; but that here one discerns a ground of meaning and value which permeates all experience, an immaterial source which promises fulfilment of being in the appropriate response to it. Concepts which spring from situations in which some transcendent reality is mediated become images which one can use to evoke specific reactive attitudes and emotions, and which may be in some sense confirmed and amplified by personal experiences.

For example, one may find a sign of the unitary, non-individual source of values which the theistic attitude is prepared to apprehend, in a situation of maternal care. The concept of maternal care may then become an image of transcendence outside the specific context in which it first arose. That is to say, it will become an image under which one conceives the non-spatial, objective, non-individual reality to which one seeks to relate oneself in and through all one's experiences, whether mediated by finite objects or in a more direct form of personal experience, which may be interpreted as an apprehension of such a reality, conceived under such an image. The image is confirmed if experiences occur which can be plausibly conceived under the image of maternal care; and it may be amplified, if the structure and context of the experience itself suggests modifications of the image—for instance, by seeming more appropriate to some aspects of motherhood than others, or by disclosing distinctive features with which the image of motherhood is unable to cope. In such ways, the image of a Mother Goddess may be constructed, by the interplay of imagination and experience, which has a definite character and structure. What is happening is not that one becomes more sure of what the personality of some limited goddess is really like. Rather, each aspect of the goddess enshrines some amplification of the original attitude which the general image preserves. Thus the ways in which the sacred becomes apparent to one are diversified and also developed towards a greater adequacy, in accordance with the development of the general tradition and one's own growing experience.

One may say that this is, in a way, a matter of evidence; but it is not evidence which is equally open to the committed and the uncommitted. In the Christian story, Christ appeared after his death only to those who loved him—except, once, to one who was desperately involved in a battle against his love. It is both unclear exactly what, as a matter of empirical fact, the resurrection consisted in, and what exactly would count as supporting belief in it. It does appear that the resurrection was not just a literal event, so that Jesus could have been seen after his death by everyone. On the Emmaus Road, he was not recognised by his own disciples; he passed through closed doors and disappeared from sight at will.[15] On the other hand, it does not seem probable that nothing happened at all, so that the stories were made up to express the value the disciples put on Jesus' life and death.[16] One has to say that certain events are revelatory, in that they demand and make possible a response of commitment and trust from the one who apprehends them. To see an event as revelatory is to respond to it in faith.

[15] Lk. 24, 16; Jn. 20, 19; Lk. 24, 31.
[16] Cf. the dispute between Moule, C. F. D. and Cupitt, D.: *The Resurrection: A Disagreement*, in *Theology*, Oct. 1972.

This means that it is not possible to see a revelation and disbelieve. Paul could not have seen Jesus on the Damascus Road and refused to respond in faith. The same empirical events may occur to a believer and an unbeliever, and be revelation for one and not the other. For the unbeliever, they will be at best strange para-normal occurrences. For the believer, they will arouse that sort of practical commitment which leads to the hope of eternal life. This is therefore not evidence in a straightforward sense. Yet the believer may say that his response is one which does unveil depths of meaning in reality; the exploration of this meaning becomes an absorbing lifelong commitment; and it leads him to posit an ultimate meaningfulness in the universe as a whole. Revelation gives insight into the fact that reality is meaningful; that there is more to the universe than combinations of material particles. And the discovery of a meaning and value in the reality one encounters through the committed response of revelation, leads one to the supposition that in some way meaning is ultimate in the universe; and that is to say that good will not be defeated. As one sees significance and value in particular empirical circumstances, one comes to believe that such value governs the universe in some ultimate way.

5

It is clear that there is a fundamental division between those who are able to interpret reality in such a way and those to whom such an approach seems superstitious or delusory. In this situation, the religious believer will regard the unbeliever as one who suffers from certain defects of vision and response, and will regard religion as an activity in which the capacity for creative response, which is one of man's most distinctive excellences, achieves its consummation, and in which man himself receives a renewal and transformation of life. He will see religion as the natural fulfilment of human life, and those who lack such belief as failing to exercise their fully human vocation. One of the great disadvantages of the process of secularisation has been that it disguises these defects as virtues. On the other hand, by clearing away many misinterpretations of religious doctrines, it has cleared the ground for a possible renewal of religious vision.

One major obstacle to the establishment of such a view of the
basis of theistic belief has been the traditional account of knowledge, given by the British empiricist philosophers. Locke,
Berkeley, Hume and their followers have held, however incon-
sistently at times, that all knowledge derives from sense-impres-
sions, and that these are discrete, atomic existents, related to each
other only in contingent ways. The knower is fundamentally a
passive observer of the occurrence of such impressions, though
he can use his imagination to combine and re-combine them in
various ways, to invent imaginery objects or generalise to un-
observed impressions. On such terms, there is no place for religious doctrine except as a revelation from a superhuman source
which cannot be directly known by men.[17] It is an unfortunate
legacy of that philosophical school that such a reductivist interpretation of revelation passed into Christian theology.

It may plausibly be held, and has been widely argued, that sense-
impressions are not the only objects of human knowledge, out of
which all knowledge, however complex, has to be built. The
foundations of knowledge are not discrete sense-data; but they
lie in the rich and complex realm of personal interaction, in which
individuals adjust and react to their environment. There is a
reality which confronts man as something to be explored and
discovered. But the way in which this reality is interpreted and
understood largely depends upon the nature of the human cognitive apparatus, and the use which is made of it by the knowing
agent. This epistemological dispute cannot be argued out here;
but it does seem that there has always been, within philosophy, a
basic dispute between those who apprehend reality as a molar,
totalistic, meaningful whole, and those who apprehend it as a
mechanistic collection of elements, a bundle of unthinking, purposeless, insignificant bits of matter or sensation. There is an
analogous division about values, too, between those who think of
values as existing over against man, to be apprehended by him;
and those who conceive values as springing solely from human
decision or desire.

There is not just one way in which these divisions are made;
nor are they always clearly made. The clearest form of the divide
is found in Absolute Idealism and mechanistic materialism. But

[17] Locke, J. *The Reasonableness of Christianity* (A. and C. Black, 1958),
p. 32 ff.

there are forms of materialism which take a holistic view of reality (the dialectical materialism of Marxist-Leninism); and there are forms of idealism which end in a reductivist notion of reality (classical British empiricism tends to such a view). Naturally, there are many sophisticated arguments on each side of the dispute, and it would be silly to brush them all aside as rationalisations of previously held prejudices. But I confess to feeling that, though philosophical arguments rage around it, the dispute is not really resolvable by arguments. Both halves of the divide express a fundamental attitude to the world, for which no further justifying reasons can be given. One either tends to view reality, from the first, as a whole which contains many levels of meaning, and which different sorts of analysis can dissect in different ways, or as a wholly contingent collocation of diverse and essentially unrelated elements.

One must start somewhere, in coming to terms with the nature of reality and deciding how to act in response to it. It is not the case that one can begin from a condition of complete neutrality, and build up a view by dispassionate syllogistic argument. One's view of reality is conditioned by the sorts of concepts one has, which govern one's approach to reality in action and apprehension. The theist begins with a conceptual equipment which predisposes him to view reality as meaningful and unitary. This is a basic predisposition, which is no more or less rational than the predisposition to view reality as a random collection of bits of energy. That is not to say that it is an irrational view; but simply that it is not derivable by inference from a more basic set of premises about the nature of reality.

A view remains rational, in one sense, if it is internally consistent, coherent with other knowledge and confirmed by relevant experiences. The requirement of confirmation is necessary, to prevent the acceptance of schemes, however fantastic, which simply do not conflict with known facts, but which there is no good reason to believe. But it is a difficult requirement, nonetheless, for experiences do not come bare and uninterpreted. The subjective act of interpretation is essentially involved in any human knowledge; so that one cannot test an interpretation by reference to the 'bare facts'. Interpretations are testable, of course. One can see if they lead to internal contradictions, when fully worked out, or if they are less adequate than alternative interpretations. But there is not one obtainable, neutral standard by which to test them; one can only say that an interpretation is supported by one's own knowledge and experience of reality.

The theist claims that, as he takes up various interactive responses to reality, he apprehends various levels of meaning and significance in that reality; and this in turn gives rise to a qualitative heightening of consciousness and creative activity. The world appears as a field of action which continually offers new challenges and possibilities of creative fulfilment, which is shot through with varieties of meaning to which one must respond openly and fully. Of course, theory and practice may become dissociated. Theists, who claim to apprehend depths of meaning in reality, may in practice deal with others as though they were objects to be manipulated—sometimes, manipulated into salvation by crude propaganda exercises. And theoretical materialists may in practice be highly concerned for others and for aesthetic and moral experience. But a clearly perceived theory about the nature of reality is one which derives from and expresses one's practical stance towards reality.

Theism does presuppose a metaphysical view of reality and of human knowledge as non-materialist and anti-empiricist; that is, as not bounded by matter and sense-perceptions. This view is not less plausible than its alternatives; and the life and experience of religion is one of the strongest factors inducing one to adopt it. Since a full consideration of these points takes one far outside the present range of debate, my suggestion is that materialist and empiricist views are incompatible with theism; and that until this is clearly grasped, theistic belief is in constant danger of misinterpretation as some sort of supernatural information, promulgated by means of extraordinary, but nevertheless, it seems, insufficient, empirical evidence.

6

That the universe is a meaningful whole, governed by absolute values, remains an hypothesis, an opinion which could be mistaken and in conflict with the facts of the case. It is an hypothesis which, though basic in the sense outlined, may nevertheless be suggested and corroborated by the occurrence of specific revelatory experiences, which unveil particular aspects of that meaning and value. The specific judgements of value one makes are shaped by the contexts in which revelatory experiences occur. So, one may say of the stories about Jesus in the Christian tradition, that one may not know exactly what he did and said; but the stories depict and attempt to re-enact the contexts in which meaning was disclosed to his followers.

An eternal destiny simply is based on historical probabilities; for faith must arise as a response to some revelation, in some historical context. The line between what exactly happened, that neutral observers could have seen, and what was revealed and expressed in symbolic language to express the revelation, cannot be drawn with certainty. But it seems quite mistaken to say, with Phillips, that the revelation is irrelevant to the empirical circumstances. That would be rather like saying that Beethoven's Ninth is quite separate from any particular manuscript or orchestra. In a sense, of course, the Ninth is not captured in a manuscript; but it involves a score and an orchestra for its performance; it does not exist apart from any empirical facts, even though it may well be said to be more than empirical.

So with revelation; it is not simply empirical; but it comes in an empirical context, which always remains important for the retelling of the revelation. The Jesus we preach from the Gospel records is the same Jesus whom the early Church found to be the locus of revelation; the stories show Jesus, as he was a vehicle of revelation; and so they give the context of this revelation. Allowing for dramatisation and defects of memory, those historical facts are sufficient for faith, because they are preserved as revelatory records, evoking faith in us as they did in the first Christians.

Certainly, such assertions involve the truth of largely unspecified empirical claims. If Jesus did not exist; if everyone suffered endlessly after death or if the wicked always prospered the main Christian assertions would be falsified. But one is not able to say, for example, that Jesus' resurrection must have happened at just 3 p.m., in just this precise way. The empirical facts are not determined exactly; but some are definitely implied. These may be of a rather general and unspecific character—namely, that Jesus perfectly expressed God's will, that good will not ultimately be defeated, and that each person will have the possibility of final fulfilment.

What is the status of a statement like, 'good will not ultimately be defeated'? R. M. Hare calls it a blik, which he defines as a statement or set of statements which 'does not consist in an assertion or system of them',[18] and so cannot be shown to be true or false by any empirical tests. However, he says, one can have normal, silly or even insane bliks. And he holds it very important to have a right blik. It is certainly true that it is logically impossible for the statement under consideration to be established as true on the basis of past experience. At best it remains a confident hope. But how are such hopes founded? It may be, on the rational argument that there must be an omnipotent and all-good creator, from which it may be claimed as a valid inference. But I think Hare's suggestion is really that it is not founded at all, on anything.

I do not think this will do. There must be some difference between a right and a wrong blik. Though he does not suggest what this could be, it must surely be that either good is defeated or it is not, in the case in question. In other words, the position would be better put by admitting that bliks are assertions, but denying that they can be evidence-based. Notoriously, one cannot prove that the future will be like the past by appeal to experience. But one can show that the immediate past was like the remote past on an overwhelming number of occasions. Such a consideration strongly supports asserting the principle now, especially if the principle is a condition of my engaging in some useful activity. So with moral optimism, one can never logically guarantee that it is justified; but one can appeal to certain considerations to support it.

For the Christian, these will include the way in which good has come out of evil in the history of the chosen people; the resurrection of Jesus (however exactly that is taken); and personal experiences of providential guidance or sustenance in moral efforts. Most importantly, the statement is not one in which one is disinterested; it is a condition of entering the Christian way, in its pursuit of the fuller vision of Christ in glory, of fuller fellowship with all the faithful and of personal fulfilment through prayer and devotion. That is, it is a practical attitude, not a dispassionate theoretical affirmation. It gives one's whole life a single aim, and governs all one's other acts and attitudes. In such a

[18] Hare, R. M., *op. cit.*, p. 100.

circumstance, one cannot wait for the results of a dispassionate empirical enquiry; especially since even such an enquiry could never be conclusive.

Theoretically, one cannot be certain that good will not ultimately be defeated, that Jesus perfectly expressed God's will or that one will finally achieve personal fulfilment. There are features of experience which suggest these opinions; but the matter is finely balanced, and so the rational course might seem to be agnosticism. But practically, one is called to involve oneself in the Christian way, and these beliefs are a condition of doing so. It is as one pursues that way that one's practical commitment becomes stronger, and increasing commitment brings an increasingly confident hope that the fulness one dimly foresees will not finally be denied.

Christian faith may be both total and falsifiable, a matter of working hypothesis and a basic commitment to a specific way of apprehending and acting in the world. These characteristics are not contradictory, and it is the peculiar nature of religious faith to hold them together. Faith is total, in that it involves life-long commitment to the life of prayer, to that pursuit of meaning and value which begins in response to a revelation of meaning in some empirical context. It is clearly extremely difficult to falsify; for if it begins from a revelatory experience which evokes committed response, it is hard to see how such experience can subsequently be denied. Nevertheless, it is falsifiable, in principle, and the tendency of subsequent experience could sufficiently gainsay it to lead to loss of faith, if faith was not corroborated by subsequent revelatory experiences. More probably, faith may not be simply rejected, but adapted in response to new experience, and this may lead to something quite different from the faith one started with (as with conversions from Christianity to Buddhism, for example). In this way, particular versions of faith are falsifiable, by reference to considerations drawn from one's extending experience and knowledge of the world.

Revelation is unique in carrying commitment with it; but it is not distinct from empirical features of the world. It originates in particular historical situations; from the first it implies statements about the nature of reality (minimally, that revelations occur; that such aspects of reality exist); and as one's appreciation of meaning and value grows, one is led to the working hypothesis that the universe is grounded in such meaning—that the good will not fail; that personal values will flourish. These are hypotheses, which could be mistaken, and which are not establishable as certain. They are not based on inference from empirical facts, but on a special form of insight into reality, given in revelation; and they become conditions of pursuing the spiritual life, somewhat as the principle of induction is a condition of pursuing physics. So one's attitude to them is not dispassionate and speculative; one commits oneself to them as practical postulates, which are supported by one's growing apprehension of meaning in the various situations of one's own personal existence.

The creeds of religion may, and often do, become restrictive systems of rigid dogmas, to be accepted on pain of exclusion from the community. But one may see their proper function as being the preservation of a sort of interaction with reality which the way of life of the community specifies by means of its paradigm revelatory images. The creeds clarify the presuppositions and implications of that way of life, in its relation to its own paradigms; but one need neither insist on one rigid interpretation of them nor claim that they embody all the inner secrets of the universe. Nevertheless, if the images really are revelatory; if they really are effective in conveying the power of the sacred; and if they do specify responses which are appropriate to the nature of reality; then some claims about the nature of the world and human destiny are involved in religious belief, however unspecific or metaphorically expressed they may be.

It is not possible to sever the ethical, ritual and spiritual aspects of religion from credal beliefs. For one's conception of the possibilities of action open to men, one's understanding of the sort of liberation religion brings, and one's concept of the objects of worship or meditation, all depend upon one's beliefs about the nature of man and the relation of the sacred to him and his world. Yet such beliefs about the world and man are not developed prior to or independently of the living out of the religious life. All these main aspects develop together, and their complex interplay produces an organic, developing form of life, in which changes in one aspect produce complex and often unsuspected changes in the others. Thus no consideration of what it means to believe in God can afford to neglect the placing of such belief in its proper context of the total phenomenon of religion.

CHAPTER FOUR

THE OBJECT OF FAITH

I

Belief in God has been characterized as primarily involving the cultivation of particular attitudes towards reality, specified by a community of faith, which maintains a set of traditions, rites and practices in which the believer participates. It is consequently accurate to say that language about God has a specific use within a particular form of social life, which may seem unintelligible to one who does not share in that community of faith. And the most adequate approach in seeking what it means to believe in God is to begin by examining the way of life which religious communities uphold. Thus far, what I have said may seem much more sympathetic to Wittgensteinian views of the nature of religious belief, as an autonomous form of linguistic activity, with its own internal norms of intelligibility, than to traditional views which take theistic belief to consist primarily in assent to propositions, which can either be established as true by reason, or reliably accepted on an authority the nature of which can itself be ascertained by reason.[1]

On the other hand, it is important to see that the autonomy in question is not that of one 'religious language-game', which is the same for all religions and believers, and can be distinguished as such on purely philological grounds. It is to be found by reference to the activities and practices of particular religious communities, each of which may have their own peculiarities and uniquenesses. And the unintelligibility in question is not simply a matter of understanding the meanings of words. It is a matter of coming to appreciate the reasons believers have for their practices, to see what it means to them to carry on their ritual activities and to appreciate what it is like to pray or meditate. In other words, it is a

[1] Aquinas, T. *Summa Theologiae* (Eyre and Spottiswoode, 1964), Pt. 2, Second Part, 1st. Number, Qus. 1–6.

question of empathetic understanding, not just of learning new words and verbal constructions.

Moreover, one must not lose sight of the fact that religious communities are communities of faith; and faith has its own distinctive object or objects. It is always sensible to ask, 'What do you have faith in?'; and the answer to that question will disclose the object of faith. The object of the Christian faith is, ultimately, God; and God can be generally characterized as that object towards which the believer, in the public rites of his liturgy, directs a complex set of dispositional attitudes—the attitudes of adoration, contrition, thanksgiving, supplication and dedication. It is immediately apparent that this is not an object, in the sense of a solid entity in space and time, which might be detected by the senses. Even in contexts where it may seem, for example, that particular objects like bread and wine are being adored, the informed believer knows that it is not the object, *qua* material substance, that he adores. For the bread is only adored in specific ritual contexts; and the same God is present in many different pieces of bread, all over the world. Furthermore, adoration is not confined to these occasions, though it may be focused there; it extends into the whole of the believer's life.

The object of theistic attitudes is thus conceived, at least in the Catholic tradition, as focused or present in certain ritual contexts; but it is not confined to any one such context, or even to all of them taken together. It can ideally be taken as the focus of one's attitudes in any and every human situation. This is part of what is meant by saying that God is transcendent; God is not limited to any specific spatio-temporal context, though he can be focussed in many such contexts, especially by ritual action. In speaking of God, one may thus be taken to be saying that there is a reality to which one can reactively respond here and now, but which could not be discovered by any enumeration of the physical objects before one. Nor is it the sum total of such physical objects. Though in the Christian tradition, that reality is believed to be known to one through physical objects and events, it is not confined to any particular set of spatio-temporal co-ordinates. However, it may be asked whether such a transcendent reality is possible, or if it is not rather true that everything that exists must be spatio-temporally locatable and identifiable? Moreover, if such a reality is possible, how could it be identified?

In answer to the first question, it seems unduly restrictive to insist that only spatio-temporal entities can logically exist. The concept of a non-spatial existent is not self-contradictory, for the term 'exists' does not analytically imply the term 'spatial', which refers to a particular mode of existing. This seems sufficient in itself to assure one of the logical possibility of the existence of non-spatial entities. Many philosophers would go further, and claim that we actually know of examples of such entities, in our experience of feelings, sensations and thoughts, which do not, on the whole, have spatial position. If such feelings are introspectible, it is certainly true that their introspectible properties do not include spatial co-ordinates—my thoughts are not in a given place, relative to my left ear. The materialist who admits introspective evidence, but wishes to assert the identity of thoughts with spatial brain-states, must establish that introspectible properties logically cannot exist without spatial properties; and he must go further and identify the two *prima facie* distinct sorts of property. I do not wish to enter into this argument; but it is worth pointing out that many philosophers would claim that mental events provide examples of non-spatial entities, or at least of non-spatial properties of entities. And this sort of example may help one to overcome the prejudice that only material objects can logically exist.

There is a serious objection which remains to be made, however. Though it may be that there is nothing self-contradictory in the notion of a non-spatial existent, nevertheless a very close connexion may be made between the concepts of existence and identification, such that a meaningful assertion of the existence of something entails the possibility of identifying and individuating that thing.[2] We may say 'X exists', and logicians cannot stop us. But if we can show no way of identifying X, or picking it out as a distinguishable thing, then our assertion becomes, not contradictory, but vacuous. It is rather like saying that an invisible, intangible, inaudable object exists, which is beyond human knowledge; if we cannot show how, in principle, that being could be identified, the assertion is useless.

Individuals may exist which may be individuated by principles unimaginable by us, and which cannot, in principle, be identified

[2] Hampshire, S. 'Identification and Existence', in *Contemporary British Philosophy*, ed. H. D. Lewis (Allen and Unwin, 1956).

by human beings; but it seems that assertions to that effect are vacuous. The question of the identifiability of God is, however, different from that of identifying finite objects. For if God is an individual at all, he is so only in a very peculiar sense. To identify as an individual is normally to pick out as one of a sort; and to count individuals presupposes denumerability, and thus the possibility of many instances of what is being counted. But one cannot, in Christian devotion, distinguish this God from that God, or say that this is the same God as that, but a different one from the other. God is not one of a class of similar beings;[3] and he is never picked out as an individual in religious practice by the sort of ostensive definition that one might use for finite objects. The believer certainly does not mean, when he speaks of God, to be speaking about an unknowable individual who is a member of a transcendent world of individuals, an object in a world of spiritual objects. To see what he does mean one must turn to the sorts of context in which talk of the transcendence of God may get started.

It may start from particular contexts in the empirical world which arouse in the believer attitudes of adoration and awe and with his refusal to identify the object of his adoration exhaustively with any spatio-temporal phenomena. This is analogous in some ways to saying that, when one enters into a relationship of love or trust with another person, one's reactive attitude is not directed solely towards the chemical constituents which comprise his material body; and it is not even directed to the sum total of such constituents, however cleverly arranged. Persons are treated differently from physical objects; and one would not normally identify a person exhaustively with the spatio-temporal lineaments of his body. Whatever it is that makes the difference, with a person —whether it is behaviour, mental qualities or the attribution of rational freedom—one naturally adopts distinctive reactive attitudes to persons, and most people are reluctant to say that a person is identical simply and solely with his observable parts.

The case of God is analogous to that of personhood, in that one adopts distinctive reactive attitudes to God—of adoration and thanksgiving—and most people are reluctant to say that God is identical with the objects in which he is manifested. The great and obvious difference is that persons are identifiable organisms, locatable in space-time; whereas there is no continuously identi-

---

[3] Aquinas, T. *Summa Theologiae*, Pt. 1, Qu. 3, Art. 5.

fiable entity which can be identified with God (the special case of Jesus, for Christians, is no exception, as will be shown later). God manifests in many ways, at many times and places, and he 'expands' to be an object of theistic attitudes throughout all one's experience. It is because God is not tied to particular locatable physical objects that one says he is non-spatial; he is not at any place, not near or far from any place, and not in any spatial relation to any spatial objects. Thus, if one is to know God, it is useless to look for him as a locatable object.

At every moment of their conscious awareness, human beings find their awareness bounded by a finite spatial frame, the segment of space-time network of which they are directly aware. Within this frame, specific objects can be located and associated with sounds, scents, tastes and tactile impressions; and one can direct one's attention to one of these objects and view it or act upon it in various ways. One can be concerned with the spatial properties of objects in a purely descriptive way. But one can also view sets of objects (for instance, a landscape) in a way which is quite different, which uses different concepts and expresses different interests; and these may be personal, aesthetic or religious. The religious interest in objects has its own peculiar concepts, among which that of 'God' has a central place. So one might say that the concept of God is a key-part of an interpretative conceptual scheme which one uses to guide one's reaction to the objects of human awareness. To understand what it is to think theistically is to see how one applies the concept of God in one's own experience, or at least how one might do so.

When one looks at the concept of God as one which is used, not to identify a locatable individual, but to interpret all experience in a specific way, learned in one religious tradition, it may well seem that it is not used to individuate at all. One may mark out specific experiences of great significance or importance or value as encounters with the sacred, which threatens human self-concern and security, but at the same time liberates to a fuller life and calls for submission to its inherent value. But what reason is there to suppose that one is dealing with just one thing in all these instances? May one not rather be dealing with many diverse apprehensions of, or claims to apprehend, meaning and value within reality, to which one responds in various ways as one seeks fuller being? Polytheistic religions do take this interpretation, and it is certainly possible to see the religious quest as one of finding significance *in* the world, rather than looking to something beyond it.

2

I think that one must take these points seriously. They emphasize the fact that, if God is an individual, he is so only in a very special-ised sense. It is not the case that the notion of the sacred is, from the first, that of one identifiable supernatural or otherworldly reality. There are those, like H. D. Lewis, who hold that true religion only begins where the mind makes 'one leap of thought in which finite and infinite are equally present'.[4] In this one intuitive leap the mind both sees what the infinite and transcendent means and also grasps that it inevitably is. Not only does one intuit something necessarily existent; but one also intuits that this reality is perfect or absolutely complete; that it is personal;[5] and that, though absolutely mysterious, it functions as an explanation of the universe, accounting for why things are as they are in some total sense.[6] The intuition itself is both unique, instantaneous,[7] does not admit of further support,[8] and is absolutely compelling.[9]

Perhaps one must admit in the end that all human reasoning must be based on principles which cannot themselves be justified in terms of further principles; so there may well be a place for intuition in human knowledge. But the real difficulty with Lewis' account lies in the number, complexity and variety of the things which are supposed to be known in one and the same intuition; and in the implicit claim that religion does not exist until such a complex intuition has occurred. Each of the notions which one is supposed to intuit seems so difficult to comprehend that it needs a long process of explanation before one could even understand it. What, for example, is meant by an 'absolutely complete' reality? Is it one which lacks no existent quality? If so, that would seem to suggest the view that the material world is part of God. Or is there a different sense of completeness, meaning perhaps, not dependent on anything outside itself? But that seems to say too little; for to

---

[4] Lewis, H. D. *Our Experience of God* (Allen and Unwin, 1959), p. 45.
[5] *Ibid.*, p. 66.   [6] *Ibid.*, p. 40.   [7] *Ibid.*, p. 42.
[8] *Ibid.*, p. 50.   [9] *Loc. cit.*

say that a being is independent is not to say anything positive about it. Perhaps one will argue that only a perfect being could be totally independent. But then the same difficulties arise over the notion of perfection. Is the notion of a being which is just perfect *per se*, without being perfect in some definite respect, meaningful? Or must one say that it is perfect in all respects? In which case, one must ask whether it is logically possible for any one being to be perfect in all respects at once—both perfectly red and perfectly green, for example.

These are old, familiar problems which arise over the typically Scholastic concept of God as a perfect self-subsistent reality. But is the occurrence of one intuition supposed to resolve all such intricate conceptual problems? It seems to me that such a suggestion is extremely implausible. And that, in turn, suggests that whatever basic religious intuitions exist must be much simpler, less sophisticated and abstract than the intuition of a necessary, perfect, complete, self-explanatory personal reality which Lewis postulates.

But the question still naturally arises: how does one know that one is not totally deluded in thinking that the basic intuitions of religion acquaint one with any reality at all? Is one ever justified in inferring, from the fact that X believes himself to experience Y, that he really does experience Y, if there is no independent test of his claim available, even in principle? To some philosophers, this problem seems unsuperable. Flew, for instance, holds that it is sufficient to undermine any claim that religious experience can be evidence of the existence of God.[10] Yet it is not clear to me that the assertion that one is never justified in positing an object of one's untestable experiences has much force at all. One must consider what sort of justification could count, in such a case.

If I say that I have just seen a black dog, is this evidence for the existence of such an animal? It surely is evidence, even if only hearsay. It could be strengthened if I could produce a photograph, or let you see the dog; if bones had disappeared and footprints could be found; if barks were heard and if I produced corroborating witnesses. There is a whole battery of available tests in such a case, but there are two basic types of test, the causal consequences of there being a dog and corroboration by other

[10] Flew, A. G. N. *God and Philosophy* (Hutchinson, 1966), ch. 6.

senses or other people. These are normal tests for the existence of
enduring material objects, which are in causal relation to other
objects, and are perceivable by humans. The tests apply because
of what material objects are; and if the tests prove negative, then
what I saw could not have been a material object—it may have
been a vision or hallucination. One need not be saying that there
was nothing which one saw; what one saw was real, but it was not,
perhaps, in causal relation with material objects, or it was not
perceived by other observers. It is therefore allocated to imagination, and denied 'objective' reality.

If there are to be any tests for the truth of claims to apprehend
the sacred, they must be appropriate to the nature of the sacred.
It would be quite inappropriate to try to make the sacred a material
object, if it is not one; accordingly, it would be wrong to make it
conform to the sorts of test we require in the case of material
objects. The sacred, as so far characterized, is knowable only by a
personal response of total commitment, in which one both submits to and is transformed by the reality one apprehends. It is
not perceivable by the senses or by neutral analysis; and it is not
an enduring spatio-temporal object, in causal relations with other
similar objects. And it is an essential part of discerning the sacred
that such discernment should depend in its detail upon idio-
syncracies of culture and character. The empirical tests of checking
by other senses or the senses of other people, or of testing for
causal consequences, are thus completely inapplicable, in the
case of the sacred.

Is any test applicable? One might be tempted to say no; but it
is true, nevertheless, that religious believers do attempt to distinguish between false and veridical experiences; and that there is
a difference between an insane or unbalanced religious view and a
sane view. So some tests, however imprecise, are actually used.
One obvious test is the general reliability and sanity of the experient. If a man cannot be independently shown to be psychotic,
neurotic or otherwise demented, and he claims revelatory apprehensions, one must at least take them seriously. If, moreover, he
is a morally outstanding individual, and if his experiences give
him the appearance of equanimity and spiritual power, this will
corroborate his reliability. So one test is that of sanity and moral
heroism—one of the basic tests of a saint in Catholicism.

A second type of test is that of agreement with other people. It is clear that there are limits to be expected of such agreement, if one expects the particular revelations to be culture and character-relative, and if one insists that revelation is only possible to those who are open to submit and creatively respond to it. But claims to apprehend the sacred will increase in probability if they tend to be corroborated, in significant respects, by others who are sincerely seeking to live well and fully. Conversely, any failure on the part of highly moral and sincere men to have such experiences will stand in need of explanation, though it will not of itself undermine claims to experience. It is clear that not everyone can be right, in this area; but one does not remove the problem by discounting all claims to such experience.

A third test is that of the ability of images which spring from the revelations of others to enrich and deepen one's own experience. This is a sort of test by corroborative personal experience; and one will tend to accept the claims of others insofar as they show illumative power in disclosing new meaning in one's own life. The Church uses a test rather like this when it lays down that new revelations must be consistent with the tradition focused on Jesus. For in that tradition a set of images has guided the spiritual lives of generations of Christians, and the appeal to consistency with authority can be seen as an appeal to the general communal experience of believers.

One is also involved here with questions of the coherence of religious claims with claims made in other areas of human life. As religious traditions develop, claims are made about the nature of the world or history which need to be assessed on their own merits; and it is one test of a claim to apprehend the sacred that what is apprehended should not be inconsistent with any otherwise known facts about the world.

There are, then, tests one can apply to help one decide on the plausibility of claims to apprehension of the sacred. But in the end one cannot prove that one really is apprehending what one claims to be apprehending. Religion stands by the claim that there are distinctive aspects of reality which can only be apprehended in this specific way; and those aspects are so defined that no independent justification could be found for such a claim. Flew appears to conclude that one must therefore withdraw all claims to apprehend the sacred; for, he maintains, one would need to know that God existed before one could claim to apprehend God.

This might be so, if one is already clear that God is a super-natural, omnipotent, omniscient individual for which one needs to find evidence. But if the roots of religious belief are in claims to discern distinctive aspects of reality in the way suggested, one can only come to know the existence of the sacred in apprehending it—just as with most other aspects of reality. Because such apprehension is person-relative and not publicly shareable (as with dreaming, perhaps), it must remain unsatisfying to one whose only paradigm is knowledge of physical objects. From the religious point of view, to hold such a paradigm is always a mistake and possibly a prejudice; and, in opposition, one must attempt to make clear the nature of the apprehension claimed in religion, and clearly assert that the lack of neutral checking procedures is, not a defect, but a condition of religion being what it is, a matter of faith, commitment and discipline.

It may now be thought, however, that the pass has been sold, in the case of God. For though one may speak, in this relatively restricted way, about aspects of reality discernible only by special techniques and distinctive uses of language, in particular contexts, this is very different from speaking of the omnipotent individual who is the Christian God. In fact, the notion of revelation has been so watered down that almost everyone must have had revelations at some time. I think this is the case; that almost everyone has had some apprehension of the sacred at some time, and felt in some experience the impact of a value which momentarily takes one out of oneself and liberates into a more creative and fulfilling realm. But if that is the case, how does it come about that some people interpret such experiences as apprehensions of God; and how can one such interpretation be rationally preferred to the many others which exist?

One must not speak as though there was just one wide gulf between theists and atheists. People may have some sorts of revelatory experience and not others; and some declared atheists may have more such experience than some avowed theists. A great depth of significance may be unveiled in apprehension of other persons, moral claims, artistic works or the wonders of nature; and though the theist will unify these apprehensions by ascribing them to a unitary, transcendent reality, they may occur to anyone, theist or not.

It may now be suspected that religion, as a distinctive phenomenon, has entirely disappeared and been merged with artistic and personal experience; and this is indeed what happens in some forms of 'secular Christianity'. But, whereas it is important to emphasize the continuity of religion with such phenomena, and to stress that such revelations are not completely other than revelations of God, the peculiar characteristics of religion must not be lost.

I. T. Ramsey, who develops an account of disclosure-situations which involve both a peculiar sort of discernment and a responsive commitment, holds that religious disclosures are distinguished from others by exhibiting 'a total commitment to the whole universe'.[11] The term 'God' is, he holds, 'a key word, an irreducible posit, an ultimate of explanation expressive of the kind of commitment' the believer professes.[12] He does not seem to think that religious disclosures are different in kind from other sorts of disclosure; but they do involve the whole of a man's loyalty, and dominate his entire life; and they operate over the whole of a man's experience, and so are, in a sense, all-embracing. Anything could be a religious disclosure if it involved total commitment and was all-embracing. The object of religion is here defined, not, as with Lewis, in terms of any intrinsic nature it may be supposed to have, but in terms of the formal criteria of totality, ultimacy and all-embracingness. Nothing at all is said of the nature of the religious object; and indeed, Ramsey might take this to be a misleading question, since all one can say of God is that a disclosure occurred along a certain route, which is then marked out by a logically odd use of language.

One might want to object to this, on the grounds that one must have some way of distinguishing between silly and sensible commitments. If a man totally committed his whole life to fishing, saw fishing as the ultimate value and talked about everything else in fishing-terms, we would, I think, want to say that the object of his religious faith (which would, perhaps, be the Infinite Fish) was irrational or misplaced. Largely because of his amusing use of such examples as fishing, penny-dropping and ice-breaking, dinner-jacket-splitting and light-dawning, Ramsey's account is in danger of trivialising religious awareness, even though this is far from his intention. There are many different sorts of awareness

[11] Ramsey, I. T. *Religious Language* (S.C.M. 1957), p. 37.
[12] *Ibid.*, p. 47.

which Ramsey puts under the heading of disclosure, and different types of disclosure may need to be distinguished more fully. Although Ramsey seems to be importantly right in focusing attention on situations in which discernment and commitment go together, and in saying that religious discernments call for a total response which can be extended to the whole of one's experience, and which should over-ride all other considerations; nevertheless, his account seems to miss some important characteristics of religious belief.

The reason for this is that he does not explicitly place disclosures in the context of a community with its rituals and disciplines of prayer and its doctrines, which determine the form of the religious life. Thus they appear in isolation from the major concerns and interests with which religion is involved. One can place moral disclosures in the context of a social life, within which men have to have some rules of interaction and some limitations on self-interest. The context which gives moral disclosures their sense is a social context, within which certain forms of human activity become intelligible. Outside such a context, moral disclosures might appear unintelligible. So, in the case of art, sense is given to disclosures by their place within general activities of making and constructing, for various purposes and within certain social frameworks. Religious disclosures, too, become intelligible only within a social context in which the concerns of religion are taken seriously, and provide acceptable forms of human activity.

3

But what are these religious concerns? A clue might be found by considering the forms which religion takes in the most primitive known forms of society. It is widely agreed by anthropologists that we do not have enough evidence to say what the origins of religion actually were, in the pre-history of man.[13] But it seems reasonable to say that the earliest forms of religion recoverable by historical investigation were tribal, and were very much concerned with significant events in tribal life and with establishing the common values of the tribe. Concern with the significance of human life and

[13] Cf. Evans-Pritchard, *Theories of Primitive Religion* (O.U.P. 1965), ch. 5.

with the values that should guide it has been a natural part of
human nature from the earliest times. In the lives of men and of
societies there are, implicit and underlying, certain basic questions
about the point of human life, which are sometimes forced to the
surface in situations of crisis or decision, or of importance for
continued existence. Human nature is subject to much the same
limitations and possibilities everywhere—men have a limited life-
span, are easily vulnerable to injury and illness, need protection in
infancy and old age, need to enter some network of social relations
to obtain the necessities of existence, and in general share the same
complex of emotions and desires surrounding sexual propagation
of the species. In almost all societies, certain moments of choice
arise which will determine one's future mode of existence and
that of those around one, and one has to choose in face of limited
information and an unknown future. So the basic problems which
men face in their lives are much the same, wherever they exist, and
form a permanent background to every human life, even if never
explicitly formulated.

If one constructs a list of the questions which naturally arise
from the main common areas of human concern, their connexion
with religious beliefs is immediately apparent:

(1) The birth of a child raises questions about how he will fare,
what his destiny will be, who he is and what accounts for his
character and personality.

(2) The fact of death leads one to ask whether it is really the end,
whether one can accept it, and what one will have achieved that
may remain for posterity.

(3) The onset of maturity raises questions about one's role—
the sort of task one undertakes and the sort of person one will
become; status—how one will be regarded by other members
of one's community; and security—how one can plan for one's
future.

(4) With regard to personal, and especially sexual relations, one
wants to know whom one should befriend, whether a liaison will be
happy and how to cope with situations of personal stress.

(5) The constant threat of pain or failure raises a set of questions
about how to cope with tensions, responsibilities and decisions,
and about the point of suffering in life. And it leads one to ask
whether one is making the most of one's opportunities, being
constructive and creative and acting in the right way.

Such questions as these arise for all human beings, and they can be raised in a very sharp form at various points in life where significant decisions, having major consequences for the rest of one's life, occur. They may be grouped around two focal concepts, those of meaning and value. Questions about value are questions about what is intrinsically and maximally worth-while, about what is the right, proper or fullest way to conduct one's life. Questions about meaning are questions about how one can cope with diffi-culties and obstacles and find some sort of creative fulfilment and freedom from care. To see the meaning of one's life is to discern one's real intentions, hopes and fears; to see that all the parts of one's life fall into an overall pattern. One answers questions of meaning by seeing what one must do, what one is aiming at, what one can hope for. One needs to achieve a picture of one's life within the wider pattern of things, and find an aim and life-style within such a pattern.

A particular event in one's experience can be said to 'have meaning' when it conveys something to one of the true nature and purpose of one's life. This use of the notion of meaning is an extension of the central use of conveying information. To see the meaning of what a person is saying is to understand what he intends to communicate—though, of course, sometimes we may know the meanings of the words he uses, but completely fail to see what he means (as when one says, 'I am not half pleased to see you', but intends to communicate that one is very pleased indeed). There is thus the complication that the meaning of what one says may not be what one intends; and there are complex cases where the sophistication of what one says makes one's meaning opaque to all but the initiated, even though all may understand the individual words being employed. But the concept of meaning is closely bound up with that of communication. We may understand what a word means when we know the dictionary definition. We may understand what a lecturer means when we can follow his line of argument or see the viewpoint he conveys. We may understand what a painting means when we apprehend what it conveys (Picasso's 'Guernico' conveys the horror of war, perhaps). Simi-larly, we may say that a piece of music conveys deep human emotions, and so tells us something about the human condition; it may put things in a new light, or suggest emphases we had not previously considered.

These are all instances of human artefacts, and may be said to be intended by some person to mean something, even though the meaning may not be what is intended. This usage is extended when and if one speaks of an event or experience as having meaning, since events are not necessarily, like products of action, intended by persons. One may speak of an event having meaning, in that it is taken to tell us something. For the Jews, the event of the Exodus was interpreted as the choosing by God of that people; and many people take events as portents or good omens, thus conveying to them implicit advice about their future actions. In a different sense, an event may be said to be meaningful if it is important, if it leads to a re-orientation of life—as when a holiday in the country leads one to take a completely new job. Sometimes experiences are termed meaningful if they are felt to be worthwhile; and are similarly said to be meaningless if they are felt to be trivial or boring. An event can have meaning if it is related to some purpose, by relation to which it comes to have a significance beyond itself—as when someone's apparently random wanderings become meaningful when we see that his purpose is to look for a lost ring. One may also say that an event has meaning if it serves as a clue to a general pattern within which my life has an intelligible place. An event like Jesus' crucifixion can be said to be filled with meaning, for as one looks at it in different ways, it continually suggests new ways of regarding human life. Its meaning is never exhausted, but can always be explored more deeply and seen in many different ways. For that event, in its constantly enlarging context, can be re-interpreted in many ways, suggesting new attitudes to human existence and new patterns of human life.

This list is not intended to be exhaustive, but simply to show that a concern with questions of the meaning of human life or events in human life is to be construed as a concern with finding a purpose or pattern in one's life which is intrinsically worth-while and which may lead to a re-orientation of conduct. In this context, it does make sense to speak of finding meaning in specific events or experiences, and of apprehending or failing to apprehend the meaning of life itself. But to say that it makes sense is not to say that such meanings can legitimately be found. It may be that one fails to find intrinsic values in life, or that one's life refuses to fit into any pattern of coherent meaning; and it may be that such is a just perception of human life, while those who pursue intrinsic

values and find a meaning in their lives are subject to delusion or
bad faith, as Sartre once christened it.[14] But men often do try to
'explain' their lives by setting them within a value-centred pattern,
by giving them a goal and a way to achieving it. Such an enterprise
is natural and likely to be universal, given the basic conditions of
human nature; but that fact neither shows nor disproves that a
value and meaning can be found in reality, by those who seek it,
which is claimed to fulfil their humanity.

4

It seems obvious that answers to the sorts of question mentioned
above would begin to be given in the most primitive societies, and
that accordingly they are at that stage unlikely to be coherent,
highly reflective or based upon scientifically accurate information
about the nature of the universe. In the religions of economically
primitive societies one finds a great number of stories, explaining
how one should live, how to find happiness, how tribal customs
began or how the world came into being. Myths, legends, sagas
and primitive scientific theories are mixed together, and closely
bound up with tribal traditions and with magical formulae for
telling the future or ensuring good fortune. These stories are
usually associated with tribal rites, which consolidate group-
feeling, give a sense of tribal identity and relate the tribe to the
sacred powers. Each element of religious life is over-determined;
that is, it does not have one clear function, but contributes in many
overlapping ways to the general life of the tribe—for example as
entertainment, force for social cohesion, superstitious observance
and vehicle of relation with the sacred. Yet a large part of tribal
life and lore is concerned with giving a meaning to human life and
finding values to which to orientate it. Questions about destiny,
good fortune, pain and happiness are answered by the provision
of a general view of the world, unsystematically expressed in
myths and legends; and personal and public rituals provide techniques for achieving fulfilment by relation to the sacred. The great
moments of birth, maturity, marriage and death are celebrated
with the invocation of the sacred powers; rituals, totem-symbols

[14] Sartre, J-P. *Being and Nothingness*, trans. Barnes, Hazel (Methuen,
1957), Pt. 1, ch. 2.

and tribal myths reinforce a sense of group identity and solidarity; and men can turn for inspiration, guidance, comfort and love to the gods, spirits or ancestors who figure in their cult.

One important point to bear in mind is that pre-scientific peoples do not have our distinction between literal fact-stating discourse and non-literal uses of language; so they conflate the two in ways which are quite unacceptable to us. It is only in recent times, and largely under the growing dominance of the experimental sciences in Western culture, that the realm of facts has been limited to the realm of the verifiable. When the Australian Aborigine speaks of the 'Dream Times', when his rituals and patterns of life were laid down by the tribal ancestors, he would be baffled by the apparently simple question, 'Did things really happen like that?'[15] He has simply not got the interest in empirical details to be concerned with what verifiable events occurred. For him, we might say, the real is the significant, the meaningful; so that many empirically ascertainable happenings, since they are trivial or insignificant, are less real than his cult beliefs. There would be nothing worth recording, from a religious point of view, in a recital of the bare facts. But he might lovingly elaborate and dramatise a significant event in the life of the tribe, until a myth is formed around which the tribe patterns its whole life. Then, however, these stories, hallowed by long tradition, may be taken by a more literal-minded age as the only true accounts of human history and destiny, which must be true in all details. Religion is turned into naïve cosmology; and perhaps the believer becomes unable to see the difference between accepting a great deal of false or outmoded historical information and preserving the significance which was communicated in one paradigm revelatory experience.

The concern of religion is thus to find a pattern of meaning and value in human life, and to establish a form of social life within which men may find fulfilment by appropriate relation to reality. This central concern is expressed in a number of different ways, reflecting the particular circumstances of the society, which govern the formulation of the universal questions about significance within a specific environmental context. The control of these important personal and social concerns usually rests with a special

[15] Cf. Elkin, A. P. *The Australian Aborigines: How to Understand Them* (Angus and Robertson, 1954).

class of holy men—shamans, witch-doctors, priests or prophets—
who control and interpret the tribal myths and rites. It is clear that
someone makes up the myths and rites in the first instance, even
if their development is gradual and piecemeal. Such creation is
usually attributed to inspiration—it may be a trance-state, a
quasi-hysterical condition or some other abnormal manifestation
which marks a man off as inspired. In such abnormal states,
religious leaders have and relate experiences of revelation, of an
unveiling of the sacred in its specific relations with the tribe. They
provide a form of imaginative symbolization for the non-human
sources of good and harm which surround human life.

These will naturally vary from one culture to another. For instance, nomadic hunting tribes are concerned with heroism,
victory in battle and the finding of satisfactory oases in the desert.
Settled agricultural tribes are concerned with fertility and owner-
ship (symbolized by the sacred places). Fishing tribes will be
concerned with good shoals of fish, clement weather and the
varying moods of the water. In such a context, talk of God, the
object of disclosure, as the Infinite Fish, becomes intelligible; for
it is here related to the central daily concerns of the tribe, as part of
their concern to be related rightly to the sacred powers, which
give meaning and value to their lives. The respective tribal
symbolizations for the sacred will naturally differ in accordance
with these different concerns and environments. One may find the
desert tribe constructing a picture of harsh or arbitrary powers
(gods) of a martial character, who give victory in return for
devotion. The agricultural tribe, on the other hand, may see the
sacred as embodied in the cyclic forces of nature, giving fertility
in return for devotion.

It is not possible to discover exactly how revelatory experiences
of the sacred first occurred to men, but it seems reasonable to
suppose that a general predisposition to discern intrinsic value and
pattern in life is given shape around particular events, places or
experiences in which some answer to the significance-questions
listed above is suggested. For instance, one may interpret one's
life in terms of a moral demand to undertake a certain course of
action, or of providential salvation from some disaster. Then the
sacred will be construed as a moral demand or a providential
power involved in the historical process. This is basically the
Judaic concept of the sacred as Jahweh; and the prophets inter-

preted significant events in the history of their people in terms of the notion of 'calling' or moral vocation. The sacred was discerned in historic events, as interpreted by the prophets. Other religious leaders have discerned the sacred, not in historic events, but in the processes of nature. One of the best examples of such a view is Taoism, which sees the meaning of life as lying in harmony with the way things go, even to the detriment of moral distinctions, which are viewed as somewhat artificial. A third main type of religious discernment is that which is typical of Indian religions, the discernment of the sacred within oneself, so that it is in the discovery of one's true inner self that one finds the limitless, transcendent, unconditioned reality which alone is of supreme value.

These different discernments give rise to very different doctrines of the relation of the sacred to the world, and there does not seem to be much point in saying that they are all discernments of the same thing, except in the very abstract sense that they all claim to speak of a non-human reality, relationship to which brings true fulfilment. But the character of that reality, of fulfilment and of the right relationship is variously conceived, and one must consider each case separately on its own merits. And one must remember that in primitive religions interpretations of the relation of the sacred to significant aspects of human life are very much bound up with fortune-telling, sympathetic and imitative magic, tribal custom and attempts at scientific explanation. There are therefore likely to be many values, vaguely centred on fulfilments of various types, and not related in a coherent rational framework.

The major world faiths now in existence arose from the reforming efforts of religious teachers, who claimed to achieve, or know or be able to obtain for others an overwhelming good, bringing fulfilment. They tended to free religion from a mechanical dependence on ritual-magical techniques and to construct a more coherent account of the sacred. Remaining within the general tradition in which they found themselves, they claimed special insight into the hidden nature of reality, which enabled them to speak of fulfilment and the way to it. Moses united the Jewish people around the notion of one unifying Law and one liberating God, known in providential encounter and the demand for absolute purity. Gautama achieved liberation from desire, and taught others the way to find such final peace within themselves.

Jesus taught the coming of God's Kingdom, a renewed society of peace, joy and love; and the Church found in his death and resurrection the beginnings of the new society. The Vedantic philosophers attempted to unite the polytheistic systems by achieving a vision of absolute one-ness, losing self in the vision of an absolute value. Mohammed taught a rigorous ethical monotheism, on the basis of divine inspiration, to unite men in the worship of one God. The founding of major religious movements is usually due to the influence of one outstanding teacher, who sums up a tradition and sets it on a new direction, with a new claim to insight and a new way for his disciples to follow. The vast majority of religious believers have to take that way on trust, after assessing it as well as they can on general grounds of plausibility, value and illuminating power.

If this is a fair analysis, it brings to the fore another aspect of religion which Ramsey does not stress, the place of authority in religious faith. Many, and probably most believers, would not claim to have had a really full disclosure, in the sense of an experience which called from them a total and ultimate commitment, as a result of some direct apprehension. They would think of themselves as on the way to such an apprehension, perhaps; but their walking is by faith and not by sight. When they join a community, they commit themselves to follow a spiritual teacher, and he is their authority for the way which they follow, in trust. I would think that most believers would not really claim a full religious disclosure at all, but they would follow a person whom they believe to have had such a disclosure.

What I am maintaining is that the revelatory insights of religion occur in the context of a seeking, in community, for human liberation; and they are grouped around the teachings of authorities, who claim to have achieved such liberation and to show the way to it. I would thus wish to distinguish religious disclosures, not simply in terms of the formal criteria of totality, ultimacy and all-embracingness; nor in terms of a definition of the religious object as perfect necessary cause of all things—which seems too restrictive—but in terms of the context of practices in which they occur. Apprehensions which may properly be called religious often occur, even though they do not dominate the whole of one's life in all its aspects. One may have such an apprehension during a time of prayer, or in a religious ceremony; and one could then say that it was religious, but not total, ultimate or all-embracing. On the other hand, it is possible to have a totally involving apprehension which applies to all one's experience which is not, in any ordinary sense of the term, religious. An example might be that of a man who is mesmerised by a particular woman, and interprets all his life in terms of what she might think. We may say, 'She is his religion', in colloquial speech; but we would probably not seriously regard him as a deeply religious man.

So I do not think one can distinguish religious revelations in the terms which Ramsey suggests. Yet it is true that certain, rather rare individuals are totally dominated by religious revelations; and their total commitment gives rise to communities which accept their claim to authority. Thus a religious life comes into being; a life to which only some individuals are fully called, but which exercises a pervasive influence on the whole society in which it exists. The traditions evolved within that life, set apart by its total commitment to the sacred, become regulative, in a modified way, for the attitudes of the society at large. In this way, spreading out from the communal religious life of a relatively few individuals, specific interpretations of the sacred become normative for whole cultures; and people tend to interpret their own revelatory experiences in the terms they receive from their religious tradition.

Revelations do not become religious because they are dominant, however; for a man can be dominated by other things than religion. It is not my intention to replace one inadequate definition of religion by another. My suggestion is only that one will decide whether to call an experience religious or not by reference to the sort of context in which it arose. It is because there do exist specific and distinctive religious practices that religious apprehension is a distinctive area of human experience.

5

It is clear that the term 'God' is not used to identify or re-identify a particular within a spatio-temporal framework. Nor can it be used to identify unambiguously one individual transcendent reality. One may say that the religious believer is one who accepts certain events or experiences as revelatory; though what is signified in such a theophany can only be expressed in the imaginative reconstruction of the experience as it occurred in a specific cultural and psychological context. Spatio-temporal phenomena, like thunder-storms or beautiful landscapes, may become epiphanies, and they may be taken by the unsophisticated as themselves gods, or filled with sacred force, or at least as expressing the acts of individual gods. On reflection, however, it appears that it is not the finite realities which are sacred, and that there are no individual sacred forces causing or underlying those realities. The world, for the theist, becomes a semiotic system, revealing the inner depths of reality in its various aspects, in ways which are directed to human liberation.

To speak of God, to use that term at all, is to affirm a transcendent depth in the world. Knowledge of God, one might say, is achieved through a specific sort of cognitive and reactive attitude to reality, which makes the being of God manifest. God is known in and through the world, as the depth and meaning of the world, encountering the man who is open to reality. One is able to affirm that God exists as one apprehends depths of value and significance in the world one encounters from day to day. Thus knowledge of God cannot be dispassionate and detached; and to assert the existence of God is not just to assent to the speculation that a first cause can be inferred to exist from the nature of the universe. Nor is it to have the complete and sudden intuition that a perfect necessary being exists.

What one encounters, when and if one comes to see elements of transcendent significance and value in the world, does not appear in one absolutely definite and clear form, whatever the cognitive and conceptual abilities of the observer may be. The agent 'sees' only what his own reactive disposition makes him capable of seeing; and he sees it as conditioned by his own past and present interests, distinctive patterns of perception and habits of thought. This is perhaps the most important fact of all to grasp; that there is not just one thing to be seen in the same way by all men; and yet there is something which demands and deserves the attention of all men. There is a reality to be known; but how far and in what way one is able to know it depends upon the conceptual tradition which has shaped one's view of reality, and the creative and original ways in which one has developed this tradition in the light of continuing experience. What is certain is that the response the believer tries to cultivate to whatever reality meets him in and through his experience, is from the first a response to transcendent being, mediated through finite reality, whether in objects or personal experience. Since this is the basic character of the theistic response to reality, there is no question of making an inference from finite reality to transcendent ground. Knowledge of the transcendent is found from the first in a specific sort of responsive attitude towards all experience. The various strands of the concept of God elucidate the various areas of experience within which such an attitude seems to find some objective correlate.

The notion of transcendence is not a particularly abstruse or difficult one. It is presupposed in all our most ordinary knowledge of a world of physical objects, other minds, the past and the laws of physics. One knows that there exists a world of physical objects, even when unperceived by men; that the past has existed, though it is irretrievable; that the future will be like the past in general ways, though we cannot know the future; that the ultimate constituents of matter exist, though only their effects can be detected, even by atom-probe electron microscopes; and that other people have experiences, which can never be known by us. All these things are known with certainty; and yet none of them can be known by acquaintance.

It might even be said that if our experience did not provide information of realities which transcend that experience, then it could give nothing but a record of purely subjective events, and each person would inhabit his own solipsistic world. This is the *reductio ad absurdum* of a rigorous empiricism, which refuses to accept any notion of transcendence, of a reality which transcends our immediate knowledge of it, but can be known in various ways and degrees by means of conscious experience. One does not, then, infer from present reality to it's transcendent cause; rather, one interprets reality by the application of the concept of a transcendent reality which is signified in experiences of value and significance. From such a basic predisposition, concepts of God or the gods are generated.

This is not to be conceived as simply a theoretical matter; for it involves the basic human concern for fulfilment and self-transcendence. Yet while the theist will say that knowledge of God expresses an evaluative orientation towards reality, he will not be able to say that those persons who lack such knowledge are blameworthy for their lack, or that all theists find greater fulfilment than they otherwise would have done. For religion as it actually appears in forms of social organization and as it is propounded by some believers can be morally, socially and intellectually offensive. And so, for many reasons, religion itself may prevent men from completing their capacity for creative response by entering into the life of worship and prayer which is the true heart of religion. Nevertheless, theistic religion claims to offer the possibility of human fulfilment by relation to a reality which is from the first considered as transcendent yet mediated in certain finite experiences. That transcendent reality is what the theist intends to signify by using the term God; and that is the object of his faith.

It may still be felt that there are great difficulties in this notion of apprehending a transcendent reality, and in justifying the theistic assertion that there is only one such reality, God. In the next chapter, I will try to show how one may speak of apprehending transcendence in a number of contexts—artistic, personal, scientific and moral—and thereby attempt to make clearer the character of those revelatory experiences which, in the context of the search for meaning and value in existence, become the basis of religious communities. I will then explore the question of what it means to say that the transcendent object of theistic faith is one. The way will then be open to examine the development of the Christian concept of God within one tradition of revelatory relationship to the sacred.

CHAPTER FIVE

THE APPREHENSION OF
TRANSCENDENCE

I

There is an initial difficulty, for those trained in the tradition of classical empiricism, in seeing what it can mean to take some thing or mental state as an image of the transcendent, as a sign of some reality beyond itself. In the end, one will have to say that experience of God, of the world as signifying transcendence, is *sui generis*; but it is possible to produce some analogies from other aspects of experience which may make the character of this apprehension clearer.

First, it is relatively clear what it means to take one thing as a sign of another. Clouds are signs of rain, and high body temperature is a sign of illness. Here, one simply establishes a correlation between two things which can be independently known; and this is very unlike the religious case.

But there are more difficult, though very common, cases where the signified reality cannot be independently known; as when bodily behaviour is a sign of some inner feeling or pain, or when physical marks are taken to convey a conceptual meaning. Whatever one's philosophical account of these cases, one can see that there is a difference between treating the signs simply as marks or movements, and seeing that they convey something further. Even the reductionist, who disavows the existence of unknowable realities, will agree that one must interpret the phenomena differently, by using a distinct set of concepts, when one takes them as signs. One does not speak of 'movements' and 'angles of inclination', but of 'actions' and 'tenderness, terseness or beauty of expression'. Whatever one is talking about, the logic of one's language, the terminology one uses, is quite different when one takes phenomena as signifying something; and one could not take them as signifying in that way without such a distinctive use of language. Thus to take something as a sign, in the sense under consideration, requires a special use of language, with its own typical concepts. Whether or not one goes on to say that such language refers to transcendent, hidden entities, that use of language, which expresses and makes possible that way of seeing, would be universally admitted to be a very important and illuminating one, in dealing with one's experiences.

A more controversial case, nearer to religion, can be found by considering a work of art, say a painting. It may be seen as a pattern of colours on a plane surface. And so it is. But is to know just that, to apprehend the reality which is before one? To see it as what it is—a painting—one must learn to interpret the picture in terms of perspective, to see the plane surface as a representation of a three-dimensional scene, to associate the coloured patches with sunlight and shadow, plane and curved surfaces. Then one must be able to interpret the expressions of face and figure, and grasp the situation which is being presented—e.g. a painting of a woman lovingly cherishing a baby she holds.

But even this is hardly the first step in appreciating the painting as a work of art. Now one needs some background information, about what the intentions and values were which went into the construction of that type of painting. Knowing that the painter was concerned with matters of representational technique, with telling a story, with conveying a sense of gracefulness, power and realism, with communicating emotions, will enable one to look at the picture in the light of such aims and criteria of success. Then, when one has learned how to look, what sorts of things to look for, one has to try to achieve an individual response to the painting by informed, intensive and dispassionate looking.

Naturally, the experience achieved by the observer will be unique; and it is one of the important things about aesthetic experience that it offers unique and unrepeatable moments of apprehension of sheer individuality. Yet this is not at all to say that such experience is quite subjective, that it reveals nothing about the object of attention. For there are things in the painting which can judge the observer and test his powers of appreciation. It seems idle to say that this must be some quality of beauty, possessed by all good paintings. The aims, methods and achievements of artists are much too diverse for that. But there is a particular way of apprehending things, which can be taught, and which will reveal what can be found in paintings, from various different perspectives. Aesthetic taste can develop and one can learn to extend it in new directions and cultivate appreciation of very different styles.

One will probably not want to say that something else exists in the painting, in addition to its observable properties. Yet one would be quite unable to appreciate it as a painting without the cultivation of an appropriate way of looking at it, in the light of certain stylistic aims and canons, which must be conveyed in the specialised language of art-criticism. And it is certainly true that the contemplation of good works of art, aided by the terminology of art-criticism, but transcending it in the contemplative experience itself, can bring the observer to a new understanding of human existence, its possibilities and its wider context. Art at its best has a revelatory function; but what is revealed cannot be adequately translated into descriptive prose. The answer to the question, 'What does it reveal?' is simply to point back to the painting itself. One can provide formal analyses of it, or let one's imagination embroider a story around it; but in the ultimate analysis, one must contemplate it for what it is, a visual array which has the power of communicating to the mind some meaning which is not otherwise expressible.

There are three points I would regard as important here. First, this communication is only given to one who has assiduously and sympathetically cultivated his aesthetic taste, and who is prepared to make a creative effort himself to understand what the painting presents. Second, the communication cannot be commanded; sometimes it will be apparent and sometimes not; it can dawn and fade again. But when it exists, it is as though we apprehend in and through the empirical properties some meaning beyond themselves —the painting can extend one's experience to include new subtleties and perspectives, and it can present images which are elusive, developing, ambiguous, multi-faceted, appealing directly to non-intellectual, non-analytical understanding. The painting may not reveal an additional, non-natural property of beauty; but it does communicate a new understanding, when the empirical properties are seen in an appropriate way. Third, this understanding is untranslatable; all that verbalising about it can do is either to prepare the mind to achieve appreciation by analysis of the form and structure—which in itself, as every art student knows, deprives art of all its power and appeal—or try to express the same sort of understanding in words, by painting a mood picture in words for example—which, in itself, if it is successful, simply creates a new literary art-work. Each work of art communicates what only it can express; and if one speaks of the spirit of the age, or the symbolization of emotion, one is just trying to express some aspect of the new understanding of man and his total environment which art has conveyed in its own terms.

It may be that this manner of regarding art is itself foreign to many people. Apart from those who lack any appreciation of art at all, there are many who would interpret their aesthetic experience in a different way, even though I have tried to keep what I said at a basic level, without importing large-scale theories of aesthetics. Thus one has the uncomfortable position that two groups of people may agree on what art is, even on which paintings are good; but their whole appreciation and interpretation of paintings may differ fairly fundamentally. This re-emphasizes the extent to which the apprehension of aesthetic objects is a very sophisticated interpretative process, which exemplifies different fundamental types of human response. All I have wanted to do is to show how art can be and is taken as a communicative sign; and I would add that there is no more fundamental way of deciding whether or not this is a rational procedure; one can only say that is how it seems, when one concentrates on and analyses one's experience as carefully and dispassionately as possible.

But one cannot analyse one's experience apart from the language one has for doing so; this language fixes the limits of one's fundamental cognitive frame. As Peter Winch has put it, 'Our idea of what belongs to the realm of reality is given for us in the language that we use . . . the world *is* for us what is presented through those concepts'.[1] Language enters into our understanding of reality in a constitutive way, so that the context in which language is used is not accurately specifiable outside the language itself; the context is defined, at least in part, by the framework of the language. So the contexts in which central concepts are used will only be accurately describable in terms of conceptual schemes themselves, and what the context is cannot be conveyed in a different language.

One may not be able to describe the context without a grasp of the conceptual structure which helps to specify it; so one cannot

[1] Winch, P. *The Idea of a Social Science* (Routledge, Kegan Paul, 1958), p. 15.

even say what the rules of the language are, or understand the concepts in question, without to some extent participating in the language oneself. This does not mean that there can be no true, objective view of the nature of reality. But it does mean that truth in this sphere is available only by the adoption of appropriate forms of language; and there is no neutral way of deciding which forms of language are truly appropriate for interpreting reality. The concepts one has will set the context in which the agent sees the possibilities of his life, of the actions and evaluations which are open to him. So it is that certain ways of apprehending the world and reacting to it depend upon the possession of certain sets of concepts, which express and make possible that form of action and apprehension, but which cannot be rationally justified or disconfirmed by any considerations external to the conceptual framework itself. The understanding of artistic experience as communicating some greater, but untranslatable, significance is one such form of apprehension, which depends upon and is expressed in a specific set of concepts, which could be used for describing works of art. In this respect, art can serve as an analogy for understanding religion, in helping to show what it is to take some empirical phenomenon as a medium of revelation which communicates a new, untranslatable understanding of reality.

.2

Another analogy for the way in which religion regards events or things as revelatory may be taken from the realm of personal relations. Though persons are undoubtedly material objects in the space-time complex, one comes to regard them as persons only when one comes to see them as imposing claims upon one. This may not be a question of positing or inferring a hidden mind behind the scenes; but it is a matter of reacting to particular physical objects in a very special way. The concepts of 'love', 'concern' and 'sympathy' define the language of personal relations; and to give them application one needs to interpret bodily gestures as signs of fulfilment or need, pleasure or grief.

Whatever such interpretations involve, they are often extremely ambiguous and difficult to judge; one can often react inappropriately though misunderstanding, misinterpretation, lack of concern or bad judgement of what response is required. As with the case of the arts, there is a consensus of opinion on what, in general, appropriate attitudes to other persons are; and in the case of personal relations, this consensus is much less culture-relative, though it still does vary enormously in particular expressions of concern or sympathy. But the attainment of such a consensus is not a detached, analytical affair; it requires involvement with others, extensive experience of them, and the development of a 'feel' or judgement which proceeds, not by analysis, but on the basis of a generally formed impression of the whole person.

The sorts of communication other people are able to make to one depends very largely on one's own character, and on what one is able to bring out of them. Moments of communication, of real understanding between people, are relatively rare and brief; and they often come when least expected, although certain sorts of loving response predispose one to be ready to accept them when they come. What is communicated is, again, not really expressible verbally; it is a new sort of understanding, which can alter one's whole attitude to life, by which one seems to know more about what underlies and motivates human action, and yet does so by means of an enrichment of sympathetic feeling rather than by a neutral registering of new cognitive data. One might say that one has suddenly come to understand another person; then, the behaviour of these spatio-temporal bits will have become a revelatory sign which carries one's knowledge and extends one's feeling to that which is disclosed in, but is not altogether distinct from such behaviour.

Yet if one asks what the body one is confronted with and to which one applies these concepts, is made of, there is a temptation to answer, material bits. The philosophical tempter here is the inheritance of classical empiricism, that all knowledge comes through the senses, and so must be of spatio-temporal objects or what can be inferred from them. So, when one asks, 'What exists here?', one begins to add up the spatio-temporal bits. The way to obtain release from this mesmerising model is to stop thinking of objects as made up of smaller spatial bits, and to take them for what they are—holistic features of the world towards which many various cognitive, affective and dispositional attitudes can be taken. Descriptions of the physical properties of objects are really descriptions of certain capacities possessed by objects, the inner

nature of which is unknown—capacities to evoke certain dis-
criminative responses in conscious percipients.

One can see this in the way the experimental sciences ignore
most of the properties which are obvious to common-sense, such
as colour, smell and texture, and concern themselves only with the
quantifiable properties of mass, position and velocity. Even such
properties have disintegrated in the hands of modern physicists
into mathematical wave-functions, eigen-values and fundamental
patterns of energy-transformation which would have completely
bewildered Galileo, with his safe, stable, solid set of primary
properties—which, he thought, no material existent could be conceived to lack.[2] The world of common-sense, of enduring three-
dimensional solid objects, is founded, not upon hard basic atoms,
but upon incredibly complex but mathematically formulable
patterns of energy. And this raises the question of whether the
common-sense world is itself not much more mysterious and
potentially revelatory than it seems, when treated as a collection
of material substances with specific properties.

Of course, we do move in a spatio-temporal world of objects,
in common with all other humans. But there is an ancient and
almost universal religious tradition that this world is somehow
'maya'—illusion or appearance. That is not to deny that it exists
at all; but it is to say that, if accepted at face-value, the world
conceals the true nature of reality, its inner meaning and purpose.
To get back to this meaning one needs to overcome the barriers
of ordinary language and achieve a more direct sort of communion with reality; and yet the way to such communion must be
taken through language. Though one may have transcended it, a
particular set of concepts will always trace the way by which one
achieved transcendence, and remain normative for one's own
experience and those of one's own community of faith.

There really are primary and secondary qualities of objects, in
the sense that, by taking up a certain line of investigation one can
bring them to light. But it would be wrong to think that these are
the only possible sorts of approach to objects, the only means
of discovering what there really is. In fact, a true understanding of
science will see it as a creative process of illumination, discovery
and conceptual innovation. There are revelatory experiences in

[2] Cf. Galileo, 'The Assayer', in *The Discoveries and Opinions of Galileo*,
ed. G. Stilman Drake (Anchor, 1957), pp. 273–9.

the creative sciences, too, as one seems to discern, by a sudden
leap of thought, a particular pattern in things or a mathematical
model which relates data in new and illuminating ways. Like the
arts, the sciences have their own distinctive concepts and methods,
and work largely by creative insights into the structure of reality,
rather than by laborious summaries of collections of empirical
data. It is far from being the case that science simply presents lists
of collected information. It is itself a particular sort of creative
exploration of reality—not the only sort. It deals with relationships, and is thus best expressed mathematically. In this sense,
science explores various sorts of intelligible relations in the universe, selecting various sets of constants, methodologies and
experimental 'interferences'. It is a quest for the intelligible
necessities in things, presupposing the affinity of the mind's
mathematising activity with various overlapping substructures of
reality. The central notions of relativity and complementarity in
modern physics make clear that the scientist is part of the reality
he explores, and his frames of reference are never total or absolute,
exhaustively determined or known with certainty. In the present
state of the basic experimental sciences, classical materialism is
dead.[3]

3

The classical materialist view rests on the assertion that the only
fundamental properties of reality are mass, position and velocity.
Reality consists of small particles possessing these properties and
forming an interacting system, within which, given the initial
state and some basic laws of interaction, everything is exactly
predictable. The position is well summarised in LaPlace's claim
that, if he knew the first state of the universe, he would be able to
predict every subsequent state with certainty, at least in principle.[1]
This assertion seems to gain plausibility from the vastly successful
advance of the experimental sciences, which has brought an un-
precedented degree of control over the environment. But it must

[3] Cf. Barbour, I. G. *Issues in Science and Religion* (S.C.M. 1966), ch.
10.
[4] LaPlace, P. S. *A Philosophical Essay on Probabilities*, trans. Truscott,
F. W. and Emory, F. L. (Dover, 1961); cf. p. 4.

be remembered that such advance has been won by a method of abstraction and generalisation. Scientists are not concerned with the unique qualities of the particular, but only with those aspects of it which can be brought under general laws. These aspects, not surprisingly, turn out to be such quantifiable properties as mass, position and velocity. But the fact that there are exactly quantifiable properties which do fall under generally formulable laws does not at all preclude the possibility that there are also non-quantifiable properties of existent things and events which cannot be brought under general laws. And if there are such properties and events, they would not fall under the province of experimental science, or into the classical materialist system.

In fact, nothing is more obvious than that there are properties and events not falling into that system. To begin with, there are properties of smell, touch, taste, colour and sound which certainly seem to exist, but are completely ignored by materialists. Various philosophers have tried to overcome this difficulty by calling these 'secondary properties', and putting them in the mind.[5] But even if in the mind (wherever that is), they still do exist in some sense, and so are characteristics of reality.

The materialist may now adopt the thesis of epiphenomenalism, that even if such properties do exist, they play no causal role in the course of events, and so are irrelevant to the causal explanation of nature. Such a theory would be very difficult to test; to establish it one would have to show that in two identical situations, events in the physical realm would be identical even though a range of mental properties was absent in one and present in the other. Or one would have to show that a persons' reactions were exactly predictable in physical terms alone. The view seems contrary to common-sense; for we say that a person goes to pick a rose *because* he sees it, its shape and colours. Here we refer to a psychic occurrence—his sight of the rose—as a causal factor in his behaviour; but epiphenomenalism discounts such causal factors, and would have to claim that what caused the person's action was simply movements of particles in the brain, of which his seeing was a useless by-product.

Epiphenomenalism places a limit on materialism; for it entails that the scientist cannot predict everything—he cannot predict

[5] E.g. Locke, J. *An Essay Concerning Human Understanding*, ed. A. S. Pringle-Pattison (O.U.P., 1924), Bk. 2, ch. 8. 10; p. 67.

what secondary properties will be produced by particular states of matter, since such properties do not enter into his calculations. He can predict only how the elementary particles will have re-combined after a certain period of time. In addition to the secondary properties, he must ignore the whole realm of living human experience, of love and grief, joy and passion, beauty and obligation. The materialist is now limited to saying that such things as consciousness of beauty may exist; and, indeed, beauty may even exist as an objective property of the world, for all he knows. He can say only that there does exist a system in which everything is predictable, and which is a closed causal system—i.e. it is not interfered with by factors outside itself—not even by his own experimenting mind! There is still some bite to his theory, however. For though he is not entitled to say, 'Nothing but matter exists', he can still say that nothing else that exists can ever act in such a way as to interfere with matter, which is, after all, a fundamental part of the world and human life.

But it is a mistake to suppose that there is just one sort of explanation in science. In physics, biology, psychology and sociology there are different forms of explanation which are complementary to each other, and which select certain features of complex phenomena, abstract them from their contexts and treat them in isolation. Although it has been claimed that all explanations could ultimately be reduced to one unified language of science, usually construed as the language of micro-physics, no such programme has been successfully worked out.[6] Each science—and the number of sciences increases from year to year at an increasing rate—attempts to formulate and explore a particular system of relations between phenomena; and all such systems are complementary and irreducible to each other. So different sorts of explanation are attempting to explain different abstracted aspects of the same total phenomenon.

Explanations work by subsuming particular occurrences under general regular laws; so they necessarily omit any consideration of the individual as such, in its uniqueness. The sheer individuality of a personal human experience is arguably the most important

---

[6] The claim is made in Ayer, *Language, Truth and Logic* (Gollancz, 1970), p. 151; and qualified in Ayer, *Metaphysics and Common Sense* (Macmillan, 1969), p. 86: 'It remains an open, scientific question, whether this reduction can be achieved.'

thing about it; and yet such individuality lies beyond any possibility of explanation in terms of regularities or general laws. Different sorts of regularity can be picked out and put in the form of laws—from movements of electrons to explanation of human acts in terms of general motive-patterns. Which regularities we pick out depends on our interests and concerns and experimental techniques, on what aspects of phenomena we are interested in. But picking on any regularity and formulating it in a law represents only part of a total phenomenon, and abstracts to a level of generality which necessarily misses much of the detailed complexity and concreteness of reality out. Moreover, such scientifically formulated laws work, or give rise to accurate predictions, only for closed causal systems—that is, systems all the parameters of which can be known and controlled, so that no unforeseen outside interferences are allowed to occur. That is why it is so important to construct laboratories in such a way that all the relevant factors can be precisely specified. In the complexity of human life, as any engineer will agree, this can never be done completely or with accuracy; so that very definite limits must be set to the ability of scientific explanations to represent adequately all aspects of concrete human experience.

For such a view of what scientific explanation is, the different levels of explanation are irreducible and complementary; none gives a complete account of phenomena; and all of them together still fail to cover the important features of individual concreteness and radical newness of actual lived experience, in human affairs. The view of the world which the progress of the sciences thus seems to suggest is very different from the mechanistic view of atomic particles obeying unchangeable laws, propagated by Newton. It appears reasonable to say that complexification of simple atomistically conceivable particulars actually produces emergent, holistic properties (what Hegel termed the transformation of quantity into quality). One might have a multi-level interactionism, with the genesis of new qualities through complexification, and their causal influence on the whole set of simpler structures of which they are built up. When the simpler parts were thinly spread out over the universe, as with interstellar gasses, they might exhibit only very simple ranges of properties and obey rather regular mechanistic laws of interaction. But as they complexify, the nature and number of emergent properties may

T.C.G.—D

increase and the laws of interaction become very much more complex and in detail unpredictable.[7] Very small statistical irregularities on the simple levels might combine to produce significant divergencies from prediction on a larger scale; and this picture seems to correspond rather closely to the situation as it exists in, say, physics as compared with sociology at the present time.

Man will have a place in this hierarchy of creative complexification, as a higher-level potentialising agent, with many lower-level systems of impulses and aims. In the process of choosing his future, he actualises some of these systems at the expense of others. And one may distinguish, in a general way, between a submergence, in which the agent is taken over by lower systems, closes himself and is trapped in limiting acts; and a creative opening out, in which lower systems are directed to higher, creative ends, and may be guided by values which the effort itself reveals ever more fully, but which are never exhaustively realised. Human freedom has an important place in this view of the world; and the old mechanistic materialism seems to have just dropped out of the picture.

Developments in quantum mechanics and field-theory make it even more fully apparent that one cannot any longer regard the physical world as being composed of fundamental, indivisible atoms of specifiable mass which obey a few general laws of motion and mechanics. Beneath the level of the atom, there have been discovered to be a bewildering number of elementary particles; not just electrons and protons, but neutrons, neutrinos, alpha particles and even quarks, a whole host of bundles of energy coming into existence and disappearing again ceaselessly. The nature and properties of these particles are so amazing as to be virtually impossible. For they do not possess the primary properties which Galileo thought to be inseparable from all matter, of size, shape, position, mass and velocity. Instead, they possess energy, angular momentum and orientation spin, which can be signified by a quantum number. Electrons themselves must be thought of both as particles and as vibratory waves which are quantized and can be described by Schrodinger wave-functions. In fact, in quantum physics, separate particles appear as temporary and partial manifestations of a shifting wave-pattern that combine,

[7] Teilhard de Chardin, P. *The Phenomenon of Man* (Collins, 1959).

dissolve and recombine at various points; and particles appear to be local outcroppings of a continuous substratum of vibratory energy. The term 'electron' is used in connexion with spinor-fields defined by linear wave-equations containing directional operators.

This is a complex technical matter, but what it means is that elementary particles can no longer be considered as specifically locatable enduring bits of solid matter. Instead, one must talk of fields of energy and sequences of vibratory patterns, which some-times act as if they were particles and sometimes act as though they were waves of energy.[8] One can express this by saying that the properties of an elementary particle system that is observed are a consequence of the character of the measurement that is performed.[9] What we call elementary particles manifest them-selves in different ways, according to what experiment is taking place. But the reality behind all our models is quite unimaginable. We can only understand it by using mathematical techniques which do not literally correspond to any model.

Modern quantum physics, then, seems to assert that there are no elementary particles, in the Newtonian sense of primary bits of matter moving according to mechanical principles. There are complex sets of wave-patterns and fields, which can be mathe-matically understood, but need to be pictured in complementary ways, sometimes as particles, sometimes as waves. In other words, when one gets down to the level of basic sub-atomic states, the mechanistic materialist view simply evaporates, and one finds oneself dealing with largely uninterpretable mathematical systems, which apply to a reality one is unable to imagine.

Moreover, the Newtonian ideal of exact predictability also seems impossible for the new physics. By Heisenberg's Principle of Indeterminacy, it is in principle impossible to predict both the position and velocity of a fundamental 'particle' at the same time.[10] All one can predict, given any physical system, is the probability of an electron being at a certain location. The future becomes indeterminate, in that exact prediction of all features of microcosmic phenomena becomes impossible. So it might be said

---

[8] Barbour, *op. cit.*, p. 279 ff.

[9] Cf. Heisenberg, W. *Physics and Philosophy* (Harper, 1958), p. 54.

[10] Cf. Williams, I. R. and M. W. *Basic Nuclear Physics* (Newnes, 1962), p. 13 ff.

that quantum physics radically undermines the old dogmas that there are fundamental material particles and that their movements can be exactly predicted in principle. Instead, one must speak of complex mathematically orderable fields of energy and indeterminate temporal processes at the microcosmic level. Physics can no longer claim to be the one basic level of explanation; for it is itself riddled with complexities and mysteries which make the old mechanistic atomistic view seem superficial. Thus while Newtonian mechanics remains an abstract model of great explanatory power for inorganic masses, it no longer poses an implicit threat to claims to apprehend revelatory aspects of reality, by seeming to erect a closed causal network which defines the true nature of reality exhaustively in mechanistic and materialist terms.

Indeed, the very reverse is now the case; for contemporary physics, however uncertain and provisional its findings, leads one to see the world as a vastly mysterious but somehow intelligible reality which underlies the world of common-sense, and which reveals itself to the mind in many different ways, according to the sort of approach one makes to it. It is quite consonant with this view to hold that in art and interpersonal relations one is able to approach reality in a distinctive and inexponible way, in such a way that reality is able, at least sometimes, to disclose a significance and meaning which is both in and beyond what one apprehends. And, in such moments of apprehension, something real and significant about the nature of being is disclosed; though it cannot be expressed in terms from a different system of discourse, based on different methods of approach to the world.

4

The religious believer should, I think, say that the concepts which are distinctive of religion, and which, for a theist, are grouped around the concept of God, express a distinctive method of approach to reality, which can be cultivated or ignored by the individual. And they can, used properly, provide a unique means of releasing the imagination to see situations in a new and deeper light. Religion provides a way of communication with the inner realities of what is encountered in experience. And two important things must not be forgotten here: first, that this communication can be achieved only by an active and creative use of the imagination; and second, that experienced reality is wider than empirical, or purely sensory experience. Such communication will usually occur only to one who is prepared to take what he experiences as an apprehension of the sacred, and who has tried to understand and appreciate the symbols of his own religious tradition—a tradition which preserves some paradigmatic revelation for one community, and which enables the imagination to be focused on a specific set of concepts or images, and use these as models for the creative contemplation of experience. The revelatory apprehension, if and when it occurs, will do so unpredictably, and in any situation; and though it gives a new understanding of and insight into reality, it is not translatable into non-religious concepts.

One of the things which distinguishes religion is that its object is not the empirical properties of the world (as with the sciences); not artefacts to be contemplated (as with the arts); and not other persons (as with morality); but it may be any situation or object in such a situation, which can become an unveiling of the reality which underlies it. There is no particular empirical religious object; the object of religion may be apprehended in any empirical context or mental state, when that situation is able to be taken as a revelation of spiritual (non-spatial) reality, which will be the meaning disclosed in its context, rather than simply an additional entity of the same sort. The revelatory experiences of religion thus embrace, and are wider in scope than, those of art, science and personal relations.

The intelligibility of religion stands or falls with the belief that there are some aspects of reality which are not experimentally testable or scientifically quantifiable, yet are nonetheless real. It is these aspects of which religion speaks, the transcendent aspects which particular things, events or experiences may come to signify. It can be misleading to ask whether the transcendent exists—an expression which can lead one to think of it as one entity commensurate with and in addition to others. But it is equally misleading to say that it does not exist—which suggests that there is simply nothing to be considered, nothing such talk is about. Perhaps the least misleading thing to say is that religious language refers to the reality one comes to know and react to, and in which one participates (since one is oneself real); but it refers to it in a distinctive way which must be accepted on its own terms. And one must not think of this as meaning that the religious aspects of reality are distinct, epiphenomenal properties of the spatio-temporal objects which constitute the material world; that they just comprise a special way of seeing that same world, a distinct perspective upon it.[11] For that would be implicitly to accept the dominance of the material model.

The way in which religious language articulates reality enables one to take some experiences as apprehensions of a meaning and value beyond themselves; a meaning which is not encompassed by empirical investigation, which is untranslatable and inexponable. It is, one might say, not a certain aspect of the world which is seen; but it is the world of experience seen in the light of a significance which lies beyond and is communicated through it. If one insists on asking how one can take the immediately apprehended as signifying something beyond itself, one must simply reiterate that the transcendence of the real is posited from the first, in all human knowledge. What the religious believer needs to emphasize is the manifoldness of approaches to this real, reflected in the different conceptual schemes for understanding it. And he will insist that religious forms of language preserve and make possible a form of approach which is able to make manifest the most comprehensive and deeply significant aspects of reality, which are communicable through a wide range of both external and personal experiences, which are elicited by the creative activity of the religious imagination, and which are preserved within a historical community of believers in the form of conceptual images which have the power to re-evoke something of the original generative insight.

Religion at its best stands opposed to the erection of any closed conceptual system, which claims to encapsulate the whole nature of reality exhaustively. It offers the continual discovery of new depths to and facets of reality, in a continuing creative dialogue with those values and challenges which are revealed in one's historical experience. Images of transcendence, which for the Christian are grouped around the notion of God, exist to make such an essentially open cognitive attitude to reality possible.

In this chapter I have tried to make clearer what is meant by

[11] Cf. the view taken by Miles, T. R. in *Religion and the Scientific Outlook* (Allen and Unwin, 1959).

finding communications or revelations of transcendent reality in the world, by taking analogies from art, personal relations and scientific exploration. And I have argued that materialism, which denies the possibility of such revelations, is an inadequate account of present scientific procedure, as well as being unsatisfying on other grounds. Thus I have held that religion stands as an autonomous activity, making cognitive claims which are *sui generis*, untranslatable and not justifiable in other terms, which can make a reasonable claim to be the fulfilment of that creative activity of discernment which is one of man's most distinctive capacities.

CHAPTER SIX

THE NON-DUALITY OF GOD

I

Belief in God is closely bound up with the perception of transcendence, as the meaning or value which lies within events or situations. Particular conceptions of it will depend upon paradigm experiences of communication, and there will be no one universal object of communication or way of relation to it. As one looks at the very various conditions of human life and history, one will find that different human groups tend to centre their religious traditions on particular sacred objects, which are thought to possess the power which they have communicated; or sacred times, commemorating historical or seasonal events of special significance to the group. Alongside such sacred occurrences there will spring up interpreters of the sacred, prophets or priests, who can discern signs and communicate them to others. And the group will form a sacred community, or church, in which the traditions are cherished and preserved.

It may thus seem that a primitive animism or polytheism is the most natural beginning of religious belief; for which the gods or spirits are poetic symbolizations of particular signs, interpreted and preserved by prophets and wise men. Such gods will come to have their own rites for effecting the desired relation between believer and the signified transcendent. But if one asks whether there really are many gods, or exactly how many gods there are, it is at once evident that there is something peculiar even in asking the question. For the question whether one knows one, or a few, or an indefinitely large number of significant realities through various experiences of the world, lacks the sort of context which could make it an answerable question.

If one wishes to enumerate things, one must enumerate things of a certain type—elements, pears, people or cars. If one says there are four things in the room, this assertion is vacuous unless one can say what sort of things one has in mind—atoms, electrons, chairs, or right-angles. So, if one asks how many significant realities there are, one must specify what sort of realities one has in mind, and how they are to be identified. But this is not possible; for human beings can only identify things by referring them to some spatio-temporal context. This is no help, when the apprehension of transcendence may come in any spatio-temporal context and is not necessarily tied to any specific context. Not only are we unable to tell whether we apprehend one or many transcendent realities; the important point is that the question does not even make sense; for where apprehensions of the transcendent are not tied to any one type of thing or sort of context, it follows that the transcendent is not denumerable; it is not logically possible to count its instances.

It certainly seems to be the case that the category of number is not applicable to God, in virtue of the fact that he is not a spatially locatable type of thing, and he is not identifiable by his constant relation to some spatially locatable type of thing or occurrence.[1] Yet the Christian does not hesitate to say that there is one God, and to speak of him, his acts, or his nature, all of which terms imply that God is singular. There are, of course, many distinct instances of apprehension of God; but only one God who is apprehended. This assertion must be taken, first, in the negative sense of excluding the proposition that one apprehends many identifiable and distinguishable gods; and second, in the positive, but non-descriptive sense of affirming that all apprehensions of significant reality can be integrated around one central concept, which can give such apprehensions a specific form, arising out of their integrated relation to each other. One must recognise the intricate logic of the language which underlies both monotheism and polytheism. It is not a question of how many supernatural beings there are, though it has sometimes been misleadingly phrased in that way. It is a question of how one is going to interpret the experiences of spiritual realities which can come to men, and attempt to make them coherent with the general range of one's knowledge.

[1] Aquinas, T. *Summa Theologiae*, Pt. 1, Qu. 2, Art. 3.: 'The unity with which number begins is not attributed to God'. But Aquinas goes on to say that we attribute to God 'the unity convertible with existence', though even this is only a way of understanding suited to our intellect, and implies no lack (e.g. of multiplicity?) in God.

This is brought out very well in Evans-Pritchard's 'Nuer Religion', where he takes an African tribe which has an apparent riot of spirits, demons and paranormal phenomena, and convincingly establishes a certain spiritual hierarchy of concepts, grouped around the central concept of Kwoth, the High Spirit.[2] In addition to Kwoth, the creator-ancestor, who is distant and unapproachable, though he can be a presence and friend, there are the spirits of the air, which can possess men in sickness, and to which libations and sacrifices are offered; the spirits of below, which are specially associated with species of animal; and, at the lowest level, nature-sprites and fetishes, which can be owned by wizards and used as talismans. In this hierarchy of spirits, cultic practices increase, the lower spirits are; and at the lowest level, spirits become differentiated into innumerable and often transitory individuals. The Nuer themselves distinguish Kwoth in terms of grammatical distinctions, by their relations of descent or by their association with particular prophets, totem-animals or fetishes. But as Evans-Pritchard points out, the Nuer would not make sense of the question whether the lesser spirits were the same as or different from the 'spirit in the sky', Kwoth. He suggests that they are best viewed as aspects of Kwoth, and points out that 'the concept of Spirit is refracted by the social structure', so that Kwoth 'is broken up along the lines of segmentation within the social structure'.[3] Yet the concept of Kwoth is not, as Durkheim suggested, reducible to the social order or 'collective soul'; 'Spirit is an intuitive apprehension, something experienced in response to certain situations but known directly only to the imagination'.[4] Religious conceptions, he concludes, are imaginative constructions which use objects and events to signify spiritual experiences. So, even in a radical polytheism, which has seemed to many Western observers to be a superstitious religion of fear, a sympathetic observer can discern elements of structure in the manifold imaginative constructions of the religion, which are grouped around the central concept of Kwoth, the creator/ancestor.

I am not suggesting, by any means, that all polytheistic systems are disguised monotheistic faiths. What I am suggesting is that the essential difference between polytheism and monotheism lies in the kind and degree of integration which can be achieved among

[2] Evans-Pritchard, *Nuer Religion* (O.U.P., 1956).
[3] *Ibid.*, p. 87.   [4] *Ibid.*, p. 321.

the disparity of images which come to be valued within a particular tradition as signs of transcendence. The monotheistic scheme of Judeo-Christianity is distinguished from many religious systems by the fact that it unifies its images of transcendence around the central notion of an absolute moral demand and enabling power; the claim is that all the various images of transcendence can be developed most fully and adequately when they are shaped by reference to the central concept of an absolute moral value and purpose.

2

The choice of the focal or controlling image is what chiefly distinguishes religions, at the most basic level; polytheistic systems exemplify either a very weak dominance of the focal image (as when the High God becomes remote and rather abstract, like Zeus in the Greek pantheon) or the complete lack of a focal image. Such complete polytheisms seem to be rather rare, in fact—perhaps because the human mind is not often satisfied with unrelated segments of knowledge and seeks to unify its images wherever possible. The search for unity and generality is one of the main sources of the scientific enterprise, and it is also characteristic of religion. Thus the religious believer seeks to unify the various attitudes which his encounters with the transcendent has called forth by relating them to one all-inclusive intentional object, which can then be said to present various aspects to men in specific situations. The essential characteristics of this object give a particular form to all images of transcendence; which, in the Christian scheme, is signified by calling them all signs of God.

One historical development of monotheism that can be traced is the rise of Judaic monotheism, in which a tribal God was construed as related to the people of Israel through the model of a covenant, a sort of primitive moral contract.[5] However primitive it was at first, the distinctive moralism of Judaism is present from the first call to Abram to leave the country of his birth, and culminates in the post-Exilic elaboration of the Torah, said to have been given to Moses in the Wilderness. This god, the moral law-giver and warrior-liberator, imposes a total moral demand on

[5] Cf. Exodus 34, 10–28.

the people, and marks them out as a chosen people, to keep his law and trust his will. Thus God is given a personalistic interpretation, as one who calls, demands, lays down the law and enforces obedience on pain of punishment and judgement. It was perhaps because of this emphasis on moral demand and obedience to the Torah that polytheism was so strongly abhorred by the Jews. Other gods would allow different ways of life and patterns of obedience; whereas the unity of the holy people demanded one law-giver and judge of all. As the demands of morality were seen to be incumbent upon all men, so Judaism became universalised, and the Jews thought of themselves as priests on behalf of humanity, and their god of the covenant as the one moral law-giver and judge of all men.[6]

Another pattern of development towards monotheism can be found in the development of the Vedantic schools in Hinduism. Hinduism remains a radically polytheistic religion; and morality is not conceived as a set of laws given by a law-giver and enforced by a judge, but as an impersonal order (karma) in the universe. But in the Upanishads the notion of Brahman is developed, as the unitary source of all reality, with which the true human self (atman) is identical.[7] This development may possibly be accounted for by the syncretistic and omnitolerant attitude of Hinduism. One can achieve monotheism by rigidly excluding every god but one from consideration; but one can also achieve it by indiscriminately accepting every god and attempting to follow every exemplary pattern of worship or spiritual technique. For it is then almost inevitable to take each particular god as simply an appearance of some further uncommunicated reality and to hold the chaos of appearances together by relating them to a unitary source, Brahman or the Absolute. The illusory character of the gods is also supported by the view that the world is a realm of suffering, illusion and death, which offers nothing positive towards human fulfilment, and is thus to be ultimately transcended. Thus one must deny all particularities ultimate reality, and this leads to a unitive conception of spiritual reality, deriving from yoga, a system of practical techniques for cultivating spiritual wisdom or insight, which reveals the transitoriness of the world and the

---

[6] Cf. Isaiah 49, 6.

[7] Hume, R. E. *The Thirteen Principal Upanishads* (O.U.P., 1931), 'Chandogya', 3. 14.

union of the inner self with that which lies beyond appearances. Though this Brahman is not, strictly speaking, one any more than it is many,[8] it is monotheistic rather than polytheistic in that multiplicity is denied of ultimate reality, and it is unlimited by anything that could make it one individual amongst others.

In this sense, of course, it is very like medieval Christian doctrines of God. It is also, to that extent, like the Buddhist notion of Nirvana which, though it means 'non-being', is spoken of in Buddhist scriptures as the final refuge, absolute bliss and supreme happiness.[9] The concept becomes explicitly monotheistic when it is combined with bhakti, the cultivation of devotion and adoration (to Vishnu or the glorified Buddha, in Mahayana Buddhism), and the absolute beyond appearances takes on a personal aspect to the believer. Here again, polytheism is ruled out because of the denial of limitation and consequently of individuality in God.

3

It is difficult, but essential, to grasp that the question, 'Is this sign a revelation of the same reality as that sign or of a different reality?' simply has no answer. One cannot say that it is the same or that it is different. Strictly speaking, both mono- and poly-theism are misleading, if that formulation leads one to suppose that gods can be individuated and quantified. How can one choose, then, between the two? The sources for answering this question lie in the differing traditions of various sacred communities, with their own rites and scriptures. It is here, and especially in the exemplary patterns of redemption which they perpetuate (e.g. the Torah, Shi'a, Mass or scriptural practice) that one will need to accept or reject various understandings of the relation of God (transcendent reality) to the world, and of human fulfilment by relation to God/ the gods. The question is answered, in other words, not by discerning numerical, as opposed to qualitative, identity among divine signs; but by evaluating differing traditions of revelatory

---

[8] Thus Sankara's Vedantic philosophy is termed non-dualism, rather than monism. Cf. Smart, N. *Doctrine and Argument in Indian Philosophy* (Allen and Unwin, 1964), ch. 7.

[9] Cf. *The Sutra of Wei Lang (Hui Neng)*, trans. Wong Mou-lam, (Luzac, 1944), pp. 80-2.

apprehension of and exemplary action and attitude towards the transcendent.

To see how one comes to interpret the sacred in terms of the concept of one God, one must study the religious life and development of the Judeo-Christian community, and the images it developed for controlling its relationship with the sacred.

There are two basic features of the Judeo-Christian concept of God which form the foundation for all the other doctrines of God's nature. They are, that God is one and transcendent. I have already held that the notion of a transcendent reality is a logically possible one; the main problem was whether it was ever meaningful to assert the existence of such a reality; and I suggested analogies from various areas of human experience which may persuade one that it is reasonable to do so.

It is clear that one cannot just say that God is wholly transcendent, meaning that he is totally and in every respect beyond the physical universe; for then one would have no way of knowing his existence. One must begin from some experienced features of the world, and assert that, in them, one has knowledge of a reality which is also transcendent in its being. This is closely bound up with the question of the unity or non-duality of God; for it is partly because God transcends every spatio-temporal manifestation of his being that he is said to be one. And it is partly because the sacred is felt to be unitary that it is said to transcend its particular manifestations.

God cannot be said to be one in the ordinary sense, that he is one among (possible) others; that he is a distinguishable individual, of which there could be two or more. When one asks whether the sacred is one or many, one cannot answer this question as one would with a spatio-temporal individual. Normally, one would say that X is the same as Y if there is some spatio-temporal continuity between X and Y; it is different if such continuity has broken down at some point. But if one asks whether one object of revelatory apprehension is the same as another, spatio-temporal continuity is not in question. What, then, is the criterion of identity?

The motives conducing to monotheism are many, though their strength and relative pressures vary from one religion to another. There may be a political motive, whereby many gods become dominated by one tribal god; and the assertion of its absolute dominance reflects the aspirations to universal dominion of that tribe. There is the intellectual drive towards unity and economy, coupled with the speculative urge to find one complete explanation for the existence of the world. There is a moral motive, by which there comes to be acknowledged one cosmic moral law, and thus one supreme arbiter of morality, over-ruling potential conflicts between gods and even blind Fate itself. And there is a soteriological motive, by which one notion of God becomes paradigmatic for specifying the saving relation of the believer to the transcendent.

In ritual contexts, the power of the sacred is offered to men; and it is natural to suppose that it is the same power in all the different ritual settings; that the power is always there, waiting to be tapped, rather than that a new power is created every time. The reality which is worshipped in one paradigm revelatory situation can be re-enacted in liturgy, and so the believer can make that revelation a present reality in his own life—as when Christians say that Jesus is present in the Eucharist. One cannot say that there is an actual spatio-temporal continuity between Jesus of Nazareth and a contemporary Eucharist. But the believer will not wish to say that the past Jesus and the present Christ are distinct individuals. The very concept of an individual becomes difficult to work with here. But if there is an object which one discerns in one's own committed response, in ritual contexts, one will wish to deny that the objects are quite diverse, on each occasion. That is, one wishes to deny individual diversity; one wishes to say that God is not two or more; rather than that he is positively one. Enumeration becomes an unworkable concept, where there is no distinguishable class of individuals which one can enumerate. So, one really wants to say that the sacred is non-denumerable, beyond number. It is not two or three; and it is not, in any ordinary sense, one either. But one calls it unitary, in order to make connexions between the original paradigm event and its re-enactments in diverse contexts.

Moreover, the aim of the religious life is to extend one's worshipping attitudes over the whole of experience. Here again, is a motive for dissociating the sacred from spatio-temporal limitations, and envisaging it as a unitary reality to which one can respond at all times. A related consideration is the desire to unify one's apprehensions of the sacred in one coherent pattern, so that the meanings and values one discerns should not be just discrete and unrelated moments, but should relate to the rest of reality and to each other in an ordered and rational way. This drive to coherence in one's imagery leads one to unify revelations around some central concept; and the concept of God functions as such a unifying key-concept, around which others can be grouped. By using that one concept for all one's revelatory experiences, one brings them into a coherence and unity which makes it possible to direct one's spiritual life in one single-minded and integrated way.

This consideration is reinforced by the fact that the notions of the many gods of polytheism do not refer to individuals in the proper sense, but symbolize imaginative aspects of reality; so they tend to merge into one another and overlap in nature and function, interchanging names and roles and interweaving in a complex pantheon; and this militates against the preservation of a full assertion of manifoldness in the sacred. For where distinctions cannot be clearly made and maintained, diversities tend to group themselves under more comprehensive hierarchies and unities; and this happens again and again in the history of religions. The discipline of prayer, too, leads to the denial of diversity. Those who advance on the path of prayer find that their worship transcends all particular notions of the gods, and expands to the apprehension of an imageless object, beyond joy and pain, hidden in a 'cloud of un-knowing', which is indescribable—and consequently not describable as two or more. Again, of course, it is not strictly describable as one; but, if we think at all, we are bound to think of God either in the singular or the plural. And in that case it is more helpful to deny plurality than to deny unity; to say that God is not two, that he is non-dual; for that makes the point that the gods are not individuals which can be played off against each other, or which are ultimately irreconcilable aspects of reality.

There do, however, seem to be irreconcilable aspects of the world, particularly in the opposition of good and evil. And there is an element of the religious life which insists on a denial or rejection of 'the world', and a withdrawal from its pleasures.[10] Because the world is felt to contain evil forces—those which cause suffering and pain—the sacred is separated off from the world,

[10] E.g. 1 Jn. 2, 15–17.

and conceived as distinct from it. Again, the demands which the sacred is felt to make upon one are often conceived to be in opposition to the present structures of the world, calling one out of the present towards an unknown future. Because one is claimed or judged, and called to change the world, the sacred is not identified with any part of the world, as immanent in it; it is rather conceived as standing over against nature, pointing to a future which does not yet exist. This is another reason for conceiving it as transcendent.

Within the Judeo-Christian tradition, further reasons for affirming the unity and transcendence of God emerge as the community as a whole meets and responds to new experiences, and incorporates them into its common life. The Old Testament records testify to the gradual evolution of the notion of a Lord of History, who uses Israel as a suffering servant to show his will, out of more primitive notions of a tribal god who protects his own tribe against all others. One can see how this development arose out of the experiences of the Exodus, the Exile and the whole prophetic tradition, coming to new conceptions of the relation of the community of faith with its object, revealing itself in historical circumstances. The unity of God appears in this tradition, not as an abstract philosophical conception, but as the developing insight that there is a unity of purpose and character, a single-mindedness, in the revelatory experiences which come to the prophets and priests of Israel.[11] God thereby comes to be conceived in terms of a personal will, a creative demand, disclosed in history, to which man must respond in action; and the unity of God is the unity of this will, as it meets one in demand.

For the Christian, this conception is fulfilled in the revelation which centred on the person of Jesus; and for the Church, the dramatic portraits of Jesus which are preserved in the Gospels are embodied in ritual practices which re-evoke that fulfilling disclosure of the sacred, as the Judaic concept was at once completed and transformed by the new revelation which occurred around Jesus. For the Christian, God is unitary, uniting all images around that of Jesus as Lord; and God is transcendent, as offering the living Lord to all men everywhere.

[11] For a brief account of the early Jewish idea of God, cf. *The Old Testament Understanding of God*, Chesnut, J. S. (Westminster Press, 1968).

4

To understand the Christian tradition about God adequately, one must know something of its historical roots in Judaism and primitive Near Eastern religion. This is not to suggest that the origins of a religion give its true or essential character, any more than the origins of chemistry in alchemy show the true nature of molecular chemistry. Nevertheless, tradition is very important in religion, for it preserves the records of what were felt to be genuine revelations, whether to inspired individuals or whole groups. To know the earliest tradition is to know how men felt able to interpret their environment and experience as signifying a transcendent meaning and reality; and to trace the development from that tradition is to see how later generations found such an interpretation inadequate or incomplete; until, in most religions, one reaches a paradigmatic point, at which the general interpretative model of significance is held to be essentially complete. Beyond that point, further development, if it remains within the tradition, is an exploration of implications of the model in new situations and in greater detail. A knowledge of how the paradigm model developed, and of how its implications have been explored, can be an invaluable help to seeing more clearly the nature of the model itself and its relevance for one's own life. But of course it is true—and was forgotten or ignored by evolutionary anthropologists like Tylor and Frazer—that one must interpret the earliest traditions in the light of one's own present experience of transcendence, as mediated in the ritual and concepts of present tradition. That is, one must judge them effective to the extent that they presage valuable elements of present practice, and mistaken or 'superstitious' to the extent that they cannot be sincerely reflected in present belief. One's guide to interpretation must always be one's own experience of transcendence, within a particular community; but one's understanding of the nature of this experience itself will be deepened by seeing its development and by setting it in the wider perspective of variant traditions and interpretations.

There has been much discussion among students of religion about the relative priority of polytheism and monotheism. Whereas

Tylor and Frazer propounded the ghost or dream theory[12]—that men first believed in ghosts, because of their dreams of dead persons, and later came to think of these as spirits; then gods; and finally one high god; Andrew Lang and Schmidt tried to show that a belief in one high God exists in most primitive tribes and that polytheism is a degeneration from such belief.[13] Apart from the purely historical question, some orthodox Christians might find a doctrinal reason for supporting Schmidt, in that the Biblical account of 'the fall' suggests a primordial direct knowledge of God, which may since have been lost. Neglecting the question of whether that story should be taken as historical fact, one may perhaps undercut the whole dispute by asking what is meant by calling God one, or by speaking of direct knowledge of God.

On the account I am suggesting, such knowledge would consist in the interpretation of events and experiences and situations as communicative signs, calling for a responsive dispositional attitude. To know God fully (or as fully as possible) would be to be able to take all experience as revelatory in this way; all pain and evil would challenge one to redemptive action; all joy and beauty would disclose new depths of value; and one would grow continually in one's response to such challenges and values. To know God deeply would be to adopt the correct dispositional attitude to the disclosed though transcendent reality. Knowledge of God would not be knowledge of an additional being, but it would be complete openness to the transparency of beings, revealing their transcendent ground.

It seems to me that one simply cannot say what was the case at that moment when the human animal first attained whatever form of consciousness was necessary to take beings as signs of transcendence. It may be plausible to suppose that acceptance of revelation was at no time just a passive acceptance of something given whole and entire. On the contrary, revelation always requires the imaginative creativity which probes depths of significance in things by making new connexions, using new models for understanding and extending models in new ways, fruitful for the

[12] Tylor, E. B. *Primitive Culture* (John Murray, 1873). Frazer, J. C. *The Golden Bough* (Macmillan, 1911–15).

[13] Lang, A. *The Making of Religion* (Longmans, Green, 1898). Schmidt, W. *The Origin and Growth of Religion: Facts and Theories*, trans. Rose, J. J. (Lincoln MacVeagh, 1931).

interpretation of new experiences. It is a false understanding of revelation which thinks of it as verbal dictation, though this has been an official view of Islam and, at times, of Judaism and Christianity. There are too many claimants to the status of revelation, however, to allow any such claim to go unchallenged. And textual criticism has often exposed the fallibility and inconsistency of certain utterances which can only be attributed to normal human agency. Thus one must see the writings in which revealed doctrine is expressed as literary works of variable merit, which convey the author's gloss of his or someone else's original imaginative response to a situation in which transcendence was revealed as communicating a *sui generis* insight and calling forth a distinctive response. There is room here, even in the best disposed human soul, for varying depths of penetration and insight, breadths of experience to give rise to a specific interpretation, resources of imaginative response, and powers of literary expression to record the impact of the situation upon one.

It is impossible to penetrate to a realm of pure experience, which is uninterpreted by human beliefs and evaluations, and which offers a sheer given element capable of being self-authenticating and of giving absolute infallibility. The sorts of discrimination and response one is able to make depend upon the concepts one has available. Although a revelatory experience is strictly incommunicable, it is not true that it is totally non-conceptual. For the apprehender always feels that some concepts are more appropriate than others to express his apprehension. There can be such a thing as a weighing of language and reality, even though there cannot be any question of establishing a one-to-one correspondence between 'facts' and 'concepts'. So, though religious experiences may lead one to modify or transform one's vocabulary, their characterization also depends upon the sort of vocabulary one already has to hand. And so one's religious beliefs will naturally reflect the ways of life and thought-patterns of one's own cultural milieu. Tradition assumes the importance it has in religion because it preserves the history of the thought-patterns which have generated one's own most general ways of interpreting experience.

5

It must be remembered that revelatory experiences need not be temporally discrete, relatively short-lasting and dateable occurrences. To take an analogy from morality, one may have many specific moral beliefs and be disposed to accept many obligations as binding, without undergoing discrete, momentous experiences of some moral reality. It would seem strange to most people to talk of experiences of obligation, even when it is not doubted that one is under obligation, and that such obligations may become more apparent or pressing at certain times. Moral beliefs are based on experience, but not usually on discrete experiences; they are based on large tracts of developing reaction to situations and other people, re-adjustments of dispositional reactions one was trained to accept and subtly changing perceptions of the character and motivations of oneself and others. So with religion, one may have specific beliefs about God without undergoing special discrete experiences of God. One may accept that events and situations in the world often signify a transcendent reality, and accept particular signs as normative for one's own understanding of the transcendent, without being able to pin-point one specific, uniquely revelatory moment. The interpretation of the world as sacramental of a spiritual reality may have formed gradually, even below the level of explicit consciousness, as one learns the language of a religious tradition; and, by increasing knowledge of the world and development of one's own personality, one comes to modify that language.

If, for instance, a Catholic grows up in a devout family, and learns to use the language of 'devotion to Our Blessed Lord', 'adoration of the Blessed Sacrament' and 'cultivation of the interior life', he will adapt this language to his own personal style, but it will condition a general way of interpreting reality which does not depend on the occurrence of unusual experiences, but which allows a special interpretation of all experience. Of course, there is the reality of the transcendent, ultimately underlying the existence of a religious category of language. But this reality may become apparent, not in some powerful emotional experience, but more indirectly, through a special way of reacting to the world.

Similarly, a Buddhist who sees all life as suffering, also claims to see the way to release from suffering; and he is able to claim this because his perception of the nature of this world involves a perception of a desireless reality (Nirvana) beyond but interpenetrating this world. But this is not a perception of some historical, temporally locatable revelation; the reality is always present, though fully perceivable only by the spiritually enlightened. There may be no dateable moment of new revelation; yet all experience may be taken as revelatory. And this will be made possible because of the language which has been fostered within a certain tradition, and which continues to make a certain interpretative view of reality natural. Traditions may lose touch with reality, and whole views of experience may simply fade away as irrelevant; but religions offer general conceptual frameworks which do not simply consist of a list of speculative or theoretical propositions about the metaphysical nature of ultimate reality. In elaborating a set of images grouped around paradigmatic revelatory experiences, they also and essentially specify an exemplary role for men, in relation to the transcendent.

Religions differ in the revelation they offer of man's situation in the face of an ultimately valuable reality, and in the exemplary way they provide for coming to possess that value. What men count as good and harm will depend on their conception of the absolute value; and their doctrine of redemption will depend on their insight into how such value can be possessed by men. Thus the doctrine of the transcendent is not a matter of simple cognition; it must also take account of and express man's desire to be related to the transcendent in a complete and fulfilling manner. The distinctive feature of religious doctrines of fulfilment is that they essentially rely on some concept of transcendence, in relation to which salvation or liberation may be defined. The rituals of religion are not simply techniques for evoking a view of the world as a system of signs; they are rites of regeneration and renewal, by means of which men seek to bring themselves into a fulfilling relationship with a reality which is communicated through the ritual action. Religion, to put it in a dangerously glib phrase, is primarily therapeutic. It offers a diagnosis of the human condition, in the light of the revelations of transcendence which have been preserved in a certain tradition; and it offers a way of healing the fragmented or broken condition which it thereby brings to light.

It is probably true to say that men do not see the necessity for redemption, and therefore of religious observances, until they can interpret their existence in the light of the transcendent to which religious language points. In this sense, religion is a closed circle; it does not offer a cure for some unsatisfactory feature of the human situation which can be apprehended apart from religion. Men may feel all sorts of dissatisfaction or uneasiness with their lives; but it is only when the transcendent becomes apparent that such uneasiness can be interpreted as sin or bondage. To see that one lacks the true good requires a prior religious understanding of what the true good is. So religion appears as a mystery, a challenge and a revelation to the secular man. It does not add something to a situation he understands perfectly well in secular terms. It speaks of his whole secular existence in a distinctive terminology which claims to reveal the hidden structure of that existence. And it then speaks of offering fulfilment through establishing a relation to transcendence.

To say that God exists, is already to accept an attitude and role, defined within the specific theistic tradition. The cognitive assertion is not possible, in the properly religious sense, without the dispositional and affective commitment to the exemplary role it specifies—thus one cannot say, 'God is Father', without committing oneself to the role of son of God. The assertions of religion therefore grow out of man's search for liberation or salvation; and the content of the assertions is primarily directed towards specifying the nature of such salvation. One might say, in theological language, that God shows himself to man in the way necessary for human salvation. Or, in more neutral language, that language about God, while it is cognitive, is also determined, in its specific formulations, by the sorts of human attitude and action it specifies. It is, one might say, true; but its truth is the sort of truth appropriate to man seeking salvation. Its point is not increase of ontological information, but the proper direction of human lives to their fulfilment. It is in this sense that it can be said that for a religious believer, to know the truth is for him to live in the truth. One grows in the knowledge of God by growing in one's appropriation of salvation; but neither God nor salvation can be properly comprehended except within the closed circle of religious images; a closed circle, however, which is open to anyone who is able to make the requisite imaginative and dispositional commitment.

6

Naturally, there are other very important features of the concept
of God of which I have as yet said nothing directly—the perfection, creatorhood and wisdom of God, for example. What I have
tried to do is establish clearly the basis for belief in God; I do not
wish in any way to deny that this concept must subsequently be
developed by rational reflection in many ways. But I am denying
that one arrives at a concept of God simply by a process of inference from the nature of the physical universe; so that anyone
who understands the nature of the world is either illogical or
stupid if he does not assent to the existence of a first cause, unmoved mover and necessary being. I am also denying that one
simply intuits or contuits the existence of an infinite perfect
necessary cause of all things, in one unique movement of the mind.

I have based my account on the occurrence of distinctive types
of experience, which I have called revelatory experiences, which
unveil something in reality which cannot be verbally expressed,
but which, when appropriately discerned, calls from the percipient
a total response of commitment and involvement. Such revelatory
experiences may occur in many ways and contexts; they become
explicitly religious when a community is formed around such a
revelation, which develops its own appropriate values and codes
of conduct, its own rituals and disciplines of prayer, and builds up
its own history and tradition. Within such communities, inno-
vators arise from time to time, who elaborate or develop the original
paradigm revelatory events in various ways, and try to bring religious experience into relation with other areas of human knowledge,
and adapt it to cope with new forms of culture and experience.

When such a developed tradition exists, it is certainly possible
to assess the plausibility of its doctrines on philosophical grounds;
to investigate its historical claims with all the means at one's
disposal; and to compare its spirituality and ethical code with that
of other traditions. It may be that one's conclusions in these
areas of investigation will prove sufficient to bring one to the
opinion that religious experience as such is delusory—if, for
instance, it is impossibly confused philosophically, historically
false or suspect, and expressive of obsessional neurotic character-
traits and of generally infantile modes of thinking.

On the other hand, a developed religion will claim that it offers a view of reality which is not contradicted by any evidence, and which, on the contrary, achieves a more coherent and comprehensive picture than any other, in dealing with aspects of reality of which the experimental sciences take no account. It will claim that its historical assertions are well-founded; and, though obviously falsifiable, are by no means falsified—for example, there are innumerable examples of answered prayers in Christianity. And it will claim that religious belief brings a higher level of morality and more integrated personality to the sincere believer, and so leads to true maturity. The most important thing of all to stress, however, is that, as I have pictured it, religion basically rests upon the claim that there is a unique and distinctive area of human experience and knowledge—that of revelatory experience; and that apprehension of such a reality is both intrinsically valuable and brings the human personality to a stable and ordered fulfilment.

Within the Christian tradition, the object of revelatory experience, the sacred, though it is strictly non-denumerable, is conceived as one and transcendent. I have tried to show that such a transcendent reality is possible; that one comes to assert it by the occurrence of revelatory experiences; and that such an assertion develops in the life of a religious tradition, as it pursues and reflects on its own way of life. To say that there is one transcendent God is not to say that there is one individual (among possible others) which exists beyond the physical universe, but interferes in it from time to time to give evidence of his existence. It is to say that the non-denumerable object of revelatory experiences, the sacred, is conceived as unitary rather than diverse, and as not limited by spatio-temporal boundaries. God is not an additional entity; but he is not just nothing; he is the ground of the meaning and value in reality, called one because comprehended under a unitary integrating image. So the sacred, in the Christian tradition, is conceived as a unitary object towards which a specific set of attitudes, generated in particular experiential contexts, can be directed, throughout the whole of one's experience. In this sense, the object of Christian faith is one transcendent God. Anyone who denies that fact, denies the central focal point of Christian faith, without which all its other doctrines lose their intelligibility and interest.

CHAPTER SEVEN

GOD IN MORALITY AND ART

I

God has been characterized as the one transcendent object of the Christian's responsive attitudes. The ways in which God may be further described will depend upon the ways in which the transcendent discloses itself in human experience, and the ways in which men are able to open their thoughts and feelings to the reality which always surrounds and encounters them. It is possible to divide up the various strands of human experience in which disclosures of God may occur; and though it is naturally possible to do this in a number of different ways, I will pick out six areas which have been of particular importance for the development of the Christian concept of God. By examining, very briefly, each of these areas in turn, the Christian concept of God can be more fully elaborated.

The areas I have selected are these: (1) the area of moral experience, by association with which God comes to be conceived as holy, as the moral demand which claims life absolutely; (2) the area of aesthetic experience, in which God is conceived as the creative source of beauty and non-moral value; (3) the area of cognitive enquiry, for which God comes to be postulated as the principle of the intelligibility of the universe and as the creator; (4) the experience of one's inner selfhood, whereby God becomes the 'dazzling darkness' at the depths of one's self and the source of regenerative psychic powers; (5) the area of personal biography, in which God is conceived as guiding and shaping one's destiny and personality within a particular, unique and definite history; and (6) the area of religious intuition, wherein one characterises God as a present reality with which one can communicate in a quasi-personal way. The Christian concept of God has developed by a process of reflection upon these various aspects of human experience, within the general revelatory tradition of the Christian community. I shall attempt to say something about each of them in turn, beginning with moral experience, which has led to the Christian description of God as holy and good.

The awareness of God as moral demand has developed from more primitive conceptions, in accordance with which certain ritual observances and social laws were set down by the gods to be obeyed by men, on pain of sickness, death or some other form of divine retribution (Cf. Exodus, 15, 26). Moreover, such observances could be contravened in ignorance, but ritual uncleanness would still follow automatically; and purification and atonement would be required before divine retribution could be avoided. There are those in our own day who believe that an absolute morality is no more than a set of irrational commands, blind obedience to which is required; and that moral motivations are nothing more than fear of the consequences of disobedience.[1] Certainly, the code of law set out in Leviticus, for example, would seem to be very much like that. And yet even that would be unfair. The Law was certainly bloodthirsty and cruel at times; and it did mix up moral, ritual and hygienic prescriptions in a confusing way. But to the believer, the Law outlined that way of life which sanctified the people of Israel, which set them apart as 'holy', as belonging to and devoted to God, cleansed, purified and, it may be, accepted as an atonement for the whole of mankind. It was bloodthirsty because its zeal for the purity and steadfast observance of the law, its sense of the absolute importance of the people's sanctification, led it to the fanatical position of exterminating opposing forms of belief. In a sense there is no excuse for this, in that there is no excuse for sin, and the transmutation of zeal into fanaticism is sin. But in another sense, there is an excuse for it, for in a generally cruel and constantly warring environment, primitive responses, in religion as in life, were almost impossible to sublimate.

There could, in principle, be lots of ritual observances, laid down by many different gods. The early Hebrew religion appears to have been henotheistic rather than monotheistic, conceding the existence of other divine powers but condemning obedience to them and stressing a peculiar relationship of possession and

[1] Peter Geach at least comes very near this view, in *God and the Soul* (Routledge and Kegan Paul, 1969), p. 117 ff.

covenant with their own god.[2] But together with the rather crude assertion that their god was jealous and exclusivist, the Hebrews also sowed the germ of the idea that the ultimate source of obligations could not be diverse and limited, even in principle. Though rules about clean and unclean food mark out this people as belonging to this god, and as set apart to him, the rules which Jesus summed up under the rubric of *agape* do not set apart any people or distinguish any one limited godly power.

It gradually became clear to the prophets of Israel that the demands of morality were unlimited, not just in the sense that this god required obedience to them, but in the wider sense that they could not logically be over-ridden by other demands. Moreover, these demands were subsumable under one co-ordinating principle of love—interpreted widely as openness to all value in things and men, concern to bring about such value, and sympathy and active friendship for those who lacked the capacity for or actualisation of such value for whatever reason. The Torah comes to divide into injunctions about the relation of men to men, which is grounded in the ultimate demand to love with active sympathy; and injunctions about the relation of men to God, which requires rituals of purification, atonement and dedication. But though these ethical and spiritual aspects can be distinguished by extrapolation (though it is doubtful if such distinctions occurred to the primitive semitic tribes) they remain intimately bound together. For *agape* is wider than love of men; it is love of being, as illumined by the transcendent; and conversely, the attainment of a saving relation to God is impossible without active love of men.

There are difficulties with each side of this dual assertion. It seems that one can love one's fellow-men quite adequately without believing in God; and many would assert that salvation is by faith, not works, so that humanitarian action is not essential to salvation. One cannot deny either of these claims outright; an atheist can love men, and an immoral man can be saved through an act of faith and repentance. But one can add this: that love is the natural outworking of faith, and the final test of its genuineness; and that faith is the natural foundation of love, faith that there is something of intrinsic value to be encouraged, conserved and revered, and

<hr>

[2] Cf. Joshua 23.

that one is absolutely obliged to realise such values; and this
faith finds its basis and fulfilment in the worshipful approach to
being which is belief in God.

There are many aspects of the moral demand, disclosed in
various developments in human relationships; but one constantly strives to find an underlying unity which binds them into a
coherent whole; and this striving is signified by the use of the
unitary term 'God', around the central characterization of which
as love all other moral values can be grouped.[3]

Thus from the primitive tribal experience of an authoritarian
code of laws or taboos, which sets the tribe apart from others and
is enforced by brutal and often materialistically conceived sanc-
tions, there slowly develops the notion of individual responsibility,
of an unlimited and unitary moral demand upon individuals which
offers the alternatives of personal fulfilment or diminishment, and
which, originating in one tradition of encounter with God, becomes universally incumbent upon all humanity. The contribution
which this tradition can still make to our understanding of morality
is that the universal categorical morality of concern for others is
founded on the being of God, conceived as unitary and absolute
moral demand; and in responding to it, one responds to the
transcendent revealed in this aspect of one's experience.

From the same tradition of the Torah, with its concern for
ritual purifications, for atonement for evil by the shedding of blood
and for the ceremonial setting apart of the holy, springs a conception of man's relation to God in which the ceremonial elements
lose importance, and the primary concern comes to be with the
new inner birth by which one is able to turn from the world and
find unity with the sacred through the inner power of grace.
Again, the change in emphasis from outer ritual to inner conversion drives one away from polytheism, in which each god could
have its appropriate rite, towards a monotheism in which man is
reconciled to the transcendent through a power which cannot be
limited to one geographical, racial or temporal group. The Christian Church, on this understanding, is not the exclusive vessel of
the power of God, as it has sometimes seen itself; it is the eternal
witness to the universal power of God to save from the dark forces
of the world and reconcile to one another. The Church's task is

[3] For a fuller development of this theme, cf my *Ethics and Christianity*
(Allen and Unwin, 1970), Pt. 1.

just to offer this witness, and never to claim exclusive possession
of the powers to which it points.

Though the early Christian communities, waiting for an imminent Day of the Lord, may have been tempted to see themselves
as set apart from the world, saved from destructive and terrifying
judgement; yet this view is in sharp contrast to the teaching of the
Kingdom of men of new hearts, in whom faith works through
love, and whose secret and often hidden power is a light and
leaven for the whole world. When Jesus took the Passover meal,
and associated it with his own death and resurrection, he transformed it from a thanksgiving for the deliverance of one tribe from
its worldly enemies, into a celebration of the reconciliation of all
men to God through love, repentance and the new life of faith in the
transforming power of God in one's inner life. The final repudi-
ation of the tribal god comes when the ritual sacrifice of atonement
is transfigured into the purification of heart which comes through
dying to the world with Christ and rising to new life in his power.
For that is not a matter of the relation of a man to his tribal god:
it is a matter of the relation of a man to the transcendent and to
the world.

2

Not only is the Hebrew conception of morality transformed by its
reliance on a transforming power which can establish a fulfilling
relationship to transcendent reality; it is also distinguished by
being purposive in a special sense. Men are commanded to adopt
particular purposes—as Abram is called to leave Ur[4]—or to
acknowledge a special role in a moral plan which transcends their
individual desires or fulfilments. A constant feature of the Old
Testament chronicles is the experience of being 'called', not only
to obedience to universal laws, but to take particular courses of
action in unique historical circumstances, and to obey particular
laws as a symbol of one's special vocation and chosenness.

The Hebrew faith qualifies the later conception of a universal
moral demand by locating that demand as in history, and in
historical interaction with men; and as choosing specific individuals
for a special vocation. All those who have heard in their own lives

[4] Genesis 12, 1–3.

the call, 'Do this', accept that this is a moral demand and that it calls them to a specific purpose or vocation. That is the way morality is experienced by some; and it is in just such a moral claim that one may come to believe that one is being called to a purpose which one did not previously know to exist, that one may come to adopt a purposive view of one's own existence, and a view of God, the source of the claim, as purposively guiding human lives.

Thus, in primitive Hebrew religion, El-Shaddai is the spirit of the mountains, who calls Abram out, promising him a country and a worthy family-line, and formulating a contract which separates this tribe as his own. This god is one who controls the destiny of a particular people, who claims its loyalty and trust, and who promises to shape its future. The primitive experience on which this belief is based, while naturally irrecoverable, may be conjectured to be the feeling that some spirit (El) was calling Abram to follow a certain course of life, and to trust that, though the journey would be filled with risk, the outcome would be for good. But it seems that both the claim and the promise were imperfectly conceived. The promise was often understood materialistically, as consisting in plenty of land, food, sunshine and leisure; and the claim was often held to involve food and cleanliness taboos, the slaughter of alien tribes and the extermination of other religions in the name of preserving the holiness and sanctity of the Hebrew people. El-Shaddai, the spirit who guided the Hebrew tribes, was judged by his results, and followed because his powers seemed to be effective in war.

At this stage, the distinction had not been made between material realities and the transcendent, and so God, as one of the spirits of the desert, was taken to require devotion and to lead into victory, to be jealous or pleased, as some tribal chieftain might be. Yet the completely anthropomorphic view never quite obliterated the knowledge that the spirits were non-human powers, with their own codes of conduct; that the demands they made and promises they offered were not totally worldly, but involved moral heroism and ritual purification, and a sort of reward that was paradoxically compatible even with earthly suffering, that they were holy in the sense of inspiring a terror and devotion quite inappropriate before any Sheikh.

In the slow development of the Torah and the Prophetic

witness, anthropomorphism was gradually discarded, to produce
the ethical monotheism of the imageless God who made the
world and controlled its history. The distinctive elements of the
theism of post-Exilic Judaism are its integration of morality and
religion—so that God is to be served by moral action—and its
conception of God as intimately involved in and ultimately controlling the historical development of men and nations.

These were elements lacking in the often competing Canaanite
religions of fertility gods, associated with the amoral aestheticism
of identification with nature in all its aspects, and being associated
with the yearly cycle of growth and decay rather than with the
historical destiny of nations. In opposition to these faiths, Judaism
condemned nature as demonic and stressed the total transcendence
of God over nature, and his power to subordinate it to a moral
purpose. Thus in the place of the images of the Baal, the Jews
placed the tables of the law, signifying that their god required
absolute obedience and sanctification, and promised in return the
overthrow of the old world-order, this world and its powers
with which nature-worship could be so easily entangled. Yet at
the same time many elements of Canaanite religion were taken
into Judaism; and needed to be so, to mitigate the rather restrictive
Puritanical legalism which recurs again and again in the history
of orthodox Judaism.

The development of the Jewish religion has always illustrated a
dialectic between the generative image of the Law and the Covenant, and mitigating or widening elements from other faiths which
could extend without replacing that primal image. So the aestheticism of the agricultural year is incorporated by being combined
with commemorations of historical events in the history of the
Jews, which revealed God's providential purpose for his people.
In thus incorporating other faiths, the god of Abraham and Moses
became the one God, ruler of heaven and earth; and his unity,
creativity and absolute superiority were expressions of the generative image of claim and promise.

All these notions arise naturally out of the Hebraic tradition,
as it responds to new environmental influences; the notion of a
holy creator, the almighty father of his people, is in the end
necessary to support the traditional belief in an absolutely over-
riding moral claim and an ultimate power to shape the destiny
of his people and bring values to realisation. This tradition

requires and allows no further development of the notion of God which is not directly related to these functions of articulating the absolute claim and promise of the experienced tradition.

Of course, the Jewish notion of God is transfigured, for the Christian, by the notion that Jesus fully reveals the nature of God in history. Both the claim and the promise are transfigured by the experience of those who witnessed Jesus' death; the claim becomes, not that of the Law, but of a renewed and loving heart; and the promise is not of a secure political state, but of a kingdom of hearts, in which the indwelling Spirit brings eternal life, releasing one from anxiety about and attachment to the world, and opening up a free relationship with the transcendent. So God is conceived as making context-dependent moral demands, as providing a peculiar sort of moral fulfilment; and he is thought by Christians to enter into history in a more intimate way, disclosing his essential character as redemptive love; and, moreover, being known in the believer as a power of moral regeneration.

In this way one can trace the development of the concept of God as absolute moral demand, source of regenerating power and the call to a historical destiny through the revelatory tradition of Judaism and the Christian Church. When it is said that God is holy and good, one signifies that the sacred demands absolute purity from men, and is able to bring them to final fulfilment. This is the way in which the sacred discloses itself in one continuous tradition of belief and in one main aspect of human experience.

3

Another important aspect of experience in which the sacred is apprehended is that which is concerned with aesthetic contemplation and appreciation, whether of human artefacts or of nature itself. In primitive religions experiences of striking or unusual natural beauty or sublime power are often construed as revelations of nature-deities. But the connexion between the deity and its finite revelation cannot be just a contingent one; as though, in two identical situations, one could reveal a god and the other could fail to do so. What is needed is a view of reality which does not see beauty as a quality superadded by the contingent presence of a god, or as a strange Moorean non-natural property possessed by substances;[5] but which sees it as a revelation of the inner glory of reality, expressed in an endless number of ways.

Beauty is apprehended by the creative response of the human agent; and though there is not just one standard of beauty, the whole business is not just a matter of uncultivated taste. Beauty itself is a misleading word; for what nature and art reveal is more diverse than that word conveys. But in every case there is illumination of some significant aspect of reality. This revelation of the gods becomes monotheistic when one sees God as the source of all revelatory beings. That is, one sees them as having one unitary source, the nature of which they reveal. This is connected with the denial that there are many independent sources of reality, or that it has no source. The issue between mono- and polytheism is, in the final resort, an issue about the limitedness of the gods. Polytheism implies that each god has a restricted field of activity, a specific set of responsibilities with regard to men, and presumably a limited revelatory function. The gods are limited because each is endowed with a specific character which excludes other characters (though polytheism typically blurs the matter of individuality by transmuting and interchanging these characters more or less freely).

In a polytheistic system, the many gods must split up various revelations amongst themselves. The god of the storm is different from the god of the sun and both differ from the god of the sea. Yet the worshipper is aware that these are not real individuals, and that the lines of differentiation are very largely arbitrary and confused, so that there is much overlapping and duplication. He is aware that his is not the only god; that it is only one aspect of a reality which may be known and approached in many different ways. Yet the gods cannot be thought of, except perversely, as competing with each other for the worshipper's favours. That is, if in the power of a storm, one feels a presence communicated through the power and terror of natural forces, a sense of purging and renewing power which demands one's submission, then this power must be understood as incommensurably great, to be a proper object of adoration. If one apprehended a being of some

---

[5] G. E. Moore discusses the notion of beauty as a predicate which depends solely on the intrinsic nature of what possesses it, in 'The Conception of Intrinsic Value', in *Philosophical Studies* (Routledge, 1922)

specific degree of power and goodness, then there might always be some other being with a greater degree of the same sort of power. But this sort of limited possession of some value, however great, is incompatible with the attitude of adoration, which bows only before unlimited value, value which cannot be overshadowed by any other value of the same sort.

Yet of course this value is found in many finite realities; indeed, it is through such finite instantiations that God becomes apprehended as the unconditioned value of which the conditioned, finite value is a faint reflection. The purging, purifying power of the storm may suggest the power of moral justice; but it will be an unlimited, perfect justice, and only so could it be an object of worship. It is not that one infers from the empirical reality of the storm that there is an unlimited justice causing it; such an inference would be unwarranted and absurd. Rather, one apprehends a transcendent reality from the first, but in the context of a storm it reveals a particular facet of its nature in relation to men—its judgement, it may be. The unlimited is apprehended from the first as unlimited, but nevertheless as revealing specific aspects of its immeasurably full and complete reality.

Since even in radical polytheism each god is unlimited in possession of the quality he represents, there can be no question of competition among the gods. But there is something unsatisfactory about positing an indefinite number of distinct absolute values, as objects of contemplative worship. Of course, values are strictly non-denumerable; it is senseless to ask whether they are in one being or are all distinct entities. A monotheistic understanding of values will, however, be one for which all values are understood as in harmonious relationship, so that there is no possibility of competition or delimitation of spheres of influence. Monotheism is akin to atheism in that it denies that there are many arbitrary or competing causal powers at work in the universe, interfering with its laws for their own ends; and it properly denies even that there is one such powerful additional being. What it asserts is that reality itself reveals features which challenge the developmental of intellectual powers to attain a pure contemplation, attained through strenuous creative cultivation, but finally transcending all intellectual effort in the delight of simply open receptivity.

Aesthetic aptitude may be characterized as that experience of immediate knowledge which has used all the tools of conceptual understanding, but discarded them to attain the pure union of knower and known. In aesthetic experience the mind meets and can accept, in creative response, intrinsic values which make their own distinctive claim on its action and apprehension, and which promise supremely fulfilling experience. As in moral experience, the mind thus acknowledges objective values in reality. But, whereas moral claims may be conceived as divorced from reality— since they are concerned with what ought to be rather than with what is—aesthetic claims must be conceived as essentially embodied in reality, which itself challenges and delights the mind. To think of these claims as one is to conceive them as grounded in a unitary source of beings.

Aesthetic experience, interpreted in a broad sense to include every contemplative apprehension of reality as communicating transcendent significance, is thus one main way of coming to see the world as dependent upon a creative reality. The basic feeling involved here is, not that everything must have a similar but greater cause; but that moral and aesthetic demands and disclosures, with the enrichment of conscious life which they bring, cannot arise from random interactions of inert matter, without the power of action, feeling or thought.

What is the force of this 'cannot'? It is not logical self-contradiction; for one can assert the lack of any cause of the universe quite consistently. What is basically required is some sort of affirmation that the mind can find new depths, challenges and satisfactions in reality which seem to reveal a supreme, transcendent value and reality. This value is both in the world and yet beyond it, so that the world seems imperfectly to embody and point to it. As one can learn to respond to and understand another person, so one can learn to respond to and understand the world itself. The fundamental element is not the theoretical assertion of the existence of a universal mind; but the adoption of appropriate reactive attitudes to what meets one in experience. Yet this does imply a theoretical assertion of some transcendent reality, to which one responds, as embodied in the world.

The idea that this reality is the cause of the world has various sources. There is the consideration that, if it were not, one could not be sure that values would ever arise or be conserved; that one's life can be empowered by such values (and so causally affected);

that one's life does offer opportunities of service and testing (which imply a causal ordering of experience); that what is morally demanded must be possible in the world; that God is able to communicate through the world at all times (which implies power over it); that life can be fulfilled by turning from the world to the reality of God (which implies that one's own existence, as part of the world, is not subject to the random motion of atoms, but has a fulfilling goal); that the world is subject to intelligible laws; that the values of beauty and love can and will triumph in the world at last. And there is the basic conviction of religious faith, that by commitment to God in trust, thankfulness and obedience, one will be sustained and brought to a final measure of perfection. In accepting one's own capacity for creative response to God in the world, one already locates the source of one's being in a reality which offers and unfolds values of intrinsic worth. To acknowledge the transcendent is not just to apprehend new properties of material things; it is already, if only implicitly, to acknowledge the ground of all things in a source of values which offer themselves inexhaustibly in the world.

Monotheism is then basically the denial that the world has many unrelated grounds, the assertion that there is a unity of values known under many different aspects. What is it to assert that the world has a transcendent cause? It is to affirm the ultimacy of values, the faith that they are always available, and can be ever more fully known. This affirmation, like the basic affirmation of inductive science and common-sense, that the future will resemble the past, cannot be independently established. Its assertion is the precondition of testing in experience the reality of God.

There are thus two main strands in the affirmation of basic theism—the fundamental axiom that the world is grounded in ultimate values, which it can progressively reveal; and the experimental realisation of these values in many aspects of one's experience, which provides a particular characterization of God. This will naturally depend upon the nature of one's experiences, upon which aspects of these experiences one stresses, and upon one's ability to comprehend, inter-relate, clarify and extend them. These strands continually corroborate and affect each other, so that the affirmation of a transcendent cause makes possible the apprehension of experience as revelatory, and the acceptance of specific events as signs reinforces belief in a transcendent ground of reality.

When it is said that God is perfect and the object of all our desires, one signifies that the sacred continually discloses itself in inexhaustible and intrinsically fulfilling values, and calls for our disinterested delight in the sheer beauty of being. So, by reference to the moral and aesthetic dimensions of experience, the concept of God, the one transcendent object of faith, is developed further as that of a holy, good and perfect cause of the world. I am not arguing that one can prove the existence of God from certain aspects of moral or artistic experience. What I am saying is that the use of the concept of God enables one to interpret these areas of experience in a distinctive way, a way which is intelligible in itself, adequate to the phenomena it interprets, and coherent with other important strands in human experience of reality. The notion of a holy, good and perfect God develops by reflection upon disclosures of transcendence in moral and artistic experience; and it functions to specify appropriate attitudes in the believer towards this experience. Belief in God is thus of direct relevance to the daily life of the believer, as it leads him to the enrichment of his distinctive human powers, in responding appropriately and creatively to the reality he continually apprehends.

CHAPTER EIGHT

GOD AS THE GROUND OF BEING

I

In exploring the articulation of moral experience in terms of the unitary concept of God, I touched on one major strand which has gone to make up the Christian concept of God. This strand is the Hebraic pattern of thought, which typically speaks of specific historical experiences of moral demand, promise, transformation and presence, experiences which generate trust in a holy, righteous power in or behind the universe. Speculative theology is really foreign to this tradition, which is much more concerned with a dynamic relationship to an experienced power in history and personal experience than with an abstract and systematic theory of the nature of ultimate reality. Yet there is a need for a supplement to the Hebraic view, which can give a wider cosmic perspective to theistic belief, and which can develop more fully what is meant by saying that God is the creator, the cause of all finite beings. This supplement has been provided by the Greek philosophical tradition, which speaks of contemplation of the general facts of change, causality, contingency, value and purpose in the universe, as generating an insight into a transcendent ground of the universe (I use 'ground' to mean non-temporal cause, avoiding the word cause only because it suggests to many the idea of an act performed once and then finished, say at the beginning of time).

The classical exposition of this approach is found in the 'Five Ways' of Thomas Aquinas.[1] The basis of his argument is that everything which comes into being can be said to pass from potentiality to actuality. But a being can be made actual only by an already existing actual being; nothing can come from nothing, and mere potentialities cannot exist unless they are founded on some actual being. So everything which comes into being must have a cause. Moreover, that which brings something into being,

[1] Aquinas, T. *Summa Theologiae*, Pt. 1, Qu. 2, Art. 3.

the cause, must be of similar nature to its effects, on the principle that like causes like. And the cause must be at least as great as its effects; a being cannot bring into actuality something greater than itself.

Since all possibilities whatsoever must be founded on prior actualities, these principles lead one to suppose that there must exist an actual instantiation of the most perfect form of every possible being and quality, which is the first and uncaused cause of all its effects. This collection of supreme perfections must be immutable; for all change is a transition from some possible state to some actual state; but since all possibilities are founded on prior actualities, these first causes must be purely actual, without any possibility, and consequently changeless. They must also be necessary in their existence, in that they cannot come into being or pass away, for that would again involve the possibility of change.

But now, the only being which can be necessarily existent is one in which essence and existence are identical. That is, existence is part of the definition of such a being, so that if one could comprehend its essence or nature, one would see that it must exist; if such a being is conceivable, then it is actually existent. But, Aquinas holds, there can be only one being in which nature and existence are identical, in which to understand what it is, necessarily entails affirming that it is. It is that being, therefore, which contains in itself the sum of all perfections, which is immutable and purely actual in its necessary existence. It can also be said to be absolutely simple in its being; for since its essence is identical with its existence, all its qualities must be identical with that existence and with each other, and all are necessary and undividedly one. It is thus simple in that it has no parts or divisions in its being. It is infinite, in being unlimited by anything other than its own unbounded plenitude of being; and it is eternal, in the words of Boethius, 'simultaneously and perfectly possessing interminable life'.[2] This being, Aquinas concludes, 'all men call God.'[3]

The concept of a simple, perfect, infinite, immutable, eternal and necessary God can exercise a great attraction. It presents one with a picture of a majestic and unlimited plenitude of being, of which the created world is an imperfect series of refractions in

[2] Boethius, *Philosophiae Consolationis*, v, prosa 6; in *Boethius*, Stewart, H. F. and Rand, E. K. (Heinemann, 1943), p. 400.
[3] Aquinas, *loc. cit.*

time, to which all things strive to return and which all by nature desire, as containing the perfection which their own greatest good dimly reflects. But the picture lives and exercises its fascination precisely by its vagueness and incomprehensibility. When the speculative philosophy upon which it is based is examined closely, it begins to crumble; and many would think that it has now disintegrated completely under the critical attacks of Hume, Kant and many more recent analytical philosophers.

The key-stone of the classical arguments is the principle of causality, assuming that every event must have a cause, that the cause must be like but greater than its effect, and that there cannot be an infinite regress of causes. Each of these propositions has been widely denied by many philosophers in the last century or so; but perhaps the most dubious is the proposition that causes must be like but greater than their effects. This axiom is necessary to the theistic proofs, for without it one might succeed in establishing a first cause, but one could say nothing whatsoever about its nature— it may be radically unlike or qualitatively inferior to its effects. In fact, evolutionary theorists would often suppose it to be true that the greater does come from the less; consciousness does evolve from unconscious matter, and that is simply how things are. There is, of course, a great difficulty in giving sense to the expression 'greater than', in this context. One way of expressing it is to say that the cause must contain at least as much reality as its effect; but this involves one in talk about degrees of reality, and one may feel reluctant to say that some things are more real than others— except in special circumstances to do with mirages, hair-pieces and hallucinations. It is even more difficult to substantiate the claim that causes must be like their effects. When a flame is produced by rubbing two sticks together, what exactly is it that causes the flame, and is like it? When one gets to God, the first cause, the problem is even greater; for surely God cannot be said to be red or hot or flame-shaped; how then is he like the flame, of which he is the cause?

The Thomist answer is that all the perfections, or qualities, which constitute the flame, are contained in God in a supereminent way. But must these super-eminent perfections not be so different in God—especially as, by the doctrine of the Divine simplicity, they are all identical with each other—that they are totally unlike their created counterparts? After all, God must not only contain super-eminent redness, but also green-ness, blue-ness and so on, for every conceivable colour. It may just be conceivable that every shade of colour should be in God, but if each of God's qualities is supposed to be identical with every other quality, one may wonder exactly what sort of green, even super-eminent, it is that can be identical with blue, brown and every other colour. The problems multiply if one asks in what way such perfections are supposed to be contained in God. It seems clear that they cannot exist in God in the same way that they exist in nature; for this would be simply to assert a doctrine of pantheism, that the world is really contained in or is identical with God. On the Thomist understanding of God as infinite, however, the being of God necessarily excludes all finite, limited realities, so that he is radically distinct from the world. It thus seems that no finite perfection can exist in God at all, and there is therefore a sense in which God cannot be said to contain in himself the plenitude of being. The whole of finite creation is necessarily excluded from the being of God, and so the created universe does add something different and new to the being of God.

Thomists who wish to avoid this conclusion, because they wish to say that God in himself is the fulness of being, which cannot be added to, sometimes claim that finite and infinite realities are incommensurable, and so one cannot add anything to the other.[4] However, in mathematics, it is evident that, though it is impossible to add a finite whole number $(2,341)$ to an infinite series of numbers $(1, 2, 3 \ldots)$, because the infinite series already contains all particular numbers in itself, other series can be constructed $(\frac{1}{2}, \frac{1}{4}, \frac{1}{8} \ldots)$ which are not included in the first series, and thus one can say that additional mathematical entities exist. So, in reality, if God does not literally include in himself any finite property, the existence of such properties adds to the number of realities in existence. Those properties are excluded from, and other than, God's being. The Thomist then says that at least such properties are in God, in an infinite mode. But this means that God contains in himself infinite heat, cold, weight, lightness, motion and rest and so on. And, since God is identical with all his properties and with his own existence, God actually is infinitely hot and cold, heavy and light, moving and at rest. The attempt to conceive of the first cause as both simple and infinite, and also as containing all per-

---

[4] E.g. Mascall, E. L. *He Who Is* (Longmans, Green, 1943), p. 102 f.

fections, collapses into meaninglessness. So far as such perfections are conceivable, God becomes the possessor of contradictory attributes; so far as they are inconceivable, one is unable to say that such perfections are in any way like their conceivable finite alleged counterparts. The Thomist concept of God vacillates between a pantheistic identification of all attributes with God and an atheistic denial that God has any particular form of existence.

2

Can anything of the Thomist concept be salvaged? The key-principle is that all possible beings and beings which come into existence must depend on an already existing actual being. David Hume simply denied this;[5] and against such a denial, no logically compelling argument can be brought. Yet, even though the axioms upon which the Five Ways are based no longer seem logically self-evident to us, there is a profound mysteriousness about the general facts of change, causality and the continuity and order of events in time, which intrigues and baffles the human mind. Change does not seem to be just a matter of 'one damn thing after another', in completely random fashion. The tree that grows from the acorn does not just happen to grow. It grows in an ordered and uniform series of stages, each of which follows naturally from the preceding and leads on to the succeeding one.

Most people are not much impressed with the sort of teleological argument that sees in the existence of noses the wise provision of God in creating platforms to rest one's spectacles on.[6] But there is a more subtle and universal form of teleology in the apparent conformity of all things to general intelligible laws of nature. What is the mysterious connexion between cause and effect which determines that the temporal process develops in just this way and no other? It seems that one must postulate some reality which ensures that the process of change is continuous and intelligible, following general, comprehensible patterns while allowing for a degree of spontaneity and creativity. That reality is such that it governs the coming into existence of things in time in

⁵ Hume, D. *A Treatise of Human Nature* (J. M. Dent, 1911), Bk. 1, Pt. 3, sect. 3 (Vol. 1, p. 81 ff).
⁶ Voltaire, *Candide*, ed. Thacker (Lib. Droz, 1968), p. 102.

a rationally ordered way, moving within the limits of an apparently necessary conformity to an integrated set of laws. If one attempts to conceive that postulated reality in terms drawn from more everyday human experience, the natural analogy is that of a rational consciousness, which can conceive future possibilities, plan the developing course of nature so as to effect the possibilities it desires, and impose order and intelligibility upon the world, while allowing scope for a certain amount of spontaneous creativity.

This analogy of a rational consciousness may be pushed more or less far in the direction of anthropomorphism. Some personalist philosophers feel little hesitation in concluding from the rational order, purpose and continuity of nature to a Divine Mind, with wisdom, power and purpose, closely patterned on the analogy of human minds.[7] Others, however, are not prepared to push the analogy so far. They would agree that these features of the universe stand in need of some explanation, that some further reality is required which can account for the rational necessity to be found in the structure of the world, which can, as it were, 'hold things together' in an ordered, intelligible way. They might agree that such a reality can be properly characterized by the concepts of wisdom, power and purpose—that is, that it ensures that the world follows an intelligible and coherent pattern (which we conceive by saying that it is 'wise', and that it 'has power' to enforce that pattern). But they might remain agnostic about the nature of that reality in itself, and refuse to say that it is really in some recognisable respect like a human mind. The application of such a term as wisdom to the postulated reality is not meant to imply any structural similarity to wise human beings, but to say simply that, as persons show wisdom in ordering things according to general rules, so this reality orders the universe according to such rules.

Such a cautious account of the cause of rational order is very much in line with the official Thomist use of the analogy of proportionality, that God's wisdom stands to God's being as human wisdom stands to human being.[8] The stock objection to this formula is that it is completely uninformative, for one knows

---

[7] E.g. Peter Bertocci, 'The Person God Is', in *Talk of God* ed. G. N. A. Vesey (Macmillan, 1969).

[8] Aquinas, *Summa Contra Gentiles*, trans. Pegis, A. C., 1,28–34, in Hick, J. *Classical and Contemporary Readings in the Philosophy of Religion* (Prentice-Hall, 1964), p. 44.

neither God's wisdom nor God's being, so that the proportional sum cannot be worked. One may reply, however, that the formula is not meant to provide new knowledge. It is just meant to point out that when one applies any term drawn from human nature to God, the meaning of that term must be qualified by its new subject, God. To say, 'God is wise' is to say that there is a reality which orders things necessarily in accordance with intelligible laws. One cannot make further inferences of the type, 'If God is wise, then he will do so-and-so . . .', for that would be to use the analogy to provide new knowledge, and to assimilate Divine wisdom too closely to human wisdom.

One does know what one means by the wisdom of God, for one applies the term to the postulated reality which accounts for the intelligibility of the universe. One uses the term 'wisdom' because there is an apparent analogy—naturally, by no means an identifiable exact likeness—between the rule-governed order of nature and such products of human intelligence as mathematical systems and mechanical devices. The process of argument is not, as in Aquinas, from every perfection to its super-eminent possession by God—which is, I have suggested, rendered vacuous by the extreme doctrine of the Divine simplicity. It is, rather, the application of an analogical term to a postulated reality, on the basis of perceived similarities between the order of nature and human artefacts. So the phrase, 'God is wise' in one sense tells one nothing new about the being of God; rather, it serves primarily to locate the use of the term God in contexts of causality, order and purpose, as the reality which is postulated or disclosed in such contexts.

Of course, in another sense the statement 'God is wise' does tell one something; for, since we describe God in many other ways, we are saying that the same object which we describe in these various ways (as holy, perfect and good) is also the principle of intelligibility in the universe. As the sacred discloses itself in moral experience as the holy one, so it discloses itself in the causality and continuity of nature as the wise orderer of nature. And one might also think that, just as one cannot move by direct inference from a neutral account of moral experience to the existence of an objective moral demand, so one cannot directly infer from a neutral account of causal order to the existence of an objective rational ground of the universe. In addition to the blunt challenge of Hume, who flatly denied the compulsion to make any such inference, there is the further consideration that the postulation of a rational consciousness does not provide what it appears to promise. What it seems to promise is an explanation of the mystery of causality—how it is that one thing can follow another in an apparently necessary and rule-following manner. And this it does seem, at first sight, to do. But when one examines it more closely, one finds that the explicans is just as obscure as the explicandum, and so can hardly function as a genuine explanation.

We may find it hard to comprehend how the universe progresses in accordance with general laws. But is it any easier to comprehend how, in the terms of the analogy used, a universal mind exists and orders nature according to such laws? It may well be claimed that, since a universal mind is quite beyond human understanding, the alleged explanation makes things more and not less obscure. It seems that at some point explanations have to stop; and at that point one is left with brute facts, which must just be accepted as they are. If that is the case, why should one not just stop with the inexplicable fact that events in nature follow general laws, rather than with the more obscure brute fact that there is a universal mind which imposes general laws on nature? It is this consideration which counts against the validity of an inference from nature to a universal mind underlying and explaining it. So it seems that the Thomist programme of establishing the existence of God as the necessary explanation of change and contingency in the world, even in its amended form, must fail. The sort of explanation offered remains so mysterious that it has no real explanatory force.

3

Philosophical theologians, however, have been perenially attracted to the idea that the concept of God functions as an ultimate explanation of the nature of the universe. Such an ultimate explanation would be one which could account for the whole nature of the universe, and for the nature of everything in it. It would attempt to answer the question, 'Why is there something rather than nothing?' and also perhaps the question, 'Why is there this world and not some other world?' Ideally, it would answer the question, 'Why is everything just as it is?' Theologians have sometimes claimed that the existence of God, and only that, is able to provide such an explanation of the world as a whole. And they have sometimes made the further claim that the necessity of some such explanation provides a demonstration of the existence of God.

Thus H. D. Lewis, in *Our Experience of God*, speaks of 'there being something incomprehensible to "account" for things being what they are'.[9] As one would expect, his treatment of this notion is subtle and complex; nevertheless, he does suggest that the world 'must have some completeness or explanation', in however unusual a sense. It is clear that this must be a very unusual sense, in which the obscure can be explained by the incomprehensible; and one may doubt whether the belief that the world has a transcendent ground is best construed by means of the notion of 'explanation'. My case is that to use the notion of explanation in such a context can be very misleading; one cannot explain the familiar in terms of the unknown. I believe that a more adequate notion is one also used by Lewis in this context, the notion of 'ultimate but sustaining mystery'. To ground the world in mystery is, I submit, to deny all possibility of explaining it in any allegedly ultimate sense. One cannot have both these concepts; one must choose between them.

James Richmond, in *Theology and Metaphysics*, also argues that finite beings are not 'self-explanatory', so that 'experience throws us beyond the empirical towards an explanation which is ultimate and absolute'.[10] He speaks of an 'ultimate explanation' as one 'in terms of a transcendent personal being . . . who exists of himself "without dependence of any kind"'.[11] Such a being will provide 'an adequate, comprehensive and compelling explanation of all experience'.[12] The main problem here is of what could be meant by the notion of a comprehensive explanation of everything, or of a self-explanatory being. Richmond seems to suggest that to explain everything would be to show 'why essence and existence are in fact united here',[13] why all things exist as and when they do. And what explains why all things exist is the reference to a personal, independent, necessary reality, which simply makes them thus.

One must ask whether this reference really explains anything

[9] Lewis, H. D. *Our Experience of God* (Allen and Unwin, 1959), p. 40.
[10] Richmond, J. *Theology and Metaphysics* (S.C.M. 1970), p. 112.
[11] *Loc. cit.*   [12] *Ibid.*, p. 115.   [13] *Ibid.*, p. 112.

at all. The existence of God will, it must be remembered, explain absolutely everything—but it can do so only in a general and abstract way. The answer to every question, 'Why is this as it is?' is the same; namely, because God made it so. When the same answer can be given to every question, it is not likely to be very informative; even if such a reply may explain why the world as a whole exists, it cannot explain why particular things in the world are just as they are. Indeed, any recourse to God's free decision in creation precludes the possibility of further explanation, in principle. Like the analogous phrase, 'I just decided to', the phrase, 'God made it' is meant to stop questions being asked; it refuses any further explanation. If one asks the further question, 'Why did you decide thus?' or 'Why did God make this world?', the fact that it cannot be answered reveals that the process of explanation has come to an end at this point; one has left God's decision to create as an ultimate inexplicable fact. That is clearly insufficient for an ultimate explanation, an explanation of everything. But what more could be provided? It seems that Richmond wants to claim that God's decision must be self-explanatory, or it would be subject to the same sort of insufficiency and inexplicability as finite beings.

It is difficult to see what that expression means. It is meant to signify more than that something cannot be explained in other terms, which would be simply to say that it was inexplicable. Richmond wants to say that, though it cannot be explained in other terms, yet it is explicable—it explains itself. What could this mean?

H. P. Owen, in *The Christian Knowledge of God*, agreeing that 'if the world is to be ultimately explicable, a self-existent God must be postulated as the final explicans', asserts that self-explanitoriness follows from the identity of essence and existence in God.[14] Holding that 'finite experience cannot be ultimately explained unless we postulate God as its ground', Owen asserts that the argument from contingent beings to the existence of a necessary cause is valid if one accepts that the world has a sufficient reason (which is not itself provable). But he concedes that the notion of a self-existent being is incomprehensible—which leads him, like Lewis, to explain the familiar in terms, not just of the unfamiliar,

[14] Owen, H. P. *The Christian Knowledge of God* (Athlone Press, 1969), p. 86.

but of the incomprehensible. He also states that, for him, ultimate explanations presuppose the principle of sufficient reason.[15] That means that everything has a sufficient reason—i.e. if the cause exists, then its effect necessarily exists, with just the character it has and no other. Since all things derive, on the theory, from one first cause, everything necessarily follows from that cause, and nothing could be other than it is. Nor could that cause be other than it is, for its existence is necessary, and its nature (essence) is said to be identical with its existence.

Owen accepts the Aristotelian equation of explicability and necessity; what ultimately explains the world must exist necessarily. And he holds that a necessary being must be infinite, so that there can only be one such being. In support of this, he follows Aquinas in asserting that a necessary being is one whose essence is identical with existence. So far as this is intelligible, it is false. A necessary being would be a being which could not fail to exist; but that is far from meaning that what it is is identical with its existing (or, even worse, with existence *per se* and in general). One can maintain a being to be necessarily existent without espousing the greater obscurities of Aquinas; but then it will appear that, since we cannot know the conditions which could make a being's existence necessary, anything or everything could exist necessarily, as far as we can tell. There is no viable argument from necessity to an infinite perfect reality.

Whatever the weaknesses of such an argument, Owen does hold that only a being whose essence is identical with existence as such is self-explanatory. The difficulty is to attach any sense to this at all. One must consider whether it is preferable to abandon the notion of a self-explanatory reality or to stretch the mind to accept the admittedly incomprehensible identity of essence and existence. It would seem to me that the incomprehensibility posited by the denial of self-explanatoriness is less disconcerting than the incomprehensibility posited by the Thomist notion of self-explanatoriness. At least one can see why the world should be incomprehensible in the former case; whereas in the latter case one is asked to accept that the apparently contradictory concept of the sum of all perfections can make the inexplicable clearer.

Some who accept that Thomist accounts of self-explanatoriness collapse into nonsense still hanker after the notion of ultimate

[15] *Ibid.*, p. 78.

T.C.G.—H

explanation. G. F. Woods, in *Theological Explanation*, maintains that God is self-explanatory and the ultimate explanation of the world, though he admits that 'divine creation remains without a full explanation'.[16] The notion of explanation which he develops is idiosyncratic; he believes that only personal explanations in terms of motives, acts and purposes are satisfactory, because only they enable one to understand the 'inner nature' of things, to know 'what it means to be the thing' one is explaining. To explain the world would be to see clearly what it ultimately is, how it is and why it exists; and an ultimate explanation will have to be personal—in terms of purposes at least analogically like ours.

It is questionable whether all explanations derive, as he suggests, by extrapolation from our knowledge of our own being. One may well hold, on the contrary, that self-knowledge is notably vague and delusory, and human conduct is best explained in terms of externally observable laws of psychology or sociology. Certainly, to complain that scientific, covering-law explanations are unsatisfactory because we do not know 'why things are in being' is to neglect the obvious fact that we do not discover why we are in being either, by introspection or any other method. In all actual personal explanations there remains the ultimate brute fact that these are our purposes. If Woods is content with that, then all he requires of an ultimate explanation is that it reveals God's purpose in creation, without explaining how or why God has this purpose, or 'what it is like' to be God, or what his 'inner nature' is. But he still does wish for an ultimate, self-explanatory reality; as though he thought that one could discover what it was like to be God, and as though, just beyond all explanations we can actually get, there is an elusive ideal of a perfect explanation, which may be achieved one day, which would leave no questions unanswered. It is noteworthy that he can offer no account of the sort of thing that would count as such an explanation; and I suggest that the desire for it should be ruled out as illegitimate.

Certainly, the sort of personal explanation Woods takes as his paradigm gives no suggestion of self-explanatoriness. It only offers, hopefully, to make plain that the world has a purpose in some way analogous to a human purpose, and that it is sustained in being by a reality in some way analogous to our personal reality. That purpose and that reality remain unexplained. This

[16] Woods, G. F. *Theological Explanation* (James Nisbet, 1958), p. 170.

is a very limited notion of explanation, by comparison with the
Rationalist or Thomist ideals. Within those limits, theistic explanation may well be possible; but it would be restrictive to regard
that as the only 'true' sort of explanation, or as an all-inclusive
explanation, and other sorts as inferior approximations. It is just
one form of explanation among others, though what it explains
(the meaning and purpose of human existence) is no doubt, the
Christian will say, the most important and comprehensive aspect
of created reality.

4

It is clear that, before one can decide whether, and in what sense,
God may be said to explain the nature and existence of the world,
it is necessary to explore in more detail what the notion of explanation is. Medieval theologians took their accounts from Aristotle,
and the Aristotelian view remains important for many contemporary Christian uses of the concept. Aristotle suggested four
sorts of explanation—one can say what sort of stuff things are
made of; what their true or essential nature is; what brought them
into being; and what their purpose is.[17] Each of these sorts of
explanation necessarily leaves something unexplained—the prime
'stuff' or energy just does exist; the (possibly infinite) set of
'forms', or sorts of being, just is what it is; the first cause (if there
is just one), which is said to be like but greater than what it
brings into being, exists without further causal explanation; the
final purpose (if there is just one) towards which all things tend
just is, without tending to a further goal. One may say of these
ultimate models of explanation that they are self-explanatory, in
the sense that, when properly apprehended, they do not stand in
need of further explanation. They do not exist contingently, as if
they could conceivably have been different; but they are in some
way necessarily what they are. Thus it becomes inappropriate to
ask for further explanation.

There are innumerable difficulties in such an account. It is not
insignificant that none of these sorts of explanation is used by the
experimental sciences, and they are all rejected by philosophers

[17] Aristotle, *Metaphysics*, trans. W. D. Ross (O.U.P., 1928), BK.A.3
(983⁹).

of an empiricist cast of mind. It seems that they are neither necessary nor helpful in helping men to understand the world better, which is, after all, the primary purpose of explanations. Moreover, even if one does assert that there is a first efficient cause of all things, few have considered it to be a sufficient cause— that is, a cause from the existence of which all things necessarily follow; so that, as LaPlace said, one could predict every subsequent occurrence from the first state of the world.[18] But if it is only a necessary cause, it does not really constitute a total explanation of reality; it only states what must exist as a condition of reality being as it is; it does not explain why things develop as they do, rather than in some other way, or why they exist at all.

Explanation in terms of final causality, or purpose, may be thought to do this. But it is not clear that absolutely everything must have the same ultimate purpose. Furthermore, if all existent realities are necessary means to bringing about a purpose which is itself necessary, then the whole universe and everything in it could not have been otherwise. But if they are simply sufficient means to a necessary end, then perhaps many other means would have done as well, or better, or more economically. And in that case, though a purpose can be assigned to everything, yet there is no explanation of why the purpose is attained in this specific way. Any attempt to provide such an explanation—for example, by saying that this is the most efficient way—simply builds 'efficiency' into the notion of the final purpose; in which case one is back to the concept of a wholly necessary world. Otherwise, one can always ask, 'Why be efficient?'. In other words, if it is a contingent matter that efficiency is a value, then there remains an irreducibly inexplicable element in one's system, a brute fact upon which further explanations can be founded, but which cannot itself be explained.

On an Aristotelian account, one might say that the limits of explanation are the limits of necessity. To comprehend a being which is necessary in its nature and existence would be to see that it could not be otherwise. Its existence would not be contingent or arbitrary, but would be self-explanatory. On this account, the world is ultimately explicable if it is wholly necessary; but not otherwise. This notion of explanation was accepted by Rationalist philosophers from Leibniz to Bradley; but it is noteworthy that

[18] LaPlace, *A Philosophical Essay on Probabilities*, trans. Truscott, F. W. and Emory, F. L. (Dover, 1961), p. 4.

such philosophers have rarely been Christian theists. For such a doctrine, a total explanation of reality will consist in seeing the unity and coherence of the world—that is, each part entails the existence of and is entailed by the existence of every other part; and all parts together form a unified whole, the nature and existence of which is necessary, in that it could not fail to exist, and it could not possess any other properties than those it does possess. One might call such a universe, as a whole, self-explanatory, in that, if one could comprehend it fully, one would see that it was not just a brute fortuitous fact, which could have been otherwise or might not have been at all. One would see that it must be, and be just as it is.

A major difficulty with this notion is that few philosophers have supposed that a finite human mind could fully comprehend the coherence of reality. It is part of Rationalist doctrine that no part can be adequately known unless the whole of reality is known, that one cannot really know anything unless one knows everything. So the ultimate explanation, which consists in seeing the logical inter-relation of all parts in a unified whole, cannot function as an explanation to human beings. It must be an act of faith that there is such coherence and necessity in reality. It may seem rather empty to say that one believes there is an ultimate explanation of the world, though it can never actually be used to explain anything to anyone. Is there any point in saying that there is a reason for everything, if one cannot, in principle, know what that reason is? Perhaps there is; but one must not think that one is thereby actually explaining anything.

The notion of a necessary coherent unitary reality is perhaps not without sense or attraction, though its difficulties multiply on analysis. But the price of supposing that there is an explanation for everything is that everything must be absolutely necessary. God's being is necessarily what it is; he necessarily creates this world, with just the nature that it has; and all human acts are necessarily what they are. If there is any event which is contingent, which could have been otherwise, then one can always ask, 'Why is it thus and not otherwise?'. But no complete explanation can be given, so long as genuine contingency remains. That is what contingency means.

If the motive for asserting that everything must be just as it is, is a desire for rational intelligibility in the universe, that is strongly counterbalanced by a motive for denying the assertion, namely that the freedom of God in creation and redemption, and of man in accepting or refusing God, would be undermined by such thoroughgoing necessity. Moreover, one may fairly point out that both rational intelligibility and the final realisation of a morally good purpose in the world can be assured without holding that everything exists necessarily. What the Christian needs to say is that, though the world and its particular properties is inexplicable, in an ultimate sense, yet it is not a wholly arbitrary concatenation of occurrences. What comes into being does so in accordance with universal, intelligible laws; there are general principles governing individual events, though they do not in every case determine those events absolutely. Moreover, whatever world comes into being will express in some manner qualities of goodness and beauty, and the world will finally be brought to moral fulfilment.

Thus the Christian will want to assert some necessity with regard to the being of God, as creative ground of the world—perhaps his necessary existence, as a necessarily holy, omnipotent, omniscient reality. But the admission of some features of necessity in God does not entail the complete exclusion of contingency from God. There is no contradiction in the notion of a being which is necessary in some but not all respects, or which is necessary in its general character (e.g. in lovingness) but contingent in the particular acts which realise this character (particular acts of love). And perhaps the Christian faith requires such a concept if it is to maintain the belief that God freely created this world and freely acted to redeem mankind, though he is necessarily a God of justice and love.

5

The Aristotelian notion of explanation is therefore not necessary to faith in an intelligible ground of and a final moral purpose for the world; and it must be unacceptable to a Christian who wishes to affirm the freedom of God and man and the contingency of the world. But it would in any case be widely rejected on the purely philosophical ground that it sets an *a priori* ideal of explanation which it is impossible and unnecessary to put into practice. A consideration of the concept of explanation readily exposes the great difficulties which lie in the way of any attempt to speak of one ultimate explanation of the universe.

Firstly, explanations, both in the experimental sciences and in history or sociology, work by appeal to regularity and generality of behaviour, and are more successful the more regular and general a form of behaviour is. So it is apparent that the uniqueness and individuality of events must necessarily be omitted by all explanations. If an ultimate explanation was supposed to explain absolutely everything, it would have to cover both the unique and the individual particularity of each event. But such a thing is impossible. It is not just impossible as a matter of fact; it is ruled out by the logic of explanation, by an understanding of what an explanation is. There just cannot be an explanation of what does not fall under any general law. Therefore there cannot logically be an explanation of the whole universe—which cannot recur—or of the particularity of events within it, which cannot be brought under general laws.

Secondly, every explanation leaves something unexplained, some ultimate law which just does exist, and enables other things to be explained in the light of it. There must be some laws of physics which cannot themselves be explained in terms of even more general laws; and so with every science. Again the notion of an ultimate explanation, which could explain absolutely everything, including itself, seems to be logically impossible, once one understands what an explanation is.

Thirdly, the notion of an ultimate explanation suggests that an explanation could be given of all features of phenomena at once. But if it is an essential part of explanation that a particular system of relations must be systematised and abstracted from the complex reality which faces the investigator, the ideal of ultimate explanation loses credibility. The more general an explanation becomes, the more abstract it also becomes; the price of universality in explanation is that much ungeneralisable information has to be omitted from consideration. It is impossible to have an explanation which is both completely universal and also fully comprehensive to all features of existent phenomena.

Fourthly, the work of Bohr and Heisenberg has made clear the extent to which our knowledge of nature depends upon the experimental techniques and cognitive resources which are available to us; so that it is no longer possible to speak of a completely objective knowledge of nature, which is not relative to human powers of apprehension and interaction with nature. We develop explanations of phenomena we find puzzling; and we are satisfied when we can interpret such phenomena in the light of what is more familiar to us. So both what we feel the need to explain and the way in which we explain it is relative to human interests, abilities and limitations. Again, the notion of an ultimate explanation which would not be relative to finite human interests and methods of observation seems to be an impossible one, except perhaps for a wholly omniscient and disinterested being.

Fifthly, the perfect explanation could only be obtained if, in the end, the universe was a closed causal system, in the sense that there were no external, uncontrollable factors to be considered, and if there were no events in it which could not be predicted with certainty, given a knowledge of all causal laws and the initial state of the universe. To the extent that a Christian believes that there are factors, however mysterious, external to the physical universe which could affect it; and that not every event in the universe is wholly predictable; to that extent a completely satisfying explanation can never be provided, in principle.

Thus an analysis of the concept of explanation suggests that the notion of an ultimate explanation is not merely unobtainable in practice, but that it is not properly conceivable even as a logical possibility. If this is indeed the case, one needs to look again at the sense in which the existence and nature of God may be said to explain the universe or certain features of it.

6

For the Christian, God, as the power making for intelligibility, beauty and righteousness, may be said to explain the universe in that he gives it meaning and intelligibility, provides purpose and significance, and so sets all things within an overall context. The typical theistic religious affirmation is that everything in the world has a place in an overall pattern which, in its general design, is valuable in itself. Thus the theist may claim to 'see the point' of the world's existence, or to 'make sense of' human life. There are three main elements involved here: first, that the world as a whole has intrinsic value, that it is good that it exists just as it does; second, that there is a rational pattern and purpose in the universe, that it is not just a chance collection of random events; and third, that there is a non-physical ground or cause of the universe, which ensures the realisation and the intrinsic value of the various purposes in the universe. To explain the world theologically is to interpret it in terms of a moral purposiveness; and God is the ground of value and of an ultimately purposive causal intelligibility.

The notion of explaining the world in terms of a moral purpose is a difficult one, and its limits must be explored. To say that the world's purpose is the glory of God is to give a final focus to all worldly activities; but it is not to explain every minute detail, in the sense of showing why it is so. It does not follow from the existence of God that there is a reason for every detail of reality being just as it is and not otherwise. If one said that the universe, or some event in it, was a necessary means to God's glory, one would be saying that God's glory would not exist if it were not for that universe. This position has usually been rejected by Christians, for it makes the world necessary to God, and thus seems to undermine God's freedom. If one said that the universe was a sufficient means to God's glory, one would allow that there could have been other ways of manifesting God's glory; but one would be saying that it followed from the existence of the universe that God was glorified. This seems to be what the theist wants, for he would hold that any created universe must necessarily manifest the glory of its creator.

So the theist must hold that the universe, taken as a whole, is a sufficient means to the moral end; but not that it, or any part of it, is a necessary means, or indeed that the moral end itself is necessary (though he must hold that there is some necessity governing the existence of a moral end—e.g. it could not be 'eternal suffering'). It follows from this that many particular features of the universe may be counter-adaptive or wholly contingent, even random. There may be many ways of manifesting God's glory; and there may be new, creative, unpredictable ways. One may explain these by giving a necessary cause (the infinite ground of being) or by giving a very general purpose (manifesting God's glory). But in the end one is simply pointing to the transcendent mystery which is the adequate cause of all beings. To say that the cause is adequate is to say that it is more than necessary, in that it alone wholly accounts for its effects, but less than sufficient, in that alternative effects are possible. To put this schematically, if X is the cause and Y its effects, to say that the cause is adequate is to say: if not X then not Y; if X then Y is possible; but not, if X then actually Y.

The belief that the world has a moral purpose, is intrinsically valuable and has an immaterial ground is such a generalised and unclear one that it cannot explain anything or give rise to any specific predictions about what the future will be like. It certainly gives no insight into the character of the adequate cause, which remains wholly inscrutable. It is not a necessary presupposition for scientific investigation; theistic explanation is unlike scientific explanation, in that it is not necessary for understanding the physical nature of things, not a condition of knowledge or technological change. Certainly, it puts the world in a new light, in the light of a transcendent reality. But it only explains in that it expresses a faith that a moral purpose lies behind reality. This is in some ways more like a new and very obscure belief than an explanation. Indeed, one may well say that to accept this sort of explanation, and even to see the need for it, is to take the decisive step of faith, to accept that life has a moral purpose and that the world is rationally ordered. Belief in a general rational and moral order cannot be plausibly said to derive by induction from empirical evidence, or from the purely speculative desire to explain the world more fully. It derives from a religious commitment to the moral and purposive ordering of one's own experience, in a particular religious tradition. And even when it is formulated, theistic belief notably fails to explain situations of suffering in any straightforward sense. True, it assures one that there is an explanation, but only of the sort outlined above—that there is a final moral justification for the pattern of events, that nothing will finally be in vain. This is still incomprehensible; but it may be accepted as true as a result of the believer's experience.

This form of explanation, in terms of God's rational ordering to a final moral purpose, is analogous to purposive explanations of human behaviour. Such explanations work by appeal to familiar action-patterns; and one is satisfied when one finds some regularity to which the act in question conforms. For instance, 'He did it because he was angry' appeals to some common behaviour-pattern. Such explanations are quite compatible with, and for some philosophers, would be held to entail, the denial of an explanation of the action in terms of sufficient causes.[19] The form of explanation used in, 'I did it because I chose to . . .' explains precisely by excluding all causal explanations. So, when explaining events by reference to God's purpose, one connects them into one overall pattern, uniting parts into a purposive whole. In this case, of course, one does not refer to a familiar, general action-pattern, since there is only one divine purpose. But one does refer to a pattern which is believed to exhibit intrinsic value, and to be governed by general laws, forming a unitary whole. The pattern must be accepted as the ultimate model for theological explanation; and, as in the case of explanations of human acts, it is compatible with, and may well be held to entail, denial of any explanation in terms of sufficient causality. One may thus find a basic, essentially mysterious spontaneity at the core of the world, a dynamism underlying a real history. There is a theistic form of explanation; but it has its limits; and these limits allow for a creative mystery which accords well with the Biblical notion of an unfathomable creator God.

One must therefore refuse to say that God has a detailed fore-ordained plan for everyone. Rather, if men exist, God necessarily lays down general limits of purpose and particular guidelines of development possible in specific situations; as evil compounds, he will yet bring all to good. The explanation involved here implies a reference to necessary moral values, free human choices, general conditions of human existence and contingent and unpredictable historical developments. For a complete, or ultimate explanation, one would need all these different strands explained in all their different aspects. That is, there is no one explanation; there are many different sorts of explanation necessary to understanding the complex world. Religion does not manage to reduce all these forms of explanation to one super-explanation. On the contrary, it adds to them the doctrine of a moral, transcendent source and goal of the universe, the foundation of both rational intelligibility and factual contingency. The belief that there is such an explanation in terms of ultimate value, rationality and purpose seems to be central to developed religion; but such an explanation is ultimate only in that it expresses the most general character of the universe,

[19] Cf. Downie, R. S. and Telfer, E. *Respect for Persons* (Allen and Unwin, 1969), ch. 4. 5.

as it is posited by the believer. Even in the unattainable ideal of the
vision of God himself, it would explain only the general nature a
world must have, if God creates one. It would not, and could
not, explain God's choice of a world, or that world's particular
nature and historical development. Here one arrives at mystery,
beyond any explanation.

I conclude that (a) it is doubtful whether the notion of an
ultimate explanation is intelligible; (b) even if it is, Christians have
an interest in denying that there is such an explanation, so as to
defend the spontaneity and mystery of God and the reality of
human freedom; (c) that God can be said to explain events by
placing them in a rational, purposive and intrinsically valuable
context; (d) the fact that there is such a context (that God exists)
cannot be established by the consideration that events are inexplicable unless there is one; for they are ultimately inexplicable anyway; and to assume that they can be explained in this way (by
reference to a moral purpose) is just to assume that there is such a
purpose, which is a matter of religious apprehension and faith.
So it seems that the postulate of a rational creator is not compelling on intellectual grounds alone. Yet it is still intelligible and
attractive, and one may still be driven to accept such a postulate,
not on grounds of inference alone, but on the basis of a revelation
of transcendent reality, which discloses itself and the existential
dependence of all things upon it, to the open and contemplative
mind as it reflects on the nature of things.

7

It is then possible to see the general facts of change, causality,
order and contingency in the universe as explained by the existence
of a transcendent reality, characterized analogically in terms of
wisdom and power. One may always take the view that these
facts, mysterious as they are, are just brute facts to be accepted
as they stand; and that the postulation of a transcendent explicans
gives rise to more problems than it resolves. The theistic explanation only forces itself upon one as and when the sacred discloses
itself in and through these general features of the universe, and
as one discerns the sacred in the necessity and intelligibility of the
processes of nature. Theistic explanation is not ultimate, in the

way that many theologians have desired; the existence of such an ultimate explanation would undermine the creative freedom and mystery of God's being. Yet it does license talk of God as the creative cause of the universe, the one who brings it into being and shapes it in accordance with rational principles.

The Thomist proofs of God's existence thus locate areas of experience which remain permanently baffling and mysterious for human understanding. They lead one to postulate an unchanging ground of change, an uncaused cause of all beings, a necessary and unconditioned ground of all dependent, contingent realities, an absolute source of values, a rationale for the evolutionary development of humanity. These areas of experience give one index of what is meant by 'God'. While the mystery remains, reflection on these facts enables one to characterize God as the transcendent cause of all beings, the creator who discloses his being in one's apprehension of the radical contingency and limitedness of all finite beings, including, of course, oneself.

Such an apprehension is not properly characterized as a valid inference or 'proof' from a neutral description of the universe. It is more like what E. L. Mascall and others have termed a con-tuition of the necessary, unlimited and unchanging ground of all beings along with and at the same time as the apprehension of the inexplicable, fortuitous, constantly changing pattern of the finite world.[20] This contuition cannot give one a license to make know-ledgeable statements about the nature of ultimate reality; and the main difficulty with the Thomist approach is that, despite its avowedly agnostic doctrine of analogy, it does advance pro-positions about the nature of the Divine being which both seem unjustifiable and in conflict with the data of Christian revelation. For example, the doctrine that God is immutable derives from the consideration that the ordered continuity of temporal change needs to be ensured by a being which is not susceptible to unfore-seeable, and possibly fortuitous, alteration. Behind the process of change the religious insight claims to discern a sustaining ground which can guarantee stability, because it is not susceptible to the possibility of change—so that it might cease to exist, or its nature might become quite different, for example. Part of what is meant by the term 'God' is a reality which is beyond all temporal change

[20] Mascall, E. L. *Words and Images* (Darton, Longman, Todd, 1957) p. 85; the concept of *contuitus* derives from St. Bonaventure.

as we know it; and this point simply elaborates the fact that God's transcendence means that he is not limited by any particular position or extent in space or time.

However, if one maintains that God is beyond temporal change, one is neither committed to the view that he is imprisoned, as it were, in a condition of static immobility, nor to the view that God cannot change in any aspect of his being. Boethius' formula for God's eternity—'the simultaneous and perfect possession of interminable life'—though it is a beautiful and evocative phrase, has had a baneful effect upon many of his successors. The conception of an unending present is still the conception of a present, if it is not to be a mere self-contradiction; and to say that something exists in the present, or simultaneously, is still to place it in time; namely, at the same time as itself. This is perfectly understandable, for human thought cannot divest itself of tensed verbs, or their analogues, so one is compelled by grammar to speak of God either as 'all-at-once' or as successive. Yet it should be clear that, just as God's transcendence of all temporal relations means that his being cannot be successive, equally it means that his being cannot be simultaneous, all-at-one-time. If God is beyond time, he cannot exist before, after or at the same time as any finite being; and his being cannot be correctly conceived by us as either simultaneous or successive.

What this means is that God's being simply cannot be conceived by us at all. We can say that, like a mathematical truth, God is timeless; and that from him all temporal things originate (in a non-temporal sense). Rather as my bodily actions can be caused by my anger, which is not in any spatial relation to my body, so temporal events may be caused by a reality, God, which is not in any temporal relation to them. If it must be said that God does not change, it must also be said that he does not remain static, unmoving. It follows that it need be no more misleading to speak of God as changing than it is to speak of him as immutable. It really depends upon the sorts of consideration which lead one to attribute certain characteristics to God, the one transcendent object of faith.

Talk of the immutability of God enables one to say that there are necessary, unchanging principles of change and rationality, governing the universe and emanating from an inconceivable sustaining reality. On the other hand, talk of change in God enables one to say that this reality interacts with finite beings, changing in its specific nature by reacting to events in the world and bringing into being new and creative possibilities for finite creatures. It also enables one to speak more intelligibly about God becoming incarnate and living as man, dying and rising again, and working in the world through the power of the Holy Spirit—all basic Christian doctrines which seem to imply change of some sort in God. Though one may say that God is unlimited in not being conditioned in his existence by anything outside himself, one must also say that he is limited in the sorts of response he makes, by the free acts of his creatures. Though God is wholly actual in the sense that all possibilities whatsoever are founded on him, yet he continually brings into being new unforeseen possibilities, as the finite world develops in various ways. One wants to say of God both that his nature is necessarily and changelessly what it is, but also that the world contains the possibility of radical newness and of Divine response to free human action.

8

It may be thought that talking of God in this way as both change-less and changing is clearly self-contradictory.[21] But many philosophical theologians, and perhaps especially Hartshorne, have argued that only such a dipolar concept of God is able to do the job which even Aquinas required of his concept of God. Aquinas wished his concept of God to express the notion of absolute perfection; and, developing the thought of Aristotle, he came to think that the perfect being must contain in himself, in a super-eminent way, all perfections simultaneously; therefore it could not change except by becoming less perfect. I have already argued that this notion of 'perfection' is incoherent, that the principles of likeness of cause and of degrees of being, upon which it is based, are insupportable, and that simultaneity cannot properly be predicated of a God who is non-temporal. Hartshorne argues forcefully that the notion of perfection as the simultaneous possession of the fulness of being, which excludes all change, should be replaced by the notion of perfection as the unsur-passable capacity to move to creative and new expressions of its

[21] Cf. Owen, H. P. *Concepts of Deity* (Macmillan, 1971), p. 82 f.

being.[22] Static immutability is precisely not perfection, he argues, for perfection implies and requires constant change and newness. Whereas for the Greeks change itself was always an imperfection, and only the changeless could be perfect, for modern Western thought the changeless is uninteresting, and constant change is a necessary condition of perfect being. Of course there must be limits to this change; a being is not perfect if it gets worse in some respect, or if it ceases to be (although even here, the loss of some desirable qualities may be necessary for the gain of others, since not all desirable properties are able to co-exist—compassion for X cannot co-exist with pleasure in X's situation, for example). Thus one must say that God is necessary in the unsurpassability of his being, and in his possession of supreme goodness, power and wisdom. But he is contingent and changing in the particular ways in which his goodness, power and wisdom are expressed. As Hartshorne puts it, there is a necessary and a contingent pole in the being of God; he is changeless in some, but not all, respects.[23] This dipolar concept of God is not self-contradictory, for one is able to distinguish the different respects in which God is immutable and changing.

The acceptance of Hartshorne's notion of the dipolarity of God does not entail acceptance of the metaphysical apparatus of process-philosophy, which has been adopted wholesale by some recent theologians. Indeed, one of the important points about the account I am offering is that one is not here engaged in an exploration of the inner being of God; that is, I have held, inconceivable. One is rather seeking to characterize the sacred as it is expressed in various areas of experience; and so it may be that the concepts which derive from diverse types of experience do not fall together to form one systematic and coherent whole. It may even be that they seem contradictory—as with talk of Divine immutability and compassion for human suffering. But if one can show how one comes to talk of God in these ways, for different purposes, such difficulties are mitigated. For one characterizes God in the way which evokes an appropriate attitude in man, not in the way which

[22] Cf. Hartshorne, C. 'The God of Religion and the God of Philosophy', in *Talk of God* (Macmillan, 1969).

[23] Hartshorne develops this conception in numerous writings; e.g. *Man's Vision of God* (Harper, 1941) and *The Logic of Perfection* (Open Court, 1962).

describes his inner being most correctly. Naturally, if one's concepts do evoke an appropriate human response, one will say that they are not misleading; they do not describe God incorrectly, by comparison with a possible more correct description. Yet the truth is that God cannot be described at all by men; so all one can ask is that one's concepts of God enable one to react to him and to one's experience at large in the right way. Concepts of God cannot describe, even analogically. They should specify attitudes to reality which are appropriate and bring human life to its proper fulfilment. If one asks what makes these attitudes appropriate, all one can say is that the inconceivable being of God does so; but what it is in God that makes them appropriate we cannot know.

This is a fairly radical agnosticism about the being of God; but it focuses attention, not on some reality which we may or may not picture accurately, but on the ways we choose to speak of the sacred, and how they determine the quality of one's character and conduct. With this in mind, one can see that there are considerations in human experience which lead one to speak of God as immutable, omnipotent, unlimited, necessary and omniscient. However, the Thomist concepts of perfection, simplicity, infinity (of pure being, without any defining, limiting, characteristics) and eternity (as interminable simultaneity), are all dependent upon the proposition that God's essence and existence are identical, so that God is fully always all that he can be, and there are no contingent aspects of his being. That proposition seems to me insupportable, since it seems axiomatic that 'to be' is always 'to be something of a certain sort'; and, while the mode of God's existence is inconceivable, it is vacuous to say that the sort of being that exists when God exists is simply existence. 'Existence' is just not an answer to the question, 'What exists?' Moreover, it is hard to see how any theory of creation can consistently hold that God is always all that he can be, containing no unrealised possibilities. For if the world is contingent, then it could have been otherwise. And if it could have been otherwise, then God could have created a different world from the one he actually did create. One can only understand that 'could have' as an admission that there are at least some unrealised possibilities in God—namely, the creation of those beings which he did not create, though he could have done so. One may add to this the consideration that, if God responds to prayers which are freely uttered by contingent creatures, then these responses must themselves be contingent—they could be otherwise, and would have been so if the creaturely acts to which they are responses had been otherwise. Thus there seems to me to be no escape from the conclusion that the being of God contains both unrealised capacities and contingent aspects. But there is no reason at all to shrink from this conclusion if one drops the identification of essence and existence, with its unacceptable corollary that everything in God must be both necessarily what it is and wholly actual.

If one does drop that identification, then it is open to one to hold that God's perfection is compatible with, or even requires, change of a certain sort; that assertions of his simplicity and infinity amount to denials that concepts which apply to finite, separated realities are applicable to God, but must be complemented by the denial that such assertions tell one anything positive about God at all, and by the recognition that it is necessary for us to conceive God as having particular properties (for example, of mercy and compassion) and as having both necessary and contingent aspects of his being. And God's eternity (his transcendence of time) in one aspect is compatible with his contingent involvement in time, as he is conceived as in response to the free acts of creatures, in another aspect of his being.

The notion of God as the creator, the necessary, omnipotent, omniscient ground of all finite beings, develops by reflection upon disclosures of transcendence in the general facts of continuous change, causality and order in the universe; and it functions to specify appropriate attitudes of dependence, reverence, awe and thankfulness in the believer throughout all his experience. The classical (Thomist) Christian concept of God belongs to this tradition of thought; and while it has sometimes seemed arid and abstract, over-concerned with purely intellectual considerations, and over-awed by the intellect of Aristotle, it does express a legitimate insight into the dependence of all things upon a transcendent reality. If the Thomist concept is modified by the doctrine of the dipolarity of God, and complemented by theistic insights drawn from other areas of experience, it remains as a compelling and perennially valid expression of the interpenetration of all things by a sustaining and incomprehensibly mysterious unconditioned reality.

CHAPTER NINE

GOD AND REVELATION

I

The sacred has been considered as it is disclosed to men in moral and aesthetic experience, and in the contingency of finite things; and the concept of God has been shown to be articulated by the application of suitable terms drawn from such contexts of disclosure. There are three further main areas of experience which help to fashion the Christian concept of God, and to develop the notion of a personal and providential presence which is so characteristic of Judeo-Christian piety. These can be touched on very briefly, as they have already been considered at various points in previous chapters.

First there is the interior life, the introspective journey into oneself which can bring one to confront an unconditioned reality at the very heart of one's personal being. This area has been mentioned in ch. 2, and there is not much I wish to add at this point. The spirituality of Hinduism and Buddhism, in particular, has concentrated on this exploration of one's own psychic being, until a stage is reached at which one realises one's unity with unconditioned being. There are various ways of construing that unitive state: for many Buddhists, it is a passing beyond being and non-being, to a state of equanimity, in which is neither joy nor pain, ease or dis-ease.[1] For Vedantists of the Advaita school, it is realisation of one's unity with Absolute Reality;[2] for orthodox Christians, it is a union with God by grace, a 'spiritual marriage' of the soul, in which there is an interpenetration but also a continued

---

[1] Rhys Davids, T. W. and C. A. F. (trans.) *Dialogues of the Buddha*, Pt. 2 (Luzac, 1910), p. 345.

[2] The Advaita philosophy of Sankara is principally based upon the later Upanishads; e.g. 'Svetasvatara Upanisad', 1, 7; in Radhakrishnan, *The Principal Upanishads* (Allen and Unwin, 1953), p. 714.

distinction of beings.[3] These different ways of interpreting the introspective experience achieved in mental prayer arise from theoretical differences about the nature of reality and human existence. So it is clear that one cannot read off from the experience the character of its object, so as to say definitively that it is personal or impersonal, distinct from the world or one with it, active or quiescent. But what one can say is that at the centre of the human self there is some form of union or encounter with a reality which is felt to be both beyond the individual self and yet somehow at the very root of one's personal being. Just as one may contuit along with external finite realities the presence of a transcendent sustaining ground, so one may find within oneself a sustaining power which is beyond one's individual consciousness and yet at the centre of one's being, and which contains inspirational and creative resources upon which the conscious self can draw.

Christianity has a particular way of construing this reality, and the way to identify with and utilize it in one's daily life. Indeed, the Christian gospel, as it is outlined in the Pauline letters, is largely concerned with the transformation of inner being, the turning from the world and re-birth in the spirit which is said to be found in Christ. Basic to the Christian message is the claim that men can be freed from slavery to desire and anxious concern with the world, and brought to a new freedom to live in hope and confidence. As Paul says, 'God's love has flooded our inmost hearts through the Holy Spirit he has given us'.[4] The Christian claims to find a new power for living by his belief that Christ lives in and through his own life. In Judaism this conversion from anxiety to hope was effected by the sacrifices of atonement; and while Christians take these sacrifices to have been fulfilled and completed in Christ, the more important point is that the sacrifice is internalised in the believer, so that, as Christ died and rose again in glory, so the believer dies to the world and finds himself raised to new life through a power which is not his own, and which comes to him through the indwelling power of Christ. It must not be minimised how important this experience of rebirth is, whether sudden or gradual, in giving rise to the trust that God can transform human conduct, and thus that he is able to bring human

[3] Teresa of Avila, 'The Interior Castle', 7, 2; trans. Peers, A. E. *Complete Works of St. Theresa* (Sheed and Ward, 1946), vol. 2.
[4] Romans 5, 5.

lives to a fulfilment, which is only imperfectly exemplified in present human experience. The man who bases his whole life on a commitment to union with a transcendent reality, may find an experimental realisation of life in God, which licenses his whole-hearted trust that the promises of God are a dependable basis for Christian living.

The Christian believes that, through faith, his life is so transfigured that Christ lives in him. That is, the power of the inner self upon which he relies is conceived in overtly personal terms, on the model of a human personality which corresponds to that of the man who was lovingly remembered in the early church as the Messiah, the agent of God's grace and judgement in men's lives. It must not be forgotten that Christianity is not just a theoretical interpretation of the nature of reality. It is a gospel, good news to bring men new power for living and new wholeness of life. Thus the starting point of a living faith is often the recognition of a lack and insufficiency in one's own personal life, an acknowledgement that one is so concerned with the conscious self and its needs that one is cut off from the creative centre of one's true being. The way to open oneself to this creative centre is proclaimed by the Church to be faith in Christ—trust in a personalistically conceived transforming reality, which works from within to empower and re-orientate one's life. This strand of experience, the recognition of one's alienation from the depths of one's true being and the return to wholeness (salvation) through the union of the conscious ego with the unconditioned, is of major importance in religion; and its interpretation by means of the images of Christ's death, resurrection and indwelling presence develops the Christian concept of God as a liberating, renewing and salvific power working in and among men to establish a community of love.

2

The second strand of experience which helps to develop the notion of a personal and providential God is that of personal biography, in which particular purposes and patterns may be discerned in one's individual circumstances. Within the Hebraic tradition there have always been those who have felt a special calling and a providential guidance in their lives, bringing them up against situations which develop new resources in them and demand specific courses of action from them. It is a deeply rooted human belief that there are purposes involved in each unique human life, which work themselves out in ways which are often mysterious, but not random or wholly pointless. The Hebrew prophets constantly interpreted the historic destiny of their own people in terms of a call from God to holiness, and judgement as a result of unfaithfulness, manifested in terms of conquest and captivity. The life of individuals, too, was seen as specifically destined by God for some purpose, and providentially ordered—as Paul said, 'I was called from my mother's womb'.[5]

There are notorious theoretical difficulties with such beliefs. As the Hebrews saw, the unjust seem to flourish and the just to be cut down; there seem to be vast tracts of human life which are barren and purposeless; and one man's rejection of God's purpose must complicate any providential plan enormously—just as in a game of chess, one unforeseen move by an opponent must change the whole strategy of the game. Doctrines of providence are difficult to reconcile both with belief in human freedom and with the recognition that nature follows general and apparently necessary laws. Yet this difficulty is not impossibility; and just as the facts of human freedom and natural law do not prevent us from forming plans and implementing them, so those same facts do not prevent God from forming special intentions for human lives, and working to bring them to fruition. It is extremely difficult to see what the Divine intention for one's life is; and history is littered with the terrible results of fanatical beliefs that individuals have been chosen by God to perform some—sometimes horrifying—task. Yet the Judeo-Christian outlook has always been that every individual, in his own particularity, is of unique and irreplaceable value. However much his life may be limited and warped by the conditions of the alienated society into which he is born, he is called to express God's glory in his own unique way.

At the heart of the Christian gospel there is an intense concern for the value of the individual, who is to be received as of supreme importance ('Whoever does this, does so to me . . .').[6] And with this concern for individuality, there is a stress on vocation—the special calling of particular people to specific ways of life. Men are

[5] Gal. 1, 15.   [6] Mat. 25, 40.

not just called to obey general moral rules. Some are called to the contemplative life, some to social service, some to teach, some to administrate. And very often in the disappointments, opportunities and achievments of life, elements of purpose are discerned which lead one to say that one's life is being guided or shaped in a specific way. Belief in such guiding, or a sense of a specific destiny, is not an inference from prior belief in a personal God. It is a basic response to the course of one's own life, as one encounters certain possibilities, faces the consequences of past decisions and seeks the pattern which is distinctively right for one's own life. This search for the truth of one's own being, as it is pursued through times of good and bad fortune, leads one to characterize God as shaping one's destiny, and so ordering the course of life that some sort of personal growth will always be possible. This basic trust in being, and acceptance of a plan or purpose which is objectively in things, and not merely self-created, is at the heart of Judeo-Christian theism. The Christian will say that it is elicited as a response to the reality of God which discloses itself in his personal history; and it enables him to speak of God as a providential power, involved causally in the universe, and responding to free acts so as to guide and shape human lives in specific ways.

3

There is a third strand of experience which contributes to the Christian understanding of God as personal. This is the direct apprehension of a personal presence, known both in prayer and in the fellowship of believers. Martin Buber has given a classical exposition of such apprehension in his philosophical poem, 'I and Thou'.[7] He sketches there the way in which one can enter into a sort of relationship which is not that of person-to-object, but which is rather that of two subjects meeting and mutually apprehending each other. And he points out that this latter 'I-Thou' relationship is not confined to interpersonal situations, but may come suddenly upon one, whatever one is doing and whatever one's environment may be. Life can thereby become a dialogue of one personal reality—oneself—with another; and this other can be permanently present throughout all experience, without being

[7] Buber, M. *I and Thou*, trans. R. Gregor Smith (S.C.M. 1937).

confined to some spatial body, like that of another human being.
Some of the things Buber says about this dialogical relationship
may be unacceptable—as when he claims that one can have
acquaintance with the 'Thou' without having any knowledge
about it at all[8]—but he has certainly emphasized a sort of experience which is common in the Judeo-Christian tradition.

In Jewish and Christian devotion, there is the commonly
attested experience of those who pray and seek the presence of the
Lord that an uplifting, surrounding, consoling and loving presence
can make itself known, sometimes with startling intensity. Such
experiences grow more or less intense, sometimes fading altogether, and sometimes—as with Brother Lawrence[9]—becoming
a constant accompaniment to one's everyday actions. To one who
has felt this loving enfoldment in a greater presence, it is thereafter one of the most significant and decisive moments of his life.
And though words fail in describing it adequately, it is clear that
such love and joy is no impersonal force, but the most deeply
personal reality one can conceive. For it conveys an overwhelming
sense of love and care, which are attributes we only predicate of
persons. Perhaps some Christians have spoken too simply and
naively about their personal relationship with God, and in consequence conceived God too literally and anthropomorphically,
and reduced the mystery of his transcendent being too drastically.
The complex concept of God must be carefully balanced by considerations drawn from many areas of experience. Yet Christians
should not be led to deny the reality of the experience of the
sacred as a loving personal reality, which adds significantly to the
general characterization of God, and which comes to them particularly through the preaching of the risen and living Christ.

This reference to the living Christ focuses attention on the
Church as a decisive place of God's disclosure to men. By the
Church, in this context, I mean the fellowship of believers,
the *koinonia*, or sharing-with one another which does, or should,
characterize those who are united in the body of Christ. Where
groups of believers share together in prayer and the sacrament,
the presence of the personal reality of Christ is known between
and among them in a distinctive and unmistakable way. Between

[8] Cf. *ibid.*, p. 11.
[9] Br. Lawrence, *The Practice of the Presence of God*, trans. Attwater, D.
(Orchard Books, 1926).

them a personal presence is felt which has been described, throughout the history of the Church, as the continuing presence of Jesus Christ, who was raised from death to be for ever with his people. It is so described because of the continuity of this experience with that of the first believers, among whom Christ, the person they had been with in Galilee and had seen crucified, was made known in a different, but indisputably recognisable way in the breaking of bread. The person whose memory is recorded in the gospels, as loving, healing, forgiving and accepting, is still felt as a recognisable bearer of such qualities, in the fellowship of the Church.

Without such a claim to apprehend the presence of a living Christ, the church would not have preserved the central belief in Jesus' resurrection which it still proclaims. It is within the fellowship of those who come together, in obedience to Jesus' call to come to him, that the sacred is disclosed as the very person who was manifest in the life of Jesus of Nazareth, and who remains among his people for ever. Again, when one speaks of a 'person' in this context, one must be careful to bear in mind that the doctrine of God's transcendence prevents this term from being literally applied to God; what is being said is that, within the community of the Church, it is appropriate to respond to the sacred as to the gospel portrait of Jesus. This is the core of the distinctive Christian revelation that Jesus is raised from death; and it is naturally only within the Church that such a characterization of God is possible. Non-Christians may and do have a sense of personal encounter with God; but it is not with God as disclosed in the person of Jesus, known as a present reality in the fellowship of the Church. It cannot even be claimed that all Christian churches effectively function as media of such disclosure; but that is part of their proper function, and enables Christians to speak of God as a personal presence among his people in a very specific way.

4

The stress in what I have said about these three areas of human life has been on personal experience, and on specifically Christian experience; and it may be argued that personal experience is too subjective, variable and disputed to be a reliable basis for belief.

Ultimately, however, all justifiable beliefs rest upon some personal experience, even though we may often accept on authority the reports of others more competent in specific fields than we are. So the objection really comes down to the point that many people fail to have the experiences in question, or have experiences which they interpret differently; and that we ourselves may reject our own past interpretations. The failure of others to experience aspects of reality which the Christian characterizes in terms of the concept of 'God' is no argument that those aspects are incorrectly seen; unless, indeed, one wishes to accept only a lowest-common-denominator view of things, which will confine itself to the most mundane common-sense assertions about tables and chairs. To do that would simply beg the question, which is whether there are aspects of reality which are not thus open to all neutral observers, but which are very important for human life. It is true that different interpretations of these aspects exist. I have tried to show how this might be the case, and how it is only to be expected, in view of men's very different levels of intellectual and aesthetic and moral appreciation, their cultural background and historical and geographical context. This is the point at which the concept of 'revelation' enters, as the continuous development of a tradition of models for articulating various aspects of experience such as the ones mentioned in this chapter, which shapes the experience of a specific community of belief and is in turn shaped by that reflective experience.

There is a sense, of course, in which the experiences of presence, regeneration and providence of which I have just spoken are universally available to men. And they may be articulated in various ways; for instance, 'presence' may be construed by a category of 'the Holy' or 'sacred power' as well as by the category of 'personality'; regeneration may be construed in terms of an impersonal life force or inner psychic power; providence as some law of Fate or Karma (an inevitable law of moral reward and retribution). It is in the Jewish tradition that the dominant notion of a jealous, wrathful, consoling, forgiving, personal 'God', develops, as the One who gives the Law and makes a Covenant with a particular people. If one wants to know how God came to be conceived in this way, one needs to examine the nature of Hebrew experience, their general patterns of interaction with the total environment, the sorts of skill and practice they possessed.

It is then not totally unfair to point out that JHVH is conceived after the model of a tribal Sheikh, harsh in his justice and fearsome, though having compassion and demanding the desert virtues of hospitality from his people. And the terms by which he is poetically conceived—as 'rock', 'fortress', 'strong tower'—are terms taken from objects significant in desert warfare. It is completely misleading to suppose that God only spoke to the Israelites, and did so infallibly, *in vacuo*, without reference to their background and culture. One must interpret apprehension of the transcendent in terms of the concepts one has, which seem appropriate for preserving such apprehension. So the model of 'God' developed through the elaboration of sacrificial ritual and historical and prophetic experience; and various aspects of experience were construed in terms of those models.

Old Testament religion cannot be our religion—our situation and culture is too radically different—but it can remain as a primordial source for our religion, since its models of transcendence have proved capable of extension and adaptation both to shape and adjust to new situations and insights. We can still stand in the tradition of the holy mountain-god, for there are elements here—of power and morality—which have not lost their force, and which carry the emotional weight of many generations of believers with them.

It may be objected that such a view sees religion as developing always from the human side; that it leaves no room for the revealing activity of God. The force of this objection cannot be clear until one sees what it means to speak of the 'revealing activity of God'. It would, I think, be totally unsatisfactory to conceive this as a series of discontinuous acts in which God either shows himself to someone or puts words into their minds automatically. Such a view is only possible when one thinks of God as one object among others in the universe, albeit a mysterious one. The Scriptures of the great religions—the Vedas, Bible and Koran—are all products of imaginative and poetic excellence; they reflect the attempts of the human mind to understand or react to a spiritual reality which was apprehended. Since God is the creator of all things, he sustains the mind as well as the physical world, and is able to order it to his purposes. So he can inspire man to the imaginative grasp of his reality, as apprehended in some aspect of human experience. In other words, given an adequate notion of

God as creator of all things, it is just not possible to oppose the development of human imaginative insight to the revealing act of God in nature. Both are under God's creative power; the acts of men are not to be divorced from the continual act of God in creation.

However, one may still ask whether these different imaginative insights can all be true; whether, therefore, they can all be inspired by God. One is really asking here which images are most adequate to characterize the transcendent. At this point one must bear firmly in mind the complexity of theistic language; it is not neutrally descriptive, so that its 'truth' can be checked against publicly accessible unambiguous data. Yet it is not therefore purely emotive, or a set of expressions of subjective emotions. Religions offer images which promise an enrichment of one's imaginative insight, together with a sustenance in sorrow and deprivation; a clarification of moral demands together with an offer of forgiveness for human failure; a contemplative loving dialogue that is offered through but beyond all contingent occurrences of fortune. Of course, religion offers psychological integration and fulfilment, strength and hope for the future; but it does so by adjusting the mind to the fulness of the reality which meets one. Religion opposes or should oppose any attempt to restrict or confine the sorts of reality which one can experience; instead, it points to a transcendent reality mediated in all the particularities of our personal history. To 'believe in God' is to receive one's existence at every moment as a gift, to explore it as a creative response to meaning, to respond to the continual dialogue of historical existence, to look to the future with hope but without attachment. 'God' is the reality one relates oneself to through and in the adoption of these attitudes. Thus belief in God can grow and fade; and to be able so to believe, the Christian will say, is a gift of grace. It is important to see that belief is not a passive acceptance of creeds or dogmas, but an individual creative activity, in which the images of faith, which evoke and clarify specific human moods and reactions, are re-worked and explored, as one's own experience and thinking develops. It is in religious belief that every individual is capable of finding depths of creativity which can and should enrich and extend his own reactions to the world. To study the language of a religious faith, in its context of ritual and cultural action, is to learn the way to the imaginative apprehension of the world which distinguishes that faith, and within which believers find the pattern of their experience and action becoming clear to them.

No man can view all religious traditions dispassionately, as if to assess their merits from outside. Such an operation is precluded by the very nature of religious belief, which requires commitment and involvement as a precondition of sympathetic understanding. One can, of course, try to understand other religions from within one's own, but even then one will be looking for differences and similarities which one can recognise in terms of the images one already has available. It is true that an image from a different faith may in turn cast a new light on one's own traditions; but, except in situations of total conversion, the matter is one of adaptation or adjustment; one's understanding is basically controlled by the patterns of thought from which one begins. So it is unrealistic to pretend to evaluate the adequacy of religious images from a position of non-commitment.

The experience of the Christian believer is bounded on one side by tradition—the long, checkered history of the community which has preserved and developed the imagery of the Christian life, and kept alive the cherished memory of a man who, it is believed, is in some sense still a presence within the framework of the community dedicated to his name. It is bounded on the other side by hope—that in some unforeseeable way the imagery, now so often obscure and latent in power, will find an adequate fulfilment, a greater clarity and comprehensiveness. Between this memory and this hope, the Christian community offers the images of its faith—images of reconciliation, sanctification and love—to the world, and in turn attempts to refashion these images so as to prompt creative responses to changing situations—responses which, though new, will still fall within the configuration of faith.

There are, however, many different types of imaginative configurations in religion; many sorts of approach to the reality they seek to reveal through the medium of a response articulated in a complex of images. Even within one religion, there exist many varieties of emphasis and interpretation. It seems to me very important that freedom to expand and intermingle should be encouraged, so that one does not look for and insist upon one true inalienable core of faith, an 'essence of Christianity'. There is an understandable tendency to try and define the things which a

Christian must believe, if he is to be counted as a Christian at all. But this tendency should be resisted; all that matters is whether what a man says is acceptable on its own terms. The term 'Christian' will be applied to signify a continuity of some sort with the historic origin of the Christian churches. But there is not just one sort of continuity. One must say that there is something valuable which has come to one in a certain tradition with which one wishes to identify oneself in some, not all, respects. This may be the life of worship, prayer and spirituality, preserved in the community which lovingly remembers the man Jesus; but it may be something rather different than this. The plurality of traditions, even within one faith, must be preserved and encouraged; as must the possibility of continual and unrestricted development to new insights and creative responses in the diverse Christian community.

Within such a perspective of a plurality of developing traditions, tracing their origins back to a number of diverse originative images, it becomes impossible to speak of religious truth as a once-for-all establishment of a perfect correspondence between concept and reality. It is more like the continuing pursuit of a greater adequacy or depth, by means of which one can come to adopt a more open, creative, imaginative response to reality. This is a truth which is in constant change, in which one lives, which one's own quality and direction of response helps to establish. But it is objective in that, in the end, one's images extend or impede one's vision, succeed in unfolding a greater reality or else close it off and restrict it. Religious images claim to reveal depths of meaning in the world we experience, by relating it to transcendence; and there is a sense in which they can be experientially verified. Images like that of God as 'father' are not precisely defined, unambiguous and based on careful analysis, classification and induction. They are creative, holistic, elusive, ambiguous, multi-faceted and developing; and they are based on experience, a lived pattern of experimental responsiveness to situations, promulgated in the first place by a religiously imaginative genius, one, as we say, 'inspired by God'. So, if one asks if religious revelations are 'true', one is asking about their illuminative power in disclosing the meanings which experience can communicate. There are clearly degrees of truth possible in religion, and one will naturally assent to that tradition in which one finds the greatest degree of imaginative adequacy. This in no way precludes one from finding enriching insights in other faiths, or from feeling unable to accept every traditional interpretation of one's own faith. While the Christian finds the Hebraic understanding of 'God' as holy father paradigmatic for his own understanding, he may well find his experience enriched by using complementary insights evoked by the Hindu notion of Brahman; and one may expect that this will increasingly be the case, as knowledge of other religions grows.

5

An important conclusion of all that I have just said about the notion of 'God' is that it rules out all confident ontologising statements about the inner life of God, saying what his knowledge is like, or whether he feels emotions and so on; and it recommends a way of speaking which confines itself to talk only of the relation of God to man—as father, king and judge, e.g.—and even then in a way which regulates human attitudes to God rather than describes modes of God's activity.

In constructing a concept of God, philosophers have sometimes tried to consider all those properties which possess intrinsic value, take them to an imagined maximal state, and define God in terms of them. One might then say that the absolute value consists in the fact that a maximally fulfilling object is known fully to itself and loved completely by itself and for itself. This is an attractive conception, which was used by Augustine and Aquinas to construe the interior life of the Blessed Trinity.[10] But it is very difficult to make it intelligible. If one negates all aspects of temporal change and all finite objects of contemplation (beautiful trees, sunsets, sounds, etc.) it may be wondered whether anything is left, or whether it makes sense to speak of a maximally fulfilling object which, as it were, contains all possible types of fulfilling experience in itself, to the fullest possible degree (though it must nevertheless exclude all finite objects and fulfilments). What is of value, for men, is the state of apprehending and appreciating objects which give fulfilment through the immanent act of understanding. This is bound up so much with creative effort, temporal change and increasing

---

[10] Cf. Aquinas, *Summa Theologiæ*, Pt. 1, Qus. 27–43; and Augustine, 'De Trinitate', Bk. 15, in *Augustine: Later Works*, trans. J. Burnaby (S.C.M., 1955), vol. 8.

depth and complexity of vision, that it is doubtful whether any humanly experienced value can be conceived as existing in God, as infinite being. Moreover, many values depend on the possession of bodies, or on the necessity of overcoming obstacles and imperfections in the world (e.g. the virtue of sympathy depends upon the existence of pain or sorrow in others); so again, it is hard to see what values would be left for God to contain. The Hegelian view that the Absolute self-consciousness includes in itself all finite realities offers an escape from these difficulties; for then fulfilment is achieved through the temporal evolution of the world-process. Unfortunately, it leads to greater difficulties of its own, raised by the proposal that all individuals are somehow included in God, as part of his being.

If one insists on saying of God only what is required by the contexts in which the notion has its natural place, one may provide a more cautious or agnostic account of these matters. One needs to say that human values are achievable only by creative response to fulfilling objects (e.g. natural beauty). Such objects are not valuable in themselves alone—a piece of music has no value, unheard by anyone. Yet that music may have the capacity to challenge, delight and bring the mind to one sort of fulfilment. In saying that God is the ground of values, one is saying that objects will be such as to provide the possibility of fulfilment, and that the mind will be such as to have the capacity to know and love such objects. When that happens, it is not the object which is loved purely for its physical properties. It provides the possibility of communicating a transcendent significance; the physical reality is so constructed that, when apprehended, it may become transparent to its creative ground. What can one say of that creative ground? Nothing; except that it is revealed to this creative response of the human mind. In revealing God, objects do not provide insight into additional truths; they bring the mind into a fulfilling communion with what is revealed in this way and no other. One may say that objects can be loved for themselves, as long as it is seen that what they truly are is not merely a sum of physical properties, but vehicles of an inner significance which is offered to complete human consciousness.

If one holds to the principle that God can be known only in his effects, one can only say that God sets the conditions of the possibility of all values and, perhaps, that he ensures their final fulfilment. One must consequently say that God has causal power over the world, that he 'knows' it and guides it intelligently. But to say these things is not to claim knowledge of the interior being of God; it is simply to say that the universe must be considered as rationally ordered towards a moral end. Talk of knowledge, power and wisdom is the only way we can make that belief picturable; but it in no way increases our understanding of the nature of the reality pictured by our concepts.

However, does this view provide the possibility of worship? Here, I think, one must take the bold step of stating that 'worship' *is* the open-ness to and affirmation of those challenging, fulfilling and judging aspects of reality of which the mind can become aware when, in the step of faith, it takes objects and situations as transparent to an undescribable, but revealed, significant reality. It may be objected that 'worship' can, as a matter of logic, only be given to a being which actually possesses every perfection unsurpassably and necessarily. One cannot worship any finite being which possesses its qualities to a limited degree. Certainly, one does not worship the objects in which one finds fulfilment. But one may be said to worship the reality which they reveal. One worships when one adopts an attitude of self-abeisance, thankfulness, submission and reverence before whatever is mysteriously revealed through—or, more loosely, in the context of—finite beings. If one would not worship a finite quality, I see no reason to suppose that one should worship the same quality, magnified to infinity—and this is apart from the incoherence of the idea of a being which possesses all properties infinitely. There is a paradoxical sense in which the attitude of worship has no object; certainly no specifiable object; as 'dread' or 'anxiety' may be a general reactive mood to all experience, so worship, the joyful and accepting heart of the believer, is a constant attitude maintained through all experience—the disposition to find and acknowledge value, and to dwell in an undescribable 'presence'.

What I am maintaining is that it does not help, in explaining the object of worship, to say that it contains all perfections to an infinite degree. Nevertheless, it is in responding to values in the world—values of beauty, morality and personal relationships—that one feels the object of worship to be most clearly revealed. One may, I think, try the analogy of the revelation of a person's moods in his behaviour. It would not help to say that the person contained in his spiritual being an infinite form of his (e.g.) joyful behaviour; yet it is in such behaviour that his joy, his spiritual nature on that occasion, is revealed most aptly. The ways in which we speak of God are developed from revelatory situations within the world, and so are limited to discourse about God as 'embodied' in the world. It does not help to say that God contains in his spiritual being an infinite form of his revealed qualities.

6

The tendency of this analogy is to make the world the body of God, and process-theologians like Hartshorne have accepted and pressed the suggestion; thus one must ask how far this analogy may be pressed.[11] After all, one may say, how can one say that a man is angry, unless there are bodily expressions of his anger? Similarly, how can one say that God is good, wise or powerful without some manifestations of these dispositions in the world? However, it is clear that the analogy of the body cannot be taken too far—for instance, the universe has no central nervous system. And men, as conscious agents, would have to be included in the 'body'; yet persons do not interact with or communicate personally with parts of their own bodies. One basic question at issue here is whether the world is necessary to the expression of the being of God, as physical bodies are necessary to human beings.

How would one decide what is or what is not necessary to God? One may certainly say that God is revealed in and communicates through the world; that the terms in which one speaks of God are all taken from aspects of the world; even that, in discovering God one is discovering the inner reality and significance of the world; these are points about the logic of 'God'. One discovers God as the comprehensible necessity of the universe; as the absoluteness of the moral claim and the depth of beauty in things; as a moral purpose in reality; and as an immediate object of the worshipful, self-transcending attitude cultivated in the spiritual life. To believe in God is to affirm something about the universe, in its present nature as sacramental of a spiritual and unitary reality

[11] Cf. Hartshorne, C. *Beyond Humanism* (University of Nebraska, 1969), p. 208. 'And we shall never understand a God of love unless we conceive him as the all-sensitive mind of the world-body.'

and in its destiny as morally orientated. These are strands of experience which tend to support a pantheistic monism.

But there are other strands which tend to support the separation of the world and God. There is the freedom and individuality of human selves; the fact that there is evil, ugliness and lack of order and purpose in the world; the fact that, in seeking to realise valuable states in himself, man responds to the being of God, as an object of faith and adoration, other than himself or any finite reality. However, I wish to pose the radical question, whether there is ultimately any real distinction between monism and belief in God's distinctness from the world. There is a clear verbal distinction; but talk about God must be so qualified and hesitant that two seemingly opposed views may merge into indistinction when each is suitably qualified. For example, those who hold that the universe is an appearance of Brahman, the ultimately real, nevertheless believe that the world is real, as illusion, and to that extent distinct from Brahman, in which there is no illusion. On the other hand, those who hold that God exists completely and perfectly without the world, nevertheless believe that the world is wholly maintained in being by God and reflects his perfections more or less adequately, and all that they say about God is said in terms derived from the world.

Hindus may say that the world exists as a necessary manifestation of Brahman, and that human destiny is to be absorbed into Brahman; whereas Christians may say that the world exists gratuitously, through a free act of the Divine will, and that human destiny is to find personal fulfilment through the redemptive conquest of evil, and in the fellowship of mutual love. But these are both fairly crude models, generated by philosophical speculation out of the fundamental realities of the personal acknowledgement of a spiritual reality and commitment to the fuller realisation of it in the adoption of a particular pattern of spirituality, prayer or meditation. It may be intellectually satisfying to build a coherent speculative system on such a basis, to make clea and precise what for faith remains vague and mysterious. But the development of speculative doctrines provides men, who perversely always seek what is new, with endless opportunities for dogmatic debate, controversy and disagreement. I think one must ask whether disputes of this nature have any connexion with the vital realities of faith at all. The guiding principle should perhaps be: only so much as is required by faith. One must always ask, of any speculative doctrine, what is its experiential basis, and how far does that basis really license one in proceeding?

Of course there are differences in patterns of human spirituality which are enshrined in speculative metaphysical differences; but the typical tendency of metaphysics is to take these differences and place them on an intellectually abstract and embracingly cosmic plane, to make them into a total world-view, defended by intricate conceptual preambles. The danger is that the intellectual debate obscures the spiritual distinction it started from. Indeed, in many doctrinal controversies in theology one finds it impossible to remember that there is any spiritual experience present even embryonically, so bitter and denunciatory do the arguments become. What is needed now most of all is the re-affirmation of patterns of spiritual experience, and their general defence against agnostic doubts and attacks.

I suppose that a Christian would see the danger of Vedantic Hinduism as being that a stress on the necessity of the world may lead to an absence of the desire to change and reform it, since all is as it must be and is as such good. And a stress on the absorption of individuals into Brahman may lead to a failure to emphasise the intrinsic worth of each human personality and the importance of realising as many positive values in the world and human lives as possible. That is to say that the pattern of spirituality preferred by Christians is one which emphasizes a positive approach to the world, affirming its basic goodness and the necessity of redemptively transfiguring the evil in it. As far as pure speculation goes, such practical beliefs could be contained in a monistic system which stressed the value of the sensory world, as part of Brahman, and posited a redemptive creativity at the heart of the world-process. But as a matter of fact they have developed within, and helped in the further elaboration of, the Judaic tradition of covenant and Divine law, with associated notions of atonement for sin through the shedding of blood—a tradition which has pictured God monarchically, as Lord and King of a world he made. Whereas Vedantic metaphysics grew around a pattern of spirituality which tended to see the empirical world as simply illusion, to be left behind, and to see human suffering as the inevitably ordained penalty for past sins.

In each case, the metaphysical world-view has taken on the

colour of its generative spiritual basis. But it is important to see the extent to which this is a contingent matter, which could easily have been otherwise. It is a profound and common mistake to treat models of God which have been speculatively developed as 'infallibly revealed' in all their technical detail. What one must see is the function in human life which the models are meant to perform; what one must avoid is the standardisation of certain models as abstractly 'true', when their living function has long been transcended and forgotten. Religions can well take up an agnostic attitude as to the possibility or success of particular speculative systems; for a religion is basically a way of life which binds man in an experimental, developing relationship with transcendent reality, as communicated in a particular historical tradition.

Some metaphysical systems (e.g. logical positivism) exclude the possibility of the spiritual life; these must naturally be opposed by believers. But do those systems which allow for the spiritual life carry any specific implications for the way in which that life is to be conceived? If one could independently establish as true, say, the Absolute Idealist conception of reality, this might have implications for religious practices; perhaps worship would be replaced by meditation. But many metaphysical systems try to incorporate religious experiences as part of the evidence for their truth; and one must always ask, of any such system, whether the evidence for it is more or less strong than the evidence of one's own experience of religious life. I would think that, in general, purely speculative considerations are rarely as strong as considerations drawn from one's own religious experience. Faced with a system which renders central elements of his devotional life irrational or superfluous (say, worship and gratitude), the Christian must reject it, unless it is more rationally compelling than his own experience—which is unlikely to be the case; but may be the case in situations of pathological beliefs or of hitherto not clearly thought out subsidiary practices of his faith. Still, it may be that there is more than one metaphysical system which will preserve the elements the Christian values; and here, he may either choose one conceding that it is not the only system adequate to Christian belief; or refrain from doing anything other than rejecting unsatisfactory systems, on the grounds of the limitations of human reasoning powers.

7

The conclusion is, then, that one can say this: the doctrine that God is Creator, for a Christian involves that God alone is the proper object of adoration and reverence; that man is wholly dependent upon God for his existence and preservation, though he is free to create his own future, within limits; that Jesus is 'one with God' in a unique way; that the world is wholly under the power of God. These beliefs exclude a crude pantheism which simply identifies everything equally with God, and a crude Gnosticism which conceives matter as an evil principle co-eternal with God, resisting his will. These exclusions are expressed by the doctrine of creation *ex nihilo*, that the world is other than God, but wholly depends on his will. Yet this doctrine gives no one positive characterization of creation; and there are various qualified senses of 'other than' and 'depends on' which can be used so as to construct an acceptable non-Thomist understanding of creation. One may say that God is the 'Real', of which the world is an appearance; or that the world is a progressively less real series of emanations from God's full reality; or that the universe of free organisms is part of God, as the inclusive super-organism. The Christian may remain agnostic between these, or choose one on speculative grounds; but it would be false and dangerous to claim that only one Christian view on the issue is possible. As so often with these debates, the time-honoured labels—pantheist and dualist—are not important in themselves, and are misleading in that they conceal so many shades and subtleties of meaning; what one has to attempt is to see the similarities and dissimilarities between God and the world which such crude labels conceal as much as depict.

The basic religious awareness underlying doctrines of 'God' as creator and father is that we are sustained in being by a present power, before which one feels existentially dependent; our life is radically dependent on God, and he has the right to order it as he wills. He is apprehended as both a moral, sustaining and dread-fully majestic, incomprehensible power, making a total claim on men; he is the one who owns men. As the Hebrew tradition develops, this God becomes a controlling moral power in history, bringing his will to pass. The world is his fiat because he is not an imminent world-principle but a moral power, erupting from without to judge and purify the world. Yet he can be approached in gratitude and confidence for his present gifts and hope of future fulfilment, and he gives a new sense of responsibility for the future, the *eschaton*, the goal of history. The roots of Christian faith lie in the ethically conceived personal experience and the history of the Jewish people, with their special sense of calling and vocation. But though that is the primordial experience of Christianity, the rational immanentism of Greek and nature-religions can be taken to complement the Hebraic insights, which must always remain in some sense dominant. And the whole configuration is re-shaped and re-orientated for Christians by the new paradigm model of Jesus. Those who wish to adopt belief in God without recourse to revelation usually fail to see how much their notion owes to a revelatory tradition, and how much weaker speculation is than experience. But if one is to appeal to revelation, one must appeal to a specific revelatory tradition, as one's own paradigm model. The reference to particularity is, I would think, essential and ineradicable; and the failure to see that has been the endemic failure of speculative philosophers.[12] But I would also wish to stress that, in the acceptance of a particular tradition, one should be prepared to allow a plurality of interpretations, a continuity of development, and a wide area of agnosticism in the formulation of one's definitive beliefs. Particularly in a largely secular culture, Christianity must affirm the centrality and rationality of revelation; but it must also clearly free itself from restrictive and limiting interpretations of the notion of 'revelation'; and it can do this by remembering that revelation is always directed to the renewal of human life, so that it must ultimately be tested by reference to the experience of the believer within the community which specifies the exemplary way of life and the power to live it.

[12] A typical example is Kant, in *Religion Within the Limits of Reason Alone*, trans. Greene, T. M. and Hudson, H. H. (Harper Torchbooks, 1960), cf. p. 55.

CHAPTER TEN

GOD AS INCARNATE

I

For Christians, God is primarily typified as 'the Father almighty, maker of heaven and earth'.[1] There are three main aspects of the image of fatherhood which deserve consideration. God is father, as the creator, the source of all being and value, as an earthly father is the source of his children's lives. God is father, as a sustaining and providential presence, as an earthly father is a source of security and guidance for his children. And God is father, as the father of Jesus Christ, through whom all men may become sons of God by adoption. All these aspects are developed within the tradition of the Church, so that particular patterns of spirituality and ontology are preserved within one community of language and ritual.

The first aspect has been explored briefly in terms of speculative concepts drawn largely from the Greek philosophers. The second has been illustrated from the Hebrew tradition of an absolute moral demand—expressed in the Torah—and a promise of fulfilment—expressed in the Covenant with the Jews, as representatives and mediators of all mankind; and also in more specific Christian revelation in the Church and personal experience. The third aspect, though is has been occasionally adverted to, must now be explored further. For it is vital to realise clearly that the Christian concept of God is essentially that of the Trinity; it is not that of a Creator, to which can be subsequently added the idea of the incarnation and then that of the Paraclete. It is, of course, true that the Christian notion is built upon the Jewish notion, in that the religious tradition from which it sprang was that of Judaism. But the Jewish concept was not simply added to by saying that the Almighty Father had, as a matter of fact, become man. It was, rather, a complete transformation of the old

[1] The so-called Apostles' Creed, recited in the Daily Office.

concept; so that God is conceived as essentially Creator, incarnate as redemptive love in the world, and empowering Spirit. The redemptive activity which is expressed in the incarnation is not added to the creation, as something leaving it unchanged and which may not have been. It is part of the creation, part of what it is for God to be truly God.

Perhaps it will be objected to this conception that God, having created the world, was free to become incarnate or not; the fact that he did so was an act of unpremeditated, unpredictable and totally gratuitous freedom. Once again, the trap of ontologism has been sprung, and one finds oneself discoursing knowledgeably about God's inner life! The question is not really as to what God could or could not do. It is about what our concept of 'God' is going to be. So, in answering it, one does not place limitations on what God can do; one simply decides what the concept of 'God' is going to mean. For the Christian, who speaks of Jesus as 'God', it must be part of the meaning of the concept of 'God' that it includes reference to historical events. Belief in the incarnation changes one's concept of 'God'; it does not give additional knowledge of what an antecedently identified God does.

The Christian claim is that, though religious understanding may develop continually in different ways, the Church's originative experience of Jesus remains a paradigm model for the reality of 'God'. In that experience, the notion of 'fatherhood' took on a new significance, in that God was then seen primarily as 'the father of Jesus Christ'. Those theologians are right who have held that the Christian God cannot be understood except as the father of Jesus Christ, and therefore only through Christ.[2] But how can we come to know Jesus as the Christ, when the historical individual is so far away in history, and the scholarly consensus as to his acts and beliefs so tenuous and often conflicting? Jesus is known as the Christ only within the community of the Church. The documents of the New Testament testify to the general impact he made on the apostles, and show the development of early theologizing about him; the history of doctrine shows the building up of various spiritual traditions on that foundation; and present experience of Christ in the Church testifies to a living force conveyed by some of those traditions. In terms of classical theology, Christ is seen as an eternal person of the Trinity, who becomes incarnate in

[2] E.g. Karl Barth, *Church Dogmatics*, 2, 1.

Jesus, teaches about the Kingdom of God, lives a life of love and gives his life as a sacrifice for the sin of the world, then rises from death, intercedes with the Father for all men, and will return in glory to judge the world. But there are other complex elements in the tradition too—the community of believers is the body of Christ,[3] all will be one 'in' him, and he dwells in the believer, bringing a new power of life. If Jesus is the eternal victim, intercessor and judge, he is also 'in' all believers, and they will at last be united 'in' him.[4] Different images qualify and extend each other, making any easily stateable doctrine of Christ's nature and work impossible to achieve.

It is not within the scope of this work to develop a Christology; my concern is only to uncover those elements of the Christian concept of 'God' which are derived from the person of Jesus. I have held that this concept has an essential reference to Jesus, and so cannot be properly understood without such a reference. But, on the other hand, the person of Jesus must be interpreted in terms of some antecedent understanding of 'God' before it can make any sort of sense to say that Jesus *is* 'God'. It seems to me quite an incredible assertion that only in that one man, and by reference to him, does the term 'God' take on any meaning.[5] It may enrich, extend and even transform the Judaic concept of God to say that Jesus is God; but the logic of that statement is much too complex to be given by a simple reference to one allegedly unique person. Jesus is recorded as having accepted the Judaic concept of God as 'holy father'. But for the Church, he came to be regarded as 'son of God' in a unique sense, so that other men become sons through adoption, by incorporation into Christ. As mystics have constantly affirmed, we are all God's sons; but this sonship is given a particular and intimate form for the Christian by being conceived as a 'growing into' Christ. We are baptised into his death, that we may rise empowered with his resurrection life; so, from being slaves to sin, we become sons of God, reconciled by Christ's sacrificial work and united with him in service and love.[6]

Jesus, as a historical individual, is remembered in the New Testament as a man who preached the inauguration of the King-

---

[3] 1 Cor. 12, 27.   [4] Jn. 17, 21–3.
[5] A position near this is taken by van Buren, P. *The Secular Meaning of the Gospel* (S.C.M. 1963).
[6] Rom. 6, 4.

dom of God with authority, and gathered around himself a group
of followers who preached repentance as a condition of entrance
into the Kingdom.[7] He was put to death, perhaps partly because
of the disappointment of those who looked to him for a political
interpretation of 'salvation', and partly because the religious
authorities felt that their authority was being attacked. Yet after
his death there were strange appearances to some of his followers,
and then a dramatic moment when the company felt themselves
empowered to proclaim that Jesus had conquered death, still lived,
and was the coming Messiah. There is a sense in which the apostles
still misinterpreted Jesus in terms of political Messianic cate-
gories, as an imminent judge of all men, as God's representative.
It was only gradually that belief in an immanent Return in glory
was superceded by a stress on the new life made possible in Christ.
There are thus at least three main strands in early Christian belief;
the call to the Kingdom of God, made by Jesus; the hope for the
Messiah, as judge and redeemer of all men, held by the apostles;
and belief in the present redemption from sin and freedom for
a new life, presented in John's gospel and the Epistles. These
should not be regarded as exclusive or conflicting; though the
particular form in which they were held was sometimes mistaken
(as in the belief that the Day of the Lord was at hand), these
strands of belief remain valid for Christians today, as complementary perspectives for understanding the new relationship of God
and man which was effected by the life of Jesus.

Subsequent theological reflection has been an attempt, with
varying success, to comprehend the place of Jesus in the new
understanding of God which is paradigmatically expressed in the
imagery of a crucified and resurrected Lord. On the one hand, it
was always stressed that Jesus was fully a man; and thus attempts
on Gnostic or Apollinarian lines to see the human body as just an
appearance of God, a form of apparition lacking full human
individuality and freedom, were always resisted by the early
Church Councils. On the other hand, Arian attempts to distinguish Jesus from God, to make him no more than a creature,
were equally resisted; so that the Church, in 451, issued the
famous, if incomprehensible, Chalcedonian formula that Jesus
had 'two natures, without confusion, without change, without
division, without separation . . . concurring in one person and one

[7] Mat. 10, 5–8.

hypostasis'.[8] This form of words is explicitly paradoxical—the two natures being unconfused and yet undivided at the same time—and because the terminology of 'nature' and 'person' reflects Platonic philosophical doctrines of existent real essences, the formula may be simply rejected as contradictory and philosophically primitive. Yet it may also manage to convey a picture which, though conceptually confused and distorted, yet safeguards and gives expression to the Christian conception of life in Christ. For it is undoubtedly the case that in the devotional life of the orthodox Christian churches, Jesus is taken as God, and as thereby transforming the Judaic notion of God.[9]

2

The vital thing to be clear about is the supreme mysteriousness of talking of God at all, and *a fortiori* of 'identifying' any finite thing with God. Many problems of Patristically influenced theology dissolve when their philosophical terminology is probed and dissected, only to recur in quite a different conceptual context. God, I have maintained, is non-denumerable, the unknowable, uncreated ground of all created beings. He must be conceived as all-knowing and all-powerful to enable us to accept the hope for a moral fulfilment of reality; but in saying these things we in no way increase our theoretical knowledge—i.e. we do not understand what God's 'knowledge' or 'causality' is like. Now, if one says of any person that he is 'identical' with God, the meaning of 'identity' here must be clearly distinguished from its normal meanings. It clearly cannot refer to spatio-temporal identity, or state that there is some spatio-temporal continuity between God and any creature; for God is non-spatio-temporal. An analogy may be sought in the notion of personal identity; for, it may be said, John Smith as a baby is identical with John Smith in heaven (after death), even though there is no physical continuity or perhaps not even temporal continuity there. It is noteworthy that this case is itself highly contentious; but let us suppose it conceivable that a person may be said to be identical with someone, even where a spatio-

[8] Bindley, *The Ecumenical Documents of the Faith* (Methuen, 1899), p. 229 ff.
[9] Cf. the Nicene Creed, said at the Eucharist.

temporal discontinuity exists between them. Presumably what one would have in mind is that some creative centre of will and knowledge is preserved from one case to the other. But even this mysterious and contentious sense of 'identity' gives no parallel to a God-creature identity; for there can be no literal identity of (e.g.) a human will and God's will, between a creaturely will faced with choices between limited possibilities and the ground of all possibilities and the absolute demand on creaturely obedience. No literal identity; yet Nestorius' suggestion that Jesus' human will had a qualitative, rather than numerical, identity with God's will, did not find favour with the Catholic Church.[10] To avoid these puzzles and confusions one must abandon the picture, which the word identity almost inevitably conjures up, of some thing or being enduring through change, and thus being identical with itself. Since God is not a thing, but the ground of all things, such a picture could never have application.

A better way might be to examine what people are engaged in doing when they assert that such and such a finite thing 'is' God. When primitive peoples, e.g. regard a totem-animal or a rock as divine, they typically offer libations to it, deck it with garlands, treat it with respect, even fear, and perform rituals around it. One can imagine them saying, 'This is a real rock, alright, not an hallucination; but it is not just a rock, or we would not treat it in this way; it is fully rock and fully God, two natures in one substance'. One might be sceptical about their philosophy; but I think one would take the point that this real rock is being treated as God by those people. The attitudes they adopt to it, and which it somehow helps to evoke in them, are here given a specific, finite object or focus; but those attitudes are particular rehearsals of more general dispositional responses to the whole of their experience, and through it all to the ground of that experience (which we might call 'God the Father or creator'). But, one might say, the important question must be, 'Is the stone really God?' What can one be asking here? Whether it made the world— including itself, presumably? Whether it knows, feels and thinks? But the answers to those questions are known; it is clear that not

---

[10] Nestorius was condemned at the Council of Ephesus, 431 A.D. But a reconsideration of his view is to be found in: *Nestorius and his Teaching*, J. F. Bethune-Baker (C.U.P. 1908), and *Nestorius*, F. Loofs (C.U.P., 1914).

everything said of the Creator can be said of the stone; so the stone must be distinguished from the creator, in some sense (so it is clear that the man Jesus, born of Mary, did not make the world, and is not omniscient and omnipotent; so 'God the Son' is distinguished from 'God the Father'). One could be asking, 'Is it appropriate to take these attitudes to this rock, to treat it thus?' Appropriate, in view of what? Certainly it would not be appropriate to treat any or all rocks like that. What would make it appropriate to react to this rock thus? We might say, given our traditions and beliefs, that nothing would; we would probably even find rock-worship positively inappropriate. This may be either because we do not believe in God—and therefore think that any devotion of this sort must be inappropriate, as probably involving mistaken beliefs about how such worship might affect the course of one's future life (e.g. protecting it from harm)—or because we regard rocks as giving only a very limited notion of the reality of God—which would be because we claimed to have a less limited notion.

It is natural to start talking of 'symbols' at this point, and to say that rocks are limited symbols of God, whereas perhaps the life of a good and holy man is a more adequate symbol. But the usual understanding of symbols is that they are clearly distinct from that which they symbolize;[11] so that one could never be said to worship a symbol, but only to use it as a means of calling to mind that reality one does properly worship. To use the word 'symbol' in this sense supposes that one is, or could be, independently acquainted with the symbolizandum; if a flag represents a country, we know that the country exists independently, and we could travel around it and meet its people and statesmen. In this sense, something could be a symbol of God if it represented a reality which was taken to exist and be knowable independently of the symbol. So the rock-worshipper might not want to say that the rock is a symbol of an independently real God, whose nature would be what it is whether or not the rock existed and who is in principle knowable more directly in other ways. He might wish to say two important things: (a) that the rock is God, in the sense that God's nature would not be the same, in important respects, if the rock did not exist—so that the existence of that rock can be

---

[11] But cf. Tillich, P. *Dynamics of Faith* (Harper, 1957), p. 42: symbols, unlike signs, participate in the reality they symbolize, Tillich claims.

called 'part of God'; (b) that God, at least in this important and determinative respect, is unknowable except by apprehension of that rock. So, with Jesus, the Christian may wish to say that the existence of Jesus makes a difference to the being of God—and not just the sort of difference which the existence of any creature makes, namely, that God's knowledge and love change in response to every contingent act of creatures. Consequently, the Christian may say, in this decisively important respect God could not be known except through the community which records the remembrance of the man Jesus. These assertions have been traditionally expressed in the orthodox doctrines that God redeems the world in Jesus and that Jesus, as the risen Lord, is a proper object of worship.

Both of these doctrines are exceedingly complex, and need to be carefully unravelled to show what they allow and what they exclude, in thinking of God. One does not worship the human nature of Jesus; that would be idolatry. One worships the 'person' of Jesus, which contains both divine and human 'natures', in virtue of the fact that it includes the divine 'nature'. It is analytic that one worships the divine nature, in that it is through analysis of the divine nature that one is able to define what worship is. I have suggested that worship is openness to and affirmation of transcendent value, disclosed in finite realities, an attitude of submission, thankfulness, love and awe towards what is revealed through those realities. It is thus a completely general attitude to all experience; but it may be focused on and shaped in its specific quality by some specific situation of revelation. That revelatory event is not just a symbol of God, as an independent and independently knowable reality. It would be more adequate, though not completely so, to say that the revelation 'expresses' the nature of God. God is what he is partly because that revelation exists, and is known to be what he is through that revelation. On this sort of analysis, to say that something has a divine nature is to say that it reveals and expresses that transcendent ground of all values. There may, then, be degrees or levels of revelation; one may hazard that a revelation is more adequate the more it evokes and specifies the attitudes which are appropriate to God. There is no clear, objective test of such appropriateness—which is not to say that there are no tests; in the end, the tests will be the experimental exploration of God through the images contributed by a certain revelatory event, as carried out in the traditions of the churches and in one's personal life of prayer. For the Christian, Jesus reveals God supremely, in that, in seeing him, one sees the character of God. One can see the Chalcedonian formula as an attempt to guard against the idolatry of giving one's unreserved allegiance to purely human characteristics, whilst asserting that the person of Jesus was the supreme revelation of the transcendent; one might say that in worshipping that person, but not that man, one worships God, for Jesus expresses what God is.

The Thomist elaboration of the doctrine of the incarnation[12] takes the philosophical terminology of 'nature' and 'person', used in the Chalcedonian formula, and presses it, with characteristic detail and subtlety, to a conceptually rigorous conclusion. The human nature of Jesus is regarded as in itself impersonal, 'having no created subject of its acts and experiences';[13] but that nature is assumed by the person of the Eternal Word. So the centre of action and consciousness in Jesus is God himself, and as such 'Christ differs not merely in degree but in kind from every other being who has ever lived or will ever live on this planet'.[14] Jesus is consequently said to possess at all times a perfect participation in the Beatific Vision of God and a permanent infusion into his human soul of all knowledge that human nature is intrinsically capable of receiving, as well as the acquired knowledge which is derived by the ordinary processes of human experience. Thomas even maintains that Jesus' beatific and infused knowledge was perfect from the beginning of his life, and thus never increased.[15] These facts about Jesus are inferred by *a priori* speculation from a particular view of what it is for God to be omniscient, and for Jesus to be identical with such a being. As must inevitably happen, the basic doctrine of God is determinative of the Christological doctrine, and the Thomist doctrine of the incarnation is worked out on the basis of a specific philosophical concept of God and of human nature.

There are naturally very great internal difficulties in the Thomist account. What, for instance, is the relation between Jesus' infused

[12] Aquinas, *Summa Theologiae*, Pt. 3, Qus. 9–12.
[13] Mascall, E. L. *Christ, the Christian and the Church* (Longmans, Green, 1946), p. 8.
[14] *Ibid.*, p. 39.
[15] Aquinas, *Summa Theologiae*, Pt. 3, Qu. 12, Art. 2 ad 1m.

and his acquired knowledge? Indeed, if he is omniscient from the first, in what sense can he be said to acquire knowledge at all? And must the omniscience of the Eternal Word not be quite different in kind from that of any human soul, precisely because it is eternal and intuitive, whereas human knowledge must by nature be temporal and discursive? But if that is so, how can one express the identity of a man and God in terms of an apparently univocal concept of omniscience? Nevertheless, the Thomist might reply that such difficulties are only to be expected of any human attempt to conceptualise the Divine; and that any adequate account of the incarnation must possess equal difficulties.

The fundamental difficulties with the Thomist account of the incarnation arise from the concepts of God and human nature which are employed. In my view, these require a radical re-interpretation, and such a re-interpretation will provide a rather different doctrine of incarnation. But the orthodox insistence on the divinity of Christ can remain intact through such a re-interpretation; and the revision may in fact bring out many elements in the orthodox tradition more explicitly and guard them more carefully. In particular, what needs to be done is to check the tendency of the Thomist account to a docetic interpretation of the humanity of Jesus, in which the willing centre of his acts and consciousness belongs solely to God, and not to the man at all. One must stress much more the social nature of the human person, and its dependence on specific social and cultural contexts. Above all, one must emphasize the very special character of language about God. The Thomist account may justly be accused of speaking too lightly of the Eternal Word as a person, or individual centre of rational consciousness,[16] and of transposing the concepts of Divine omniscience and omnipotence too directly onto the plane of Jesus' human personality. Despite his expressly stated qualifications of these concepts in a very agnostic direction, Thomas nevertheless proceeds to employ them in Christology as if they retained their full force. What needs to be clearly seen is that such concepts as omniscience, when applied to the transcendent, cannot be simply transposed back onto the finite human plane. Consequently, one cannot express Jesus' identity with God by ascribing to him Divine omniscience and omnipotence, while saying that he remains completely human. By this method, one

[16] *Ibid.*, Pt. 1, Qu. 29, Art. 1.

only succeeds in anthropomorphising the concepts of omniscience and omnipotence unacceptably, and turning Jesus into an extra-terrestial Superman who does not share the human condition of ignorance and helplessness, intellectual struggle, weakness and moral striving at all. I have suggested a radical interpretation of the orthodox doctrine, according to which one can express Jesus' divinity by saying that the proper reaction to Jesus is a particular-ised form of the appropriate response to transcendence, so that Jesus can be said to express fully the nature of God.

3

But there are two major problems to face at once. First, though an inanimate being might be used by God as an expression of his nature, since it is wholly passive, how can a free and active human life express God truly? Second, how can the Christian claim that this expression is a final and complete revelation of God? May there not appear other men who reveal and express the being of God in the same way? In answering these questions, one must turn to emphasize the historical, contextual character of reve-lation. The Christian revelation is what it is because of the his-torical Judaic tradition in which it stands; one cannot tear the person of Jesus out of its historical context, and try to treat it in isolation. Perhaps it is one of the main disadvantages of the heritage of Greek philosophy that Christian doctrines were for-mulated in terms of an ontology of being, which tends to be static and universal, abstracting from historical change, and possibly conveying the impression that Jesus could be considered as 'Son of God' in abstraction from his historical situation, simply by framing abstract sequences of substantive nouns, like 'nature', 'person' and 'substance', which could equally well serve to define him as the unique son of God in any or even no historical context.

This sort of view raises insuperable problems about the relation of human and divine natures in Jesus. For if Jesus was fully man, then he was free at any time up to the moment of his death to make an evil choice; denial of such freedom would amount to a denial of Jesus' humanity. But Jesus could only be fully God if he was totally sinless, for the divine nature cannot sin. It thus seems to follow that the incarnation was always in doubt, until Jesus' death; for had Jesus sinned, the incarnation would at that moment have ceased. The incarnation could have started and then stopped again—a supposition which seems very unpalatable. Two things are wrong with this sort of account; first, a lack of appreciation of the discontinuity between the being of God and that of all temporal creatures; and second, a failure to grasp the historical nature of Christian revelation. One of the peculiarities of history is that if one looks back with the benefit of hindsight, the process of history can seem to embody an inevitable plan. In the context of Jewish history, God called Abraham, arranged the exodus from Egypt, the exile to Babylon, the fall of Jerusalem and, perhaps, the return to Palestine. He prepared the way for the coming of his Son by sending the Prophets, and by using John the Baptist and Mary to fulfil his plan. When his Son had been revealed, he prepared and called Paul to spread the gospel of redemption throughout the world. The picture here—and it is a familiar one—is of God arranging the processes of history according to an inevitable plan. But what happens to human freedom in such a picture? One can say that it does not exist; but that seems to count against the experience of decisive choice with which Christianity claims to confront man. If one admits human freedom, one must then ask, what if Abraham had refused God's call? Or if Moses had? Or Mary? Or Jesus? Or Paul? Clearly, Christianity, if it existed at all, would be quite different from what it now is. Suppose that Jesus at Gethsemene had decided to flee from Jerusalem before he was captured. One may presume that he would then have become just one unremembered religious teacher or possibly a claimant to Messianic status among many others. The 'Son of God' would then not have been revealed; or at least not in that way. More correctly, the very concept of the 'Son of God' would not then have developed. This brings home the point that God's revelation is contingent; it is always at risk, and it is always contingent, to an extent unpredictable, that it takes place as it does. That is to say that God constantly reveals his being to men, but such revelation depends on men's full, imaginative and committed response to it; it does not take place despite all human disabilities, ignorances or perversities. Does this mean that God never acts, that he never interferes in the course of the world? Here again what is needed is a sensitive approach to the logic of such utterances. What God does is how the world is, in its drive towards fulfilment. God and his acts cannot be publicly located in the world, as though he did this but not that, and could be picked out and ostensively indicated as one agent among others. Even to point to Jesus and say, 'There is God' is incorrect; and it is quite different from saying, 'God is in Christ, reconciling the world to himself'; for one can *point* only to the humanity of Jesus.

Once again, to see what it means to say that God acts, one must look back to the Hebrew conceptualisations of God. As we have seen, they felt themselves called to specific acts and vocations, as being sustained by an inner power and as involved with a quasi-personal presence throughout their lives. To say that God acted was not to say that some objective change could be unambiguously attributed to a specific agent, God, but to say, from the standpoint of faith, that God disclosed himself and helped to shape their social and personal lives. In this sort of quasi-personal interaction, the response of the believer is vitally important. What one is able to discern of God partly depends on the quality of one's own response to his call in one's own experience. Jesus, Christians would say, acted in response to God's call to him, though he need not have done so; and, in his particular historical context, he in turn became the vehicle of a new act of God, which at once revealed something of God and claimed the lives of men. A stress on the discontinuity between God and men would ensure that one did not think of the incarnation as a particular causal sequence directly and inevitably inaugurated by God; a stress on the historical nature of revelation would ensure that one emphasized the contingent character of this disclosure of God in Jesus, and its dependence upon a specific and growing situational context.

I am not suggesting that one can talk of acts of God, whatever the world is like, or affirming that God makes no empirically discernible difference to the world. Certainly, if there is to be a moral goal of the world, not any empirical events can happen—though the possibilities of what might happen are extremely wide, and cannot be predicted in detail. If there are special moral vocations in individual lives, again the empirical facts must be such as to allow those vocations to be implemented, to some extent and in some way. If the Christian asks God for help, he expects that his prayers may make some empirical difference, though not necessarily the one he expects. These beliefs in God's purpose and providential rule are not primarily hypotheses about empirical facts; they are primarily directed responses—of trust, hope and confidence—to the reality of God, apprehended in but beyond the world. Nevertheless, such responses would be impossible or inappropriate if all empirical facts counted against them—if prayers were never answered, vocations never achieved, or if Jesus became a political agitator. So, to see in Jesus the act of God, though this was a direct response to transcendence as revealed in his life, involved certain empirically distinctive features in his life—perhaps his performance of miracles, his transfiguration, his evident spiritual authority, and eventually his resurrection. And if these features had not existed, or suddenly ceased to exist, one would have to qualify or abandon acceptance of him as a revelation of God. In this sense, it was only when the earthly life of Jesus had been completed that one could confidently speak of his life as a whole, and therefore of his person as such, as the revelation of God. One might say that a personal life of self-sacrificial love is the best possible expression of God's being: it does not complete revelation in the sense that there is nothing left to learn about God; but it is final in the sense that this personal form is the most adequate possible general characterization of God towards men. Other men may perhaps express such love in their lives; but they can never stand in the context of a 'sacred history', which enabled Jesus to become the unique representative of God to men and men to God; they can never have the same functional placing in history as Jesus. So they may be perfect men; but they cannot in the same way be revelations of God; for to be such a revelation depends upon the whole religious tradition of imaginative interpretation in which it occurs.

In view of this consideration of the contingency and context-dependence of Jesus' divine sonship, one might be tempted to say that Jesus became God only in his resurrection, or that he is never really identical with God in his own being. It would be a mistake to yield to that temptation. What is true is that men can only speak of the person of Jesus as God after the resurrection, and that, had that not occurred, vindicating the whole life of holiness that preceded it, they would not have so spoken. Yet Jesus was not, at one time simply a man, and at a subsequent time also God. His whole life is the revelation of God; God is non-temporal, and thus cannot simply be added to a man at a certain stage. To identify man and God is just to assert that Jesus expresses God;

that is what identity means here; not that a new reality is added to
the humanity of Jesus. This is the point the Chalcedonian formula
puts clumsily by speaking of the union of divine and human
natures in Jesus as 'without change'. It is true that Jesus reveals
God only because of his place within the wider context of Jewish
history; but individuals are what they are because of the wider sets
of social relations of which they form part; so that Jesus' individuality, as revealer of God, can only adequately be seen in its
context. Jesus reveals God, then, in that his character expresses
the character of God; and it does so both in virtue of his own moral
perfection and, equally importantly, in virtue of the spiritual
tradition in which he stood, from which the images for interpreting
his life—images of sacrifice, covenant, Messiahship and Kingdom
—could be taken, and re-formulated around his person by the
new community inspired by him.

4

As well as being the revelation of God, Jesus is believed by
Christians to have exemplified the redeeming act of God, in his
life and especially in his death.[17] He is the redemptive act of God.
How is this conceivable? Here one must recall the Judaic view
that God's acts are primarily the personal addresses made to men
by God. Jesus has come, both because of his character and context, to have the function of God in such personal addresses.

In the first place, Jesus makes the same claim on men as God
does, for total obedience and a call to a special way of life. The
Synoptic Gospels portray him as presenting men with the choice
of entering the Kingdom of God or opting for rejection;[18] and
John's Gospel portrays Jesus himself as the sign, by reaction to
which men would place themselves irrevocably in relation to God.[19]
In the preaching of Paul, the proclamation of the crucified and
risen Lord is again conceived as placing before men the option
of being redeemed from this wicked age.[20] In the preaching of the
Church today, Christ is presented as the one who died for the sins
of mankind, and who is now glorified at God's right hand; the
response to the preached Christ is taken as a response to the claim

[17] Hebrews 9, 14.   [18] Mk. 8, 34–8.   [19] Jn. 3, 18.
[20] Rom. 8, 1–3.

of God upon one. Jesus is the one who sets before men judgement and blessing, and demands a choice; the proclamation of his risen presence places a decisive judgement before men. In this respect, Jesus functions as the character of God, active in relation to men, calling them from worldliness to new life in him.

Secondly, through his cruel innocent suffering and death, Jesus offers the forgiveness of God to men, and the reconciliation of men to God. The Judeo-Christian understanding of human existence is that man is alienated from God, and is unable to achieve that true repentance which consists in a sincere turning from the world. Although there are strands of Hebrew thought for which God is a familiar friend, to be argued with, chided and cajoled, there is one major strand—and it is a definitive one for Christian thinking—for which God is the holy and terrible one, to be approached only through sacrifice and priestly mediation. There are many complex elements in the idea of sacrifice: one may be feeding the god, propitiating its anger or offering it a token of submission and esteem; one may be expressing one's gratitude for life, with all its gifts; one may be destroying a valued object, as a symbol of one's commitment to god; one may be symbolically destroying one's own sins and imperfection, or offering a perfect life in place of one's own imperfect life; one may be offering a substitute victim to be punished in one's own place; or one may be offering suffering in the hope that it may have a redemptive purpose in bringing men to a higher quality of life. Sacrifice may be held to honour the god worthily, to reconcile one with the god, to cleanse oneself from sin, to thank the god, to receive his power, and to express the cleansing and deifying action of the god himself. In the case of the Jewish Passover, the chief element was of thanksgiving for bringing the Israelites safely out of Egypt;[21] and early Christianity developed a pregnant union of the common meal of thanksgiving and the sacrificial elements of consecration, destruction, offering and communion, as models to interpret the life, and particularly the death of Jesus. Jesus was seen as the priest who could mediate between God and men; for he still lives to intercede for men.[22] But he was also the victim, the destruction of which wipes out the past, breaks down the barriers between God and men and opens up a new life of creative freedom. Of course, it is not just the fact that a man died that does this.

[21] Ex. 12, 26–7.　　　　[22] Heb. 8, 1.

Rather, that human death expresses an eternal suffering and self-giving within the being of God. The Christ-story shows that God suffers to reconcile the estranged world to himself; he is involved in the process of history; in some way, his own being is given, sacrificed and renewed in the world's making. Men can unite themselves with this sacrifice, by dying to the world; and they can be assured that between them and God there stands no gulf. One might say that 'God the Son' expresses the general character of history, of God transforming himself in the human drama. To believe in 'the Son' is to identify oneself with the ground of history, as suffering, redemptive love.

Thus the distinctively Christian doctrines of the incarnation and atonement, while susceptible of different interpretations, maintain that the nature of the ineffable and absolutely transcendent reality is fully and definitively expressed in the life of the man Jesus; and that the life, death and resurrection of Jesus accomplish the reconciliation of the world to God, establishing the fulfilling relationship to transcendence which perfects human life. With the introduction of these notions the Judaic concept of God is transformed, and the dominant model becomes that of the suffering God who participates in the travail of his creation. The Greek notions of immutability and impassibility have to be radically revised, to allow for God's entrance into time and human sorrow, while remaining changeless as source of all being and value. And the Hebrew notions of omnipotence and holiness have to be radically revised, in view of the fact that God's power is revealed in the weakness of the Cross, and his terrible holiness has been replaced by the intimate indwelling of Christ in the heart of the believer. So, for Christians, the image of the Cross conveys a new understanding of the reality of the transcendent which builds upon both Hebrew and Greek notions, but refashions them both around the central model of an incarnate and actively reconciling creator of all being.

CHAPTER ELEVEN

GOD AS REDEEMER

I

A central claim of the Christian religion is that Jesus expresses or reveals the nature of the transcendent in relation to men fully and adequately; and that in Jesus God acts decisively to reconcile the world to himself. This notion of the life of Jesus as God's act is clearly paradoxical; for if all Jesus' actions were brought about by his own finite centre of knowledge and will—as they must be, if Jesus is fully man—how could they also and at the same time be directly caused by God? Two suggestions have been briefly made in this respect; namely, that Jesus functions in place of God, in presenting men with the alternatives of blessing and judgement, in the acceptance or rejection of him; and that Jesus offers God's forgiveness to men, and expresses the nature of God as redemptive love. But there is still a problem of the sense in which one could be entitled to speak of God as acting uniquely and specially in Jesus. For God in one sense does everything, since all created beings exist solely by his power.

One might exempt human acts from this, by saying that God leaves men free to act as they choose; so one might limit God's acts to those things he does voluntarily and intentionally, freely, with knowledge and for a purpose. One could then speak of a special class of God's acts, which were segments of nature exemplifying a special purpose. God still causes everything; but some of these things express special purposes—thus one could speak of God's act in answering prayer, if the course of events looked at once purposive yet contingent. It seems to be quite conceivable that God should contingently express special purposes in nature. Thus if I pray for a sign, and a volcano explodes, I can take this as purposive (answering my prayer) and contingent (it could have been otherwise in form or existence)—as a miracle. Of course, God does not just confine his acts to miracles; he does everything;

but in most cases his finite effects conform to general purposes and necessary laws of nature. The difference—and it is important to see this—is not between God's action and his inaction, but between his special contingent purposes and his necessary general purposes (e.g. the redemption of the world). One must further distinguish between what God intends, what he approves and what he permits;[1] for instance, he intends the movements of the planets, but permits misuses of human free will. He may be said to permit those things which are involved as possibilities in implementing his general purposes, but for which he does not lay down a specific form, and which he does not forbid. He can be said to approve those things which positively contribute to his purposes, but for which he decrees no specific form. He can be said to intend those things which contribute in a general way to his purpose (i.e. he permits human agents to sin; he intends them to realise positive values; he approves of the specific ways in which they do so). Often God may intend specific acts—e.g. a specific action in the course of an individual's life—but we cannot usually be certain of what he intends, as distinct from what he approves. God may intend a man to live a certain life, permit him to do so, and approve of him when he does. But both permission and approval are wider than the range of intended acts. In general, one may say that God's intentions leave open a set of specific acts which are permitted or approved.

When one speaks of Jesus as God's act, one does not merely want to say that Jesus does just whatever God intends that he should do. That sense of intention (X intends Y to do A) is more like the sense of 'wish' or 'desire'; for the intended act is not wholly within God's power, due to his permission of human freedom. One can only intend, in the primary sense, to do what it is within one's own power to do. Here an asymmetry between human and divine action appears; for God could not, on this account, be said to intend to become incarnate in Jesus, since, as we have seen, such incarnation depended always on Jesus' free choice, and so could not be complete until Jesus' death. But God could take that completed life and use it for a special contingent purpose, within the context of his universal purpose for the world. The redemption of the world must be considered as God's universal purpose. It is

[1] The distinction is made in many Patristic and Scholastic texts; cf. Aquinas, *Summa Theologiae*, Pt. 1, Qu. 22.

both intellectually and morally unacceptable to speak of God (as Luther did)[2] as changing his mind and suddenly deciding to redeem men instead of damning them. God cannot change in his moral character; and his decision to create the world must already be seen as incorporating the decision to redeem it, if necessary. So the very being of the universe is the redemptive act of God; it is unthinkable that God should fail to redeem his creation. It is perhaps worth pointing out here that one makes this assertion about God as a result of accepting the revelation of his nature given in the life of Jesus; it is not an *a priori* speculation. What I am saying is that the sort of God who is revealed in Jesus is a God who must necessarily, being what he is, redeem the world; and that denials of this truth amount to denials of the fulness of the revelation given in Christ. Yet it is a contingent matter that Jesus, by his perfect obedience, revealed God's nature fully, in the context of the Judaic religious tradition. It must therefore also be a contingent matter that God acted to redeem the world in Christ.

What alternative means of redemption there could be we cannot speculate; but the orthodox Christian view is that God did something in Jesus which removed sin, and so redeemed mankind. Perhaps one can say that he took the life, death and resurrection of Jesus, in its place in the context of Judaic and Messianic images, and used it to release men from the power of sin. This process is contingent (another means might have been chosen) and purposive (it applies the general purpose of redemption to particular cases, in answer to specific human needs). Each application of Jesus' death to a person's sinful condition, to heal and annul it, may be called a special act of God, directly intended by God, a redemptive act accomplished in Jesus' death. But, one may ask, is the orthodox concept of the atonement not that it is an objective act—i.e. something was accomplished by God on Calvary, once for all, whatever men think? And wasn't the passion and death of Jesus itself the act of God, not just something that could later be taken and used by God to address men personally?[3] The

---

[2] Cf. Theilicke, H. *Theological Ethics*, 1; ed. Lazareth, W. (A. and C. Black, 1969), p. 98: 'Luther makes . . . constant reference to the fact of conflict in God, the fact that God had to wring from himself the resolve to love.'

[3] This is perhaps a danger of Bultmann's account; cf. 'New Testament and Mythology', in *Kerygma and Myth*, ed. Bartsch, H. W., trans.

answer to both questions is simply, 'yes'; the fact that they arise
as worries is a symptom of the difficulty of grasping the logic of
such expressions as 'act of God'.

Many Christians conceive their faith in the form of fairly simple
pictures—of God the Father sending his Son down from Heaven
to save men, of Jesus' death as something which relieved men of
some sort of punishment, and of Jesus as now somehow sitting
bodily in Heaven. Such pictures may be misleading, but they may
also give insight; and for many people they may be essential, if
treated circumspectly. But they miss altogether the complexity of
even the Chalcedonian insistence on Jesus' full humanity. To see
the crucifixion as the paying of a penalty by the innocent on
behalf of the guilty is (apart from its moral unacceptability) to
see the atonement as much too external to man, almost as a
magical, automatic process. The crucifixion was the act of God
because God effects by means of it a special, contingent purpose,
a particular way of redemption; it was not just later used by God,
as though the means was only accidentally related to the sort of
effect to be produced. On the contrary, the means is conceptually
related to the effect of redemption; what redemption is conceived
to be is so conceived because of that death, taken in its total context.

But to say that God effected human redemption, as it is now
conceived by Christians, in the crucifixion, is not really to suggest
that this could be so, however men reacted to that event. Bluntly
put, redemption cannot be intelligibly said to be accomplished
unless people are actually redeemed. Even in the old Anselmian
picture, though the price of sin had been paid on Calvary, individuals still had to accept baptism into Christ's death before
they could actually obtain the release procured for them. Moreover, in the Catholic Church the mass was considered as the
presentation of Christ's eternal, even though once-for-all, sacrifice, so that it could not properly be considered as unrepeatably
finished in some past time. So the point to be preserved is something like this: that Christians do not have to wait for some further
and perhaps doubtful divine act to be performed before they can
be assured of reconciliation; everything on God's side has been

Fuller, R. (S.P.C.K. 1953), p. 42: 'The real Easter faith is faith in the
word of preaching which brings illumination.'

done; only their joyful acceptance is required. This point is completely preserved by the account I have suggested, whereby Jesus' death remains for ever the means of effecting redemption; and more, the generative model for the Christian concept of redemption, that which specifies the true character of redemption; yet it can be continually presented by the Church in the Eucharist and offered anew to each generation to release men from the power of sin.

It is not only that Jesus' death must be construed as the redemptive act of God solely in terms of a prior concept of what such an act could be; but that death itself helps to redefine and establish what is meant by speaking of a divine act of redemption. The notion of God as acting had arisen with the Hebrew belief that events in their history were being shaped so as to express a continuing divine-human dialogue. Indian religious thought notably lacks this sort of belief; the world emanates from impersonal Brahman and is governed by the immutable law of Karma and bound to the wheel of rebirth. Even when Hinduism begins to talk of avatars of Vishnu, and Buddhism of incarnating Boddhisattvas, there is little or no concern for the historicity of such figures. It is considered to be sufficient to say that they are personal aspects of Brahman or Nirvana; an attention to history is not important. For the Jews, however, God is continually present in the events of life, acting towards and in reaction to men; so history, as the record of such spiritual transactions, takes on great importance. By the time of Jesus, the hope of many individuals in an oppressed and fragmented Israel was that God would decisively intervene in history, in the form of a political Messiah; they looked for a decisive act of God, to save them in a political sense as well as a spiritual one from their oppressors. So strong was this hope that the apostles immediately looked for an imminent return of the risen Christ in glory, to bring this wicked age to an end. Yet they were able to see that the crucifixion was itself the decisive act of God for man's redemption—not a political solution, but a spiritual victory in the midst of material weakness. And in this apprehension the concept of a divine act was transformed. This can be clearly seen in the light of the Jewish belief that the redemption has not yet been accomplished; for the Messiah has not yet come with power. Christians have not abandoned the hope of a return of Christ in glory, the achievement of God's moral purpose for the world, conceived in terms of the fulfilment of Christian imagery. Yet God's action in this present age is revealed in a context of weakness, rather than of power; the act of God lies in his suffering for and with mankind, rather than in his absolute, passionless power. The desert God of jealousy and power becomes transmuted, for the Christian, into the suffering God, who takes upon himself human sin and sorrow, and reconciles the world to himself. Christians take Jesus' life of perfect obedience as also the act by which God removes the burden of their sins; the suffering of the man expresses fully—and so is identical with—the redemptive suffering of God on our behalf, the suffering of the 'Lamb of God' whose obedience is accepted in place of our disobedience. And this is no external transaction; for we can be actually incorporated into the obedience of Christ, through baptism, becoming members of the body of Christ, and so redeemed from the world into the worshipping community of believers.

So the fatherhood of God takes on new depths of meaning when this is seen as the fatherhood of Jesus Christ, the Lamb of God. God is involved and suffers with the world, and through and arising from the life and death of Jesus he has fashioned the Church, which offers forgiveness and sanctification to men, by their incorporation into the 'body of Christ'. Forgiveness is actually effected when a man, in penitence, accepts his baptism into Christ's death, either in baptism or its reaffirmation and reapplication in absolution. The power of sin is broken as a man brings his life before the cross; and in its place the presence of the risen Lord begins to grow in his life.

God has made the death of Jesus the way to our redemption, to the establishing of the truly fulfilling relation to the transcendent which all religions attempt to convey. It has provided the paradigm images in which redemption should be conceived, and claims to offer the power which can enable men to incorporate these images into their own lives, as exemplary patterns. But it is a mistake to treat the crucifixion in isolation from the resurrection, and the completion of the process of redemption in the daily experience of the Church, where the forgiveness of sins is proclaimed.[4] It is not simply one human death which is efficacious

---

[4] This stress on the continuing work of atonement is characteristic of many modern treatments. Cf. Hodgson, L., *The Doctrine of the Atonement* (Nisbet, 1951), esp. ch. 6.

for salvation; it is a death resulting from a life of total obedience
to God, in a particular context of religious aspirations and expec-
tations, transforming old images of redemption and giving birth
to a new community, the Church, which is able to develop, by
reflection on its originative experiences, a whole complex of images
which at once fulfil and transform the tradition and bring release
from evil and new life to its members. It is this total historical
pattern which is important; and no moment can be isolated as
objectively efficacious of itself alone. Yet, though it is untrue that
Jesus' death is efficacious, if (impossibly) taken in complete historical isolation, it is nevertheless true that it is objectively
efficacious, when considered in its proper total historical perspective; for it is only in that total perspective that its real character
can become apparent. The moment of Jesus' death is the objective
act of the decisive liberation of men from sin; but it can be seen
under that description only from the proleptic perspective of the
end of time—within the total context of history, as the act of God
in creating and redeeming his world. That, one might say, anthropomorphically, was what God intended and what he accomplished
by direct volition; but that can only be affirmed by faith, within
the universal perspective of the redemption of mankind; it is not
a description which could be correctly affirmed as a result of an
inspection of a limited segment of space-time. It is this truth
which Anselmian theories of atonement neglect; and, in consequence, they become impossible to reconcile with doctrines of the
nature of God as the transcendent creator of space and time, much
less with Thomist doctrines of his nature as changeless and
impassible.

2

It goes without saying that no conceptualisation of what happens,
in atonement, will be adequate. A riot of rich images, which
continually qualify each other, having the general effect of putting
each one slightly out of focus, have been used to interpret Jesus'
life and death and resurrection. Christ is at once the crucified
eternal victim and the triumphant risen King; he is the intercessor
for all men and yet the judge of all men; he dwells in the believer
and yet is present among the faithful; his body is eaten and yet all
believers are parts of his body; he is in heaven, in the heart and on

the altar. Some theologians have selected one image to the exclusion of others, literalised it and in consequence have produced distorted forms of Christian belief—Anselm's doctrine of atonement as a price paid by one man for another's sin, of which God cheats the Devil at the last moment, is a case in point.[5] Yet the image of Jesus dying in my place is an indisputably powerful one. A different picture is of Jesus fighting Satan and the hosts of evil on the cross, and winning in the apparent defeat of refusing to use sheer force.[6] The picture of the warfare of good and evil is also powerful; the cross as the crux of history, when Satan fell at the moment of his greatest power; this is a sublime picture. Again, one can take Jesus as showing what man does to God by his sin; and that death can be a powerful force for changing men's hearts and bringing them to see what they are and need redemption from. Or one can take Jesus as showing how God suffers to the utmost to recall men to himself. To take on oneself suffering and to face the temptations and assaults of evil, and to accept all this as from God and offer it to God, that is the utmost reconciliation of estranged nature to its ground. The voluntary acceptance of the utmost risk and destroying power of evil is a lived prayer which has an efficacy which is unsurpassable. Or one may stress the crucifixion as what makes the resurrection possible—the natural consequence of a life of total obedience in an evil world, which becomes the means of unleashing the Pentecostal experience of the risen Lord—Jesus' death releases from sin because it is the means of bringing the power of Jesus into our hearts; for Jesus rose and became the vehicle of the Holy Spirit only because he was fully obedient, thereby revealing man's natural hostility to God and his need for positive reconciliation. The cross shows the need for forgiveness—for it shows what one's acts do to God and to oneself—and expresses the offer of forgiveness—for it expresses the lengths to which God goes to reconcile men to himself, and it presages the means of reconciliation, the power of the risen Lord. Forgiveness is not the juridical remission of penalty; nor is it just God saying, 'I won't hold it against you'; it is a positive reconciliation, by which alienated humanity is made one with God, even while remaining in the world of alienation.

[5] Anselm, *Cur Deus Homo*, in Deane, S. W. *St. Anselm, Basic Writings* (LaSalle, 1962).
[6] Aulen, *Christus Victor* (S.P.C.K. 1953).

These are various models for conceiving the atoning action of God in Christ, and they have all been used in the Christian tradition. What one must remember is that religion does not present a 'just-so' ontology, even though it often seems to do so. It sponsors images which aim to make possible a creative response to the molar aspects of reality, a growth in love which is also a discovery of significant reality. One is not saying that religious images have no objective referent, and merely specify attitudes, that they induce a constant state of pretending that things are thus, when in fact they are not so. And one is not saying that they refer to some being in a literal fashion; the doctrine of God as creator and the inconsistent character of the images, when taken literally, rules this option out. Nor is one saying that they refer in some analogical way to God, who is like creatures, though one cannot say exactly in what way. What I have suggested is that one may assert a transcendent, mediately revealed reality, apprehended in specific finite events. Religious images basically celebrate these historic revelations, attempting to re-create the new relation to reality they originated. Thus the events of the life and death of Jesus were meditated upon, and inspired the general images of incarnation and atonement—God becoming one with and redeeming man—which have been preserved in the Church. These general images give rise to a great number of subsidiary images for articulating further the appropriate dispositional responses of men to the transcendent as revealed in this historic tradition. It is important to see that there is no question of the images referring to anything, in a straightforward sense. Their use is to specify and sustain distinctive attitudes; and, taken in the ritual context of the mass, the complex images of sacrifice, triumph, communion, pleading and submission, which were worked out in the Jewish tradition in the models of Lamb, Priest, Judge and King, specify the attitudes of repentence, thankfulness, contrition, adoration and dedication which characterize the Christian response to 'God'. All these images are applied to Christ, as the focal and transforming point of this revelatory tradition, the originative experience of the Christian way of life.

There is an important sense in which these images cannot be conveyed by a conceptual system or theology; they mean something beyond themselves, but only in virtue of what they untranslatably are. They do provide cognitive insight; and this is insight into the nature of the transcendent in relation to man; but one cannot further express this insight except by calling attention to the generative experiences from which those images sprang, as a creative response to a revelatory apprehension. Images do not merely provide cognitive insight; they provide exemplary patterns of living, ways of seeing one's own acts and situation, as one lives in constant interaction with one's environment, and they convey charismatic power to achieve fulfilment. The Christian life thus becomes a sort of drama in which the roles constituted and defined by these images can be played out. One conceives oneself as, and acts as, a redeemed son of God, indwelt by the liberating Spirit and incorporated into the body of Christ. Thus it is not possible to speak of the Christian concept of God as an abstract notion arrived at by detached contemplation; it is a complex concept which has, as an important part of its function, the specification of roles which the believer can play, which embody a specific understanding of the human situation in relation to 'God'. Thus it is proper for the Christian to say that man comes to the Father through the Son in the Spirit; he turns to the transcendent, as articulated by these images, focused on Jesus, as media of dialogue, and empowered by the Spirit's charisma. By construing God under these images, salvation is to be attained.

3

But one may still object: is there not something objective that is being discussed? Is God not really like this? Did Jesus not rise from death, and will he not come again to judge the world? Of course, there are implications about the nature of the world in the Christian images. Christianity is indeed founded on the miracle of the resurrection;[7] and whatever exactly happened then, it was an extraordinary event which expressed a special purpose of God in the world. So the Christian is committed to the view that God acts in extraordinary ways and for special purposes; in particular, to establish the Church as the New Israel, the Covenant people. This, as I have suggested, is not the creation of a privileged few, but the call of a community to witness to God's redemptive concern for all men. But belief in incarnation and atonement implies

[7] 1 Cor. 15, 14.

more than this: it implies that God is involved within the universe immanently and redemptively, so that it is no longer satisfactory to characterise God as the ethical demand or the distant Lord of history. Greek philosophy has often been accused of distorting the Hebrew view of God as the living Lord of the Patriarchs. But a more basic and important conflict is between the Greek idea of an impassible, immutable perfection and the Christian faith in incarnation. This faith is opposed to both Greek and Hebrew concepts of God. The Christian God is not either the passionless unmoved mover or the Lord of Hosts, expressing his judgement and grace in the events of history; he is the co-sufferer, redeeming and reconciling the dark possibilities of the world to himself. This God does not rest complete in his own beatitude, drawing all things to himself by desire; nor does he interfere cataclysmically in history, using men for his own purposes, destroying and blessing whom he will; this God expresses his being in weakness, but gives his strength as an inner transformation, renewing the world by patient reconciliation.

There are definite beliefs about the nature of the world involved in this view; it is entailed that reality has a moral purpose, that human nature is to be fulfilled in a certain way, that the historical Jesus has an essential part to play in the fruition of this purpose. But one must realise the complexities involved. Jesus is conceived as a resurrected person, who can enter into personal relationship with the believer; yet he can enter into such relationships with thousands of people at the same time. Thus one cannot say that his living presence is confined to a spatially locatable resurrection-body; the believer also takes it to be on thousands of altars and in thousands of hearts throughout the world. The risen Christ is not to be literally identified with the spatially locatable body of the man Jesus, now 'in heaven'. Of course, there are problems about whether there are spatial relations in heaven, and if so, how they relate to spatial relations on earth, which makes the assertion of bodily continuity questionable in any case. So to say that Jesus sits at God's right hand is perhaps to say that death was not the end for the man Jesus, and that his personality has been so united with God that it now serves as the communication between man and God; it is a model for God's relation to us. There is a living presence, available in the Church, which is conceived under the model of the remembered person of Jesus, and the conception of which originated in the historical life and death of Jesus. But does Jesus not now reign in heaven, and will he not come again to judge the world? Yes; but the physical body of Jesus does not now sit anywhere; and the Judgement will not be the return of that body into the upper atmosphere! So one can see that the Christian is bound to believe that there is a real personal presence offered by the Church and that there will be a culmination of historical existence which will confront men with judgement on their acts; and these are beliefs about the course of the universe, in its physical detail. But the exact manner of these happenings is left completely unspecific, and the images (of Jesus as present King and future Judge) in terms of which Christians think of them have the primary function of regulating one's attitudes to present experience, and as such are founded upon creative insight and special revelatory experiences in a specific tradition, centred especially on the life and death of Jesus. The point is that those insights, and the attitudes which embody appropriate response to them, would be illusory if the nature of reality offered no confirmation of them at all. But both insights and attitudes are directed primarily to the reality of the transcendent, which is beyond any and all empirical situations.

I would still want to deny that religious images give any knowledge of the inner life of God. One can only speak of the world, as illuminated by transcendence. If one maintains that God is the suffering redeemer, one is not really making a statement about the inner being of God—e.g. that he literally suffers pain. One is saying that it is in the acceptance of suffering and its use for a redemptive purpose (out of Jesus' death, the community of the new life, the Church, sprang) that one finds the heart of reality, the deepest level of significance in reality. That is what one means by speaking of 'God' in such a context. One may construct a picture of the universe as a self-giving of God, involving suffering and evil, but becoming reconciled again to God in history. In some way, God incorporates suffering and evil into his own being, for he knows things in such a way that they become part of his being; and he will draw this alienated world back to himself, by being present in the world as a creative striving towards good. This striving cannot completely overrule creaturely freedom; it is a work which depends on obedience; but God can place such limits on creatures that his plan will not entirely fail, and he gives himself as a sustaining and empowering reality to those who turn in obedience. This inward force is the Holy Spirit, who can eventually bring each free individual to express the creative love of God, expressing God's love of himself, in his beauty, wisdom, power and holiness—a love expressed in creative response and advance. God is thus the beloved, the lover and love itself—an insight incorporated by Augustine into the doctrine of the Trinity.[8] The interior love of the Trinity is an asymptotic ideal for the universe; for the universe should express this love by the creative appreciation of all values. Insofar as things attain their true integration, fulfilment and satisfaction, they move towards this ideal; conversely, as they move away from the ideal, they become disintegrated, unfulfilled and dissatisfied, and, one may say, less fully 'things' at all.

One has here constructed an all-inclusive and coherent picture of the whole universe, in which the various strands of the concept of 'God' are woven together around one central unifying image of the Trinity, as the self-giving, suffering and reconciling ground of reality. When the Christian speaks of God the Father, he has in mind the generative power which effects a moral purpose in the world, the final moral cause; when he speaks of God the Son, he has in mind the historical process of the estrangement of the world, which is accepted and shared by God; when he speaks of God the Spirit, he thinks of the empowering force within himself prompting him to a fuller relationship with God. This complex master-image defines the roles of man with regard to the transcendent, the relation of gratitude to the Father, identification with the Redeemer, and obedience to the Spirit which is exemplified in the Church, as the continuation of the incarnation and the means of grace to men. By using this complex image, man is able to see himself as a creative individual centre through which positive values can be realised, through which the glory of God can be expressed; yet as a being fallen, through its autonomy, into estrangement, and called to reconciliation by a God who accepts his suffering and works in the world to bring about the eventual triumph of one universal saving purpose.

From the originative experience of Jesus as the risen Christ, the pattern of creation—fall—redemption—glorification has been preserved in the working-out of the doctrine of the Trinity, as the

[8] Cf. note 10 to ch. 9.

paradigm model of transcendence. The model has a documented origin, a real history. Yet what it now conveys is what Christ has meant to generations. What we need is not, as some have held, a de-mythologisation to get rid of these mythical models;[9] we need to learn to think mythically again, and know that the realities conveyed were moulded on actual encounters in history, now unrecoverable. Now they exist autonomously, as images governing man's conception of himself in relation to transcendence, and one may be agnostic about many of the details of what really happened so long ago in history. In all this, of course, there is the possibility of error. Jesus may not have been as he seemed, or he may not have existed. If this is so, then Christians are mistaken in the specific set of images they use for the spiritual life; for those images are conceptually related to the historical events in which they originated. More seriously still, God may not exist. This is like saying that one may be mistaken in one's basic moral beliefs, in one's fundamental commitments. The basic commitment to God is evaluative, and the commitment to Christian images is one way to articulate this commitment—Christians believe, the way with richest possibilities, truest insights, most fruitful results in personal life.

So one may say that the truth of the Christian faith does depend upon certain historical claims; though it seems permissible to draw the limits of these as widely as possible—to say simply that Jesus must have been the sort of person whom it would be appropriate to take as the revelatory act of God, without committing oneself to the literal inerrancy of every biographical detail in the Gospels. And it does make definite historical claims—that the Church will not fail, that there will be the triumph of a moral purpose in the universe, and that all men will receive a clearer vision of God— though again the details of these are presented only in picture-language, and cannot be worked out from revelation. Beyond this, the central claim of Christianity is that it provides a set of images which specify the appropriate attitudes of men to the transcendent reality which has been revealed in specific historical situations; that it provides a set of exemplary roles for men to adopt to that reality; and that it offers the charismatic power to live out these roles more fully. If one asks whether those images refer to some being, the answer must be no; for the transcendent is not a being.

[9] Cf. Ogden, S. M. *Christ Without Myth* (Collins, 1962).

But, while recognising the limits of human speech, which render one unable to speak at all of the inner nature of God, and while recognising that the function of religious language is to specify attitudes to experience, one must also recognise that those attitudes are claimed to be appropriate. That is, we can only conceive God in human terms; and we must use the terms we do if we are to be rightly related to God; and these terms are licensed by the reve-latory situations in which they originate. The Christian must hold both that God in his own nature is completely unknowable in human concepts; and that it is perfectly correct and necessary to speak of God as a personal Father, working out his saving purpose in the person of Jesus Christ, and reconciling the whole of creation to himself through the activity of the Holy Spirit. To paraphrase St. Paul, the new life which Christianity offers is to be found, not through the construction of a speculative theory of the nature of reality, but through the acceptance of God's revelation of his nature in the cross of Christ.[10] And that is not merely an intellec-tual acceptance; but the adoption of the exemplary role of dying to the world and rising to new life, relying on the power of God which is offered in the sacraments of his Church.

[10] I Cor. I, 21.

CHAPTER TWELVE

THE CONCEPT OF THE
TRINITARIAN GOD

I

The Christian concept of God has been definitively formulated as the concept of a Trinity, three persons in one substance, co-equal and co-eternal, not confused one with another, and yet not three Gods, but one God. The Son is begotten by the Father, and the Spirit proceeds from the Father and the Son (except for the Orthodox Churches), and yet no person is before, after, greater or less than another. Those who, on the appropriate occasions, recite the Athanasian Creed, affirming that 'He that will be saved must thus think of the Trinity',[1] may be forgiven for thinking that salvation must be virtually impossible of attainment. And those who read the elaboration of Trinitarian doctrine in Augustine and Aquinas[2] must feel at once awed by the immense ingenuity expended on making the whole intellectual puzzle fit together and puzzled as to how a faith which spurned the wisdom of the Greeks[3] could find itself so entangled with Greek philosophy and so knowledgeable about the interior life of God.

Yet the doctrine of the Trinity remains central to the Christian faith, and if the methods and concepts of Greek philosophy are to be abandoned, some way must be found of guarding against those views which the Fathers were concerned to exclude by the use of the terminology available to them. One intention of the classical formula was to deny that there are three distinct gods, three possibly conflicting sources of finite being and goodness. But that denial must be taken alongside the insight that God is non-denumerable; so that asserting his unity serves mainly to deny plurality of gods rather than to assign a number to him. Then, the classical formula was concerned to deny that the persons of the

---

[1] The Athanasian Creed, recited at certain times of the liturgical year.
[2] Cf. note 10 to ch. 9.   [3] 1 Cor. 1, 23.

Trinity are merely aspects of God, or modes of his acting, which express an underlying identity; that is, that God is in himself straightforwardly one, but appears to men under three different phases of activity. Against such a view, the Fathers wished to hold that some distinction between Father, Son and Spirit always remained in God, even though they were not distinct self-subsisting beings.

It should be clear that, on the general account I have given of theistic language, it is not possible to express that concern in the same way at all. To do so contradicts the more perceptive notion of the Scholastics that God cannot be known in himself, but only in his relation to the world.[4] What one must say, instead, is that 'God' is to be conceived under three distinct models, which are not reducible to each other or to anything else; but these models are to be ascribed to the 'one' or non-denumerable reality of the transcendent. One thus avoids tritheism, by denying the existence of distinct, self-subsistent sources of being; and one avoids unitarian monotheism, by denying that one's basic models for 'God' are reducible to a unitary model, even in thought. In the old terminology, one is neither distinguishing the substance nor confounding the persons; for one is talking of the transcendent in relation to man, as properly conceivable under three irreducibly basic images.

These images are founded on certain originative events which are taken as giving decisive clues to the nature of reality. And this is not an inferred reality, depicted as it is in itself, apart from all relation to our experience or our conceptual forms. It is reality as it is disclosed to the creative imagination and apprehended through conceptual forms available to us in our culture. The images are grouped around the central unifying concept of God, and enable one to adopt a specific way of apprehending events and of acting out one's existence in accordance with an exemplary role.

The first basic image which constitutes the concept of the Trinity is that of the Father, the origin of all things, guiding his people but demanding absolute obedience, controlling history and drawing it to a final moral purpose, awesome in mystery and power, but revealed as the concerned consoling and sustaining,

---

[4] Aquinas, *Summa Contra Gentiles*, trans. Pegis, A. C. in Hick, J. *Classical and Contemporary Readings in the Philosophy of Religion* (Prentice-Hall, 1964), p. 47.

father by the life and teaching of Jesus. The origin of this image has been briefly traced in the history of the Jewish people and the speculative constructions of the Greeks; and it is dramatically modified by the Christian doctrine that all men can become sons of God by incorporation into the body of Christ, which is his church.

The second basic image is that of Jesus Christ, who expresses the nature of God fully in human form, and who has become the means of reconciliation between God and men. A whole cluster of subsidiary images have arisen to articulate the person and work of Christ. He is conceived as the perfect Lamb of sacrifice, the only Son of God, the Messiah, the King of Glory, the Crucified suffering servant, the eternal High Priest, the Judge of all men and the Good Shepherd. Underlying these images is the fundamental thought that it is proper to take the treasured remembrance of Jesus as the full disclosure of God's nature; that God includes the sorrow and suffering of the world in himself; and that the repetition in oneself of the exemplary role of dying to the world and rising to new life and the entrance into the Church, the community of Christ, is the way to that fulfilling relationship with transcendence which all religions seek. This complex set of images originates in the early Church's reflection on Jesus' life and teachings, as it interpreted that life in terms of images already present in the Judaic tradition, though not unified around one focal figure. We cannot be sure how many of these images originate with Jesus himself, though it seems reasonable to believe that he accepted a special place for himself in the working out of the Divine purpose. The resurrection appearances and the Pentecost experience assured the apostles that release from estrangement, negative love-lessness and futility into a new life of fulfilment, happiness, love and meaning had come to them through Jesus, who presented the forgiving love of God and his living power. So the concept of 'God' was expanded to incorporate the notion of the appropriateness of speaking of 'God' as human (suitably qualified) and of the redeeming, reconciling act of God in history, offering through the Church, the continuing body of Christ, the exemplary role of death and new life by which man can find true fulfilment.

The third basic image in the concept of the Trinitarian God is that of the Holy Spirit, the continuing renewing and creative power of God within the world, drawing it into unity with himself.

This image originates in the experience of the Church, as it felt itself empowered by a force arising within individuals, yet somehow other than them. But it can be taken in a much broader sense than that of a psychological force in human lives within a specific community; for it comes to represent the work of God as an immanent power, present in the whole of creation, active in bringing it to its final goal. Thus the Spirit is said to brood over the waters at creation,[5] to inspire artistic or literary works, to guide men into all truth, and to co-operate in the historical process, bringing all things to good. This is no place to develop a theology of the Holy Spirit; and I must confine myself to sketching the outlines of this image, as part of the total concept of the Trinity. My only concern here is with what the concept of 'God' means; but of course it is impossible to do this for Christianity without stressing that doctrines of Christ and the Spirit are integral parts of, not addenda to, the Christian concept of 'God'.

2

One may say, summarily, that, whereas the Father is the source and goal of all things, ineffable, always beyond and absolute; and the Son is the one who supremely reveals the nature of God's action, as freeing men for a new relationship with transcendent reality; the Spirit is the impulsive drive within the world, moving to ever-changing consummations of present reality, producing a creative drive towards new and fuller expressions of being. The image of the Spirit qualifies the Hebraic notion of the radical otherness of God; and it does so by introducing the complementary image of God as working immanently within history and human life.

In the creative inspirations of the sciences and the arts, it is very easy to think of a genius, muse or inspiration which can take over one's own personality and produce new insights and visions. Similarly, in morality it is possible for one's inadequate personality to be taken over by a positive power which can bring new insights and capacities of positive action. To construe this experience a distinction is needed which could be made in various ways, but

[5] Gen. 1, 2.

which I will draw as between the power of choice and the creative will. The power of choice has only two basic modes—that of subordinating itself freely to the creative will, or that of electing for autonomy and independence. Ironically, the latter choice turns out to be the choice of slavery, while the former, the choice of obedience, turns out to be the way of true freedom. For once the self chooses autonomy, it severs contact with the sustaining power which holds it in being, and it comes under the sway of the passions, which quickly establish dominance. The supposedly independent self is really governed by its needs and desires, which grow by what they feed on, and which bind the self more and more closely to the world and its structures. In this way, the self gradually loses its integrity and unity; and, at the extreme, becomes a bundle of conflicting desires, unable to aim coherently at one object or to achieve peace in the attainment of a final satisfaction. However, if the self chooses obedience rather than independence, then a new power of creativity is released, which frees one from all past attachments and rigid patterns of behaviour; one becomes fully free when one's power of choice is made, to be obedient to the creative will within one.

This distinction has been made in Hinduism as between atman, the true self which is identical with Brahman, the supreme reality, and the empirical ego, under the illusion of its separate individuality.[6] St. Paul made it between reason, which is usually impotent, and the flesh (sarx); and he holds that the Spirit can empower the rational self and release one from slavery to desires. However the distinction is made, the Christian will certainly say that he does find a new power for living, as he brings his life before the cross, and asks the risen Lord to break down his attachment to sin and build up new attitudes of love in him. And he will find this power renewed as he participates in the sacraments. The doctrine of the Holy Spirit asserts that this creative power, which seems to arise from within oneself and yet to be something which one must allow to work through oneself, is to be regarded as the act of God within the human self. It is as though the autonomous self is given up in favour of God's action in one, as though one can become transparent to God, allowing

---

[6] Cf. 'Maitri Upanisad', in Radhakrishnan, *The Principal Upanisads* (Allen and Unwin, 1953), p. 793 ff.

him to conform one to the image of Christ,[7] and love himself in the human soul, whose only autonomous task is that of obedience.

It seems that one must say that, not only is God the ground of objective values, assuring their presence and constancy; he is also the ground of that creative apprehension which brings these values to fulfilment as consciously apprehended. The creative pursuit of values is itself the work of God, in which both the subject's apprehension and the object's presentation of material for apprehension must be taken together for the value to be realised. This is a radically different view from that of the Thomist concept of an immutable self-complete being; but it seems to be a direct implication of Christian belief in God as Spirit. Values do not just lie in objects; God is not just the 'Thou' which encounters man in various situations. They lie in the creative loving contemplation of objects; God is thus equally the creative source of apprehension through which value is realised. The historical process must thus be seen as the progressive realisation of new values, all grounded in the mysterious beyond of God, yet realised only in the interaction of subject and object. God is present in both poles of this relationship. He is not the object *simpliciter*; he is the object, conceived as containing levels of meaning, containing many possible values. He is not the subject *simpliciter*; he is that creative force which the subject allows to come to be in itself. So God works through the subject and through the object to produce the realisation of intrinsic value. Man is the vehicle for this continuing historical process, which is the action of God, in contributing to God's general purpose in specific and contingent ways. The interior work of grace differs from miracle only in that it is not specifically expressed in extraordinary external events. It may nonetheless indirectly give rise to extraordinary manifestations of sanctity or spiritual power; and for this reason, those who are most closely united with God through their obedience are often taken as vehicles of extraordinary works of God—usually miracles of healing—wrought through intercession to God through them.

So in saying that the power of the creative will is the action of God, one is characterising it as a power to which one must freely submit, yet which issues from the depths of one's own subjective being, and which realises contingent and special purposes of God,

[7] Rom. 8, 26–9.

in the self-conscious realisation of values. And this act of God is the effecting of human salvation; for it brings fulfilment and integration to the human person, and delivers one from the power of worldly desires and attachments. The old self, which is the set of traits and dispositions arising from the option of the power of choice for the world, must be continually crucified with Christ, so that the new self, the creative will, may operate fully and freely.

3

The doctrine of the Spirit confirms that one must not think of God and the world as in external causal interaction; such a view would in any case transmute God into a creature among others. One must think of God as acting continuously in the world, sustaining it and working from within, creatively and without perpetual causal discontinuity; yet nonetheless remorselessly shaping it to a moral purpose and using human purposes and intentions wherever possible to reveal and implement that purpose. God is both the striving and the goal of the world; as the world's striving, he is a particular, creative, adventuring, groping impulse to fulfilment and enrichment; as the world's goal, he is the general archetype upon which all things are patterned. To use a rather crude model, one might see the world as God's adventure in expressing his own nature. The creative striving in time, in which values evolve and develop by overcoming the recalcitrant powers of inertia and passivity, in which alienation and objectification lead to final return; all this, under the aspect of eternity, is the expression of God's love, by the bringing to be of creatures in whom it can grow and be reflected.

The image of God as creative Spirit entails that there is an important sense in which God is in time, and changes in response to events in the world. But one must here recall the function and limits of theistic language. It is tempting to think that one can make affirmative statements about the real nature of God. But, if God is beyond time, the sort of being he may possess just cannot be expressed in a tensed language. It would be equally incorrect to say either that God changes or that he knows and wills all things at once—for the notion of simultaneity is temporal, too! The only ways in which we can properly speak of God are ways which spring from imaginatively apprehended originative experiences, taken as revelations of transcendence, and used to specify responsive attitudes and roles. So we must say that God is changeless in power and goodness and wisdom and mercy—for trust, hope and obedience are appropriate attitudes to the reality disclosed in the Christian tradition, and they rule out a radical change in the character of God. But we must also say that he perpetually acts within the world, as the creative inspiration of the spirit, and responds to particular changes within the world: to the obedience of human selves, to prayer and to particular human acts, all of which could have been otherwise, and so are contingent. It follows that these acts of God in the world are contingent; so that the being of God could have been other than it is, in detail. It seems to me necessary to say this, if it is not also to be said that everything in the universe, and the existence of the universe itself, is necessarily what it is. However, all one can ultimately say here is that, though talk of God as acting contingently in response to the world is appropriate, in specifying correct attitudes to the reality of God, it cannot be said to be appropriate—since no talk can—as a putative description of the being of God as it really is. One must conceive the action of the Spirit as making a real difference to the world, as transforming human lives; and so Christian belief is committed to the assertion that the being of God makes particular causal differences to the world.

4

This must be true also of belief in miracles, prayer and providence. It is an important part of orthodox Christian belief that prayer can bring results; that spiritual awakening in a church, or healing, or even tangible material results can be brought about by prayer. The pattern is, of course, very unspecific; one cannot say in advance how one's prayers will be answered. It is also vital to remember that the first object of prayer is God; it is not to be conceived as a spiritual technology, to replace surgery or planning and activity. The first thing in prayer is to bring all one's life, including one's concerns and interests, before God. In praying for a church, or a person, one brings that concern before God, asking that his will may be done; one remembers it before God. Just as one must remember God before men, by directing all one's thoughts and acts to him; so one must remember men before God, by thinking of their needs in his presence, and asking that they will be met.

In doing this, one believes that one's prayers are not in vain; not that they will bring about the effect one desires, whatever others may wish or do, or whatever the state of the world and the possibilities it presents; but that they will enter into the considerations which determine what the future state of the world will be. One should not think of prayer as a form of sympathetic or imitative magic, bringing about some result by the expression of a wish, or by telepathy, without reference to God. Nor should one think of it as asking a Person for a favour; which he must then turn over in his mind, until he decides whether or not to grant it; God is not an arbitrary and whimsical Genie.

Prayer is the offering to God, characterized for Christians by the person of Jesus Christ, but also creator, co-sufferer and creative Spirit, of one's intentions for the world. God has given men freedom to work creatively to help others or to opt for a course of selfishness and obstructiveness. Most human intentions can be directly expressed through bodily action, which may or may not accomplish the desired effects. One of the important human freedoms is the freedom to pray, to direct one's thoughts and acts to God. And part of prayer is to remember the needs of others before God. This is not a direct expression of intention by telepathic action; it is a bringing of the needs of others to God. This, the Christian believes, will affect the future of the world, so that things will not be as they would have been had one not prayed. One can suggest a parallel with prayers for oneself. The Christian does not believe that these are merely techniques of auto-suggestion, ways of making oneself a better or more confident and secure person. In prayer, one brings oneself before God, offers oneself to God, and asks for one's needs to be met, so that one can serve God more fully. The act is more like 'asking' than like 'intending' or 'trying to effect'; though even asking is only an inadequate analogy for the presentation of one's needs in trust and dependence to God. And the Christian expects his prayer to be answered, by the meeting of his needs, perhaps in unexpected ways which may reveal that he has been mistaken about the nature of his deepest needs. One must not think of God wondering whether to 'answer' or not; the presentation of prayer will elicit a response; but one cannot tell what this will be, or how the acts and intentions of others may affect it.

Prayer is one of the ways in which the world is redeemed; it is the co-operation of man with the action of God. One cannot say how it accomplishes its effects; and no direct causal link between prayer and response can be traced. For it is not always clear, until long after the event, what the response has been; nor is it known what other intervening factors must be considered; nor is there any causal mechanism involved, which could be independently investigated. Yet, though one cannot experimentally check on prayer, one would expect there to be some empirical evidence for its efficacy, in that one would expect many people to claim 'answers' to prayer; and so they do.

However, one of the strongest objections to intercessory prayer is that God would always do what was for the best in any case; so, if one prays for his will to be done, one prays only for what will inevitably be. And God would surely not penalise those for whom no prayers were offered, by refusing them the grace that he could give them, and would give them, if someone prayed for them. In reply, it must be said that this view of God is too anthropomorphic. God has created a universe in which creatures exercise their freedom by caring, or refusing to care, for one another. Intercessory prayer is one form of caring. The difficulty arises when one thinks of prayer as arousing God to do something which he could have done anyway, but would not otherwise have bothered to do. The same difficulty arises in the cases of miracle and providence. If God can work one miraculous cure, why does he not cure everyone? Or if God can providentially save one man from death, why does he not save everyone in a similar way? In general, if God can causally interact with the world, why does he not right evil and cure and redeem all men, without the paraphenalia of the incarnation, crucifixion, miracles and the painfully slow spread of the Church?

5

When the question is posed in these terms, it is apparent that something has gone radically wrong with the notion of God.

Augustine's classical formulation of the problem of evil—if God
is omnipotent, he could remove all evil and if he is infinitely good,
he would wish to do so; so it follows that the existence of evil is
incompatible with the existence of an infinitely good omnipotent
god[8]—depends for its force upon a particular interpretation of the
concepts of omnipotence and goodness, as applied to God. But
if those, and similar, concepts, are interpreted along the lines I
have suggested, the problem becomes less intransigent, though of
course it remains a problem for the theist. Along those lines, to say
that there is a God is to say that there is a transcendent ground of
the world, a mysterious and unknowable source from which all
finite realities, good and evil, flow. God, as the source of all beings,
must be the source of good and evil alike. We cannot say why this
world should flow from his being; and we are not entitled to say,
as Leibniz thought, that this must be the best of all possible
worlds.[9] To say that God is omnipotent is not to say that he can
do anything which is logically possible; it is to say that he is the
unfathomable power, than which none can be greater, which produces the world and which will bring it ultimately under a moral
purpose. There is no power which is greater than the power of
God, and his power is finally inexorable; but one is not entitled to
say that God can suddenly decide to do anything which is logically
possible. We simply cannot say what the limits of freedom and
necessity are, within the being of God; we can only say that this is
the world which God creates, and his purpose will be accomplished in it.

Similarly, to say that God is infinitely good or loving is not to
say that every created thing, considered in itself, must be supremely
good. It is to say that God is the moral standard and goal for all
creatures, the source of all values and the guarantor that all
things will ultimately work together for good; that personal values
will not be thwarted. One must abandon the Leibnizian picture of
God considering every possible world and choosing to create the
best, as though there was a fixed realm of possibilities and God
was necessitated by his own goodness to select only one set of them.
One must start from the world one has, and say that this is the
world God has made, and that a moral purpose will be realised in

[8] Augustine, *Confessions*, trans. E. B. Pusey (Dent, 1907), Bk. 7, ch. 5;
p. 124.
[9] Leibniz, G. *Monadology*, trans. Latta, R. (O.U.P. 1898), p. 267.

it; that, taken as a whole, it is of intrinsic value, though not necessarily the greatest possible intrinsic value. One might be tempted to say that parts of the world could have been better—less painful, perhaps—than they are. That is true; but it would always be true, in any finite world, that some particulars could be better than they are. For to be finite implies having a limit, and some limits could always be less severe than they are. Perhaps, then, one protests only that the amount of suffering in the world seems disproportionately high. However, what is the standard of comparison here? One must remember that the Christian belief is that there is an existence after earthly life which is so glorious that it makes any earthly suffering pall in comparison; and that such eternal life is internally related to the acts and sufferings of worldly life, so that they contribute to, and are essential parts of, the sort of glory which is to come. The Christian paradigm here is the resurrection body of Jesus, which is glorious beyond description, but which still bears the wounds of the cross.[10] So the sufferings of this life are not just obliterated; they are transfigured by joy, but always remain as contributory factors to make us the sort of individual beings we are eternally.

This must be true for the whole of creation, insofar as it has sentience at all. If there is any sentient being which suffers pain, that being—whatever it is and however it is manifested—must find that pain transfigured by a greater joy. I am quite agnostic as to how this is to happen; but that it must be asserted to be true follows from the doctrine that God is love, and would not therefore create any being whose sole destiny was to suffer pain. In the case of persons, the truth of this claim requires the existence of a continuous personal life after death. The Christian will then say that his sufferings, whatever they are, help to make him the unique individual he is. To wish for a better world is to wish for one's non-existence, as the person one is. Often one may indeed wish for that; but the Christian would say that, if one could clearly see the future which is prepared for one, such doubts and fears would disappear; and the resurrection of Jesus is given to confirm this faith.

Perhaps, then, one would not really desire that only the best possible world should exist; for then one, as the precise person one is, would not be a member of it. We cannot assign a reason

[10] Jn. 20, 27.

why this particular world exists; but we can say that it comes solely from God, whose being contains the possibilities of all the good and evil things alike which we see around us. The appropriate response to this knowledge is, like Job, to bow in acceptance before the unfathomable ground of being.[11] Perhaps all possible worlds, an infinite number of them, do exist; we do not know; we only know that this one, not the best or the worst (if those superlatives make any sense), exists. And we believe, as Christians, of this world that, taken as a whole, taking into account life after death, it is better that it exists than not; and that every sentient creature in it which wills to do so will find an appropriate fulfilment within which, as an integral part, its own sufferings will contribute to the unique character of its final joy.

This condition must be qualified in a complicated way by the fact of creaturely freedom to choose self-interest, and so bring harm to oneself and others. This may naturally seem to bring an element of fortuitous and even possibly unredeemed evil into the world. For my freely chosen course of evil may, on some understandings of the matter, bring eternal harm to myself; and may inflict evil on innocent bystanders. The theist must simply say here that freedom is such a great good as to outweigh these possible and actual evils which ensue from its possession. And, however complex a detailed working-out of these problems must be, the general thesis I have suggested must remain true, if a Christian concept of God is to be rationally supportable.

We also believe that there is an absolute moral demand on creatures, and a moral goal for them, which we construe by speaking of God as good, or as infinite goodness itself. And we think of God as sharing in the pain and sorrow of creation, as well as its joy and happiness, and thus, by his omniscience, as participating in the creative expression of his own reality which is creation. These assertions are, it seems to me, necessary if the theist is to face at all adequately the fact of the very great evils which exist in a world which he claims to be the expression of the love of God. And in saying all this, it is most important to bear in mind the character of assertions about God, as grounded in situations of revelation and transformation, and aimed primarily at specifying correct attitudes towards the transcendent.

[11] Job 42, 1–6.

6

God is not adequately conceived as a Person deciding to make a world which he can interfere with as he chooses, and which is quite external to his being. The fact that the Christian feels able to take the person of Jesus as a model for God does not license him in adopting a God's eye view, assuming God to be a person related to the world as a workman is related to his products. The doctrine of the Trinity has as one important function the qualification of one model of 'God' by others, which prevents an over-crude deployment of any one image. And the workman or playwright model of God, as controlling his creation completely from outside, is appropriately qualified by the notion of the Spirit, the life-giver, the breath of God within the world, actively working to create new levels and complexities of consciousness in creatures. God is the inward power sustaining the reality of the world, as well as the value drawing it towards fulfilment; and 'miracles' are those 'clear points' in which the purpose and value of reality become apparent. This is not to say that they are wholly subjective, in that God is equally apparent at all times, but his becoming known lies only in the increased perceptive power of human beings. For some events really are more significant indicators of the being of God than others—the death of Jesus really is intrinsically more revelatory than a thunderstorm. It is not that God interferes dramatically in an otherwise closed causal system, adjusting the clockwork by external manipulation. It is rather that the world, in its essential being, is an ongoing process of overlapping, creative and often conflicting freedoms; and the presence and power of the Spirit is always guiding and shaping this process to advance the fulfilment of new values and purposes of love. Within this overall pattern, specific and often unusual events taken in special contexts and apprehended by faith, can become revelations of a Divine purpose. Whatever exactly happened at the resurrection, a man appearing after his death in any form is a very rare occurrence. It is clear that it was not used by God as evidence to convince all people of his existence and plan for the world; Jesus appeared only to the first disciples, and then often in ambiguous circumstances.[12] And it seems to be a general characteristic of miracles that they are

[12] Mat. 28, 17.

ambiguous, taken as evidence—the Egyptians probably did not think much of the Reed Sea incident! An event, however unusual, becomes a miracle only when interpreted within a tradition of faith and prayer, as conveying a special revelation within that tradition.

Similarly, providence is not an artificial adjustment of an otherwise smoothly working causal framework. It is the possibility that every new situation can be used in positive and creative ways; that lives and purposes interweave and are moulded together to produce fulfilments unpredictable in detail but already implicit in the contingent interdevelopment of free purposes in the world. A providential occurrence is one which advances the fulfilment of values or purposes in human lives by the provision of challenging and suitable circumstances. Prayer, too, is not the influencing of a master-mind who can fiddle with the predestined course of things. It is the openness of minds to each other at a deep and often unconscious level.[13] In presenting one's intentions to God one helps to sustain a creative reservoir of spiritual energy, and so one becomes an instrument of God's purposes. Prayer is a means of grace, it conveys a power which may be used or refused by the individuals for whom prayer is offered. It is not that man adds to the limited amount of grace that God gives; but that prayer is one of the ways in which God wills to give grace, just as he wills to heal through the human development of medical science. Indeed, prayer at its deepest levels is often characterised as God praying in one; so that it represents, in some degree, a continuation of the incarnation of God in the world, using our personal energy to apply to the whole human community. It would seem that the prayers of some people would be more efficacious than those of others, as they become more transparent to God and more advanced in the psychic abilities which often accompany growth in the knowledge and love of God. But though paranormal powers of healing and telepathy are often involved in prayer, intercession for a Christian must remain just one part of a total orientation to God, and that relationship to God must remain paramount.

What I have been briefly trying to do is to show how the being of God does make causal differences to the world; God could not be the same God, whatever the world was like. In the work of

[13] For a brief sketch of such a view, cf. Price, H. H. *Essays in the Philosophy of Religion* (O.U.P. 1971), ch. 3.

grace, in prayer and providence and miracle contingent occurrences are involved, which could have been otherwise, and which exemplify a contingent response of God to the acts of his creatures. Yet one must reject the view that God interferes episodically in a pre-ordained mechanistic causal order. The doctrine of the Holy Spirit suggests instead a picture of an interior, striving, creative, guiding power at the heart of temporal reality, God as the guiding co-adventurer with man and all creatures in the unfolding process of the world's development. But the wider doctrine of the Trinity reminds one that this picture of God as in process, striving within his creatures to bring all to good, is not the whole story. As well as picturing God as active in striving love, one must picture him as absolute, eternal and the unfathomable ground of all reality, including time itself. Both models must be used of the Christian God; and one cannot say that one is more correct than the other; or that either is more correct than the model of the incarnate, crucified and risen Christ. To affirm the Trinity is to affirm that these models, taken together as complementary and irreducible, define the way in which the Christian must conceive 'God'. And God is the transcendent reality which is mediated in certain historical events, which thereby specifies dispositional attitudes to the whole of one's experience, and which offers a fulfilment of human life by the adoption of that specified role.

7

Why should the Christian assent to this three-fold specification of 'God'? He does not do so on the basis of abstract speculation or metaphysical argument. And he does not do so simply by inspecting his own personal experience of prayer and worship. Yet I have throughout insisted that personal experience must be the starting-point for belief in God. I have no desire to retract this view; but it is clear that personal experience is always shaped by some conceptual tradition, whether one is conscious of it or not; and that it may well be rather idiosyncratic in some respects—no one man can embody the full range of possible human experience, or anything like it, in religion or anything else. So experience needs to be shaped by adherence to a particular tradition and complemented by a fund of communal experiences within that tradition. The

Christian Church claims to be a community of loving concern, bringing peace and reconciliation between men, developing human gifts and possibilities, offering friendship and culture, in the best sense. And it is maintained by the personal commitment of its members to the development of love, humility, detachment, joy and peace in their lives, to the pursuit of a life of prayer, conceived in the widest sense as a fulfilment of humanity in the loving relationship to God. This personal commitment, while contributing to the life of the community, is itself nourished by the community, especially by the liturgical re-enactment of the paradigm originative events upon which the community was founded. For the Church is a community which is founded upon the memory of historical events—especially the life of the man Jesus —revelatory experiences defining the tradition which has now become authoritative for the individual experience of its members. And those events are continually re-enacted, so as to preserve the revelatory communications they enshrined.

Historical remembrance is notoriously subject to uncertainty and distortion; and for that reason many philosophers, especially in the eighteenth century, felt that acceptance of the intrinsically improbable events recorded in the Christian Scriptures could not be an essential part of faith in the eternal God.[14] It is true that we cannot know exactly what happened in the life of Jesus; and the Scriptural accounts are notably not concerned to provide a neat and chronologically accurate biographical picture. But Christianity uncompromisingly asserts that God has revealed himself in history, and has finally, completely, uniquely and unalterably revealed his nature as love in the life of Jesus of Nazareth. That is, whatever exactly happened, one must assert that the images used to express the original interpretation of those events were appropriate expressions for revelatory disclosures, evoking a new insight and practical responsive commitment, both for those who first apprehended them and for us.

One may assess the acceptability of the Christian faith, the set of revelatory images it offers, in a number of ways. One may ask whether they do give insight into the meaning of the world, and extend and illuminate one's vision of reality; whether the way of life they specify does fulfil and transform human lives, and bring

[14] E. G. Lessing (cf. note 3. 8); Kant (cf. note 9. 12) and Fichte, *The Way towards the Blessed Life* (Chapman, 1949).

a new power of joy and love; whether the attitudes to reality they enjoin seem appropriate and lead to a growth in personal fulfilment.

Again, one may ask whether there are any empirical claims or entailments which we have good grounds for taking to be false, or which cannot be reconciled with findings in other fields, such as the sciences or philosophy, and whether any confirmation in experience is available for at least some of the basic claims of the faith. One may ask whether the general view of reality they provide is internally consistent, coherent with other beliefs, intellectually satisfying and adequate to the whole range of human experience. One may bring to bear all the critical apparatus of rational criticism on the historical evidence and the general reasons and presuppositions offered by believers. One may attempt to assess the sanity, integration and moral performance of believers, asking whether the Christian images seem to present a superior wisdom and moral insight, which may transcend our natural understanding but does not simply contradict it.

These are all criteria for assessing a religious scheme, and as such are important for rational beings to take into account. But it is even more important to see that they are not criteria for constructing a religion. One cannot create a revelation on such grounds as these; revelations just occur; and while one must attempt to judge between them by using rational criteria, in the end the revelation stands as an objective challenge.

So Christianity stands by the claim that the life and resurrection of Jesus, recorded in the New Testament, is the historical revelation of God. It is complete and final, in that no further revelation can surpass that of the love which was in Jesus. It is unique, in that the whole historical context of that life, and the community which was founded upon that memory, is, in an unrepeatable way, the means by which God wishes to bring all men finally into communion with himself. The Trinity is the definitive model of God because it grows, in a rather complex way, from an actual historical locus of particular experiences which produced paradigm images of transcendence. To reject, change or add to these central images would be to deny their historicity, to treat them as a free-floating system, to replace revelation by free imaginative invention. So, while Christian faith leaves a large place for the creative personal appropriation of faith, in different approaches to and understandings of it, it nevertheless presents an objective claim, in the memory of the events of the life of Jesus, re-enacted in the Church, which offer to men a new insight, a new way of life and a new power of fulfilment, forgiveness and hope. The personal experience of the Christian must therefore always stand under the authority of revelation, under the acceptance of the claim that a real historical revelation of the nature of God has been given; for his present life is the constant re-enactment of the memory of that one individual moment in time when the ineffable ground of all being was fully revealed in the grief and pain and glory of a human life. The Christian concept of the Trinitarian God is meant to preserve the full historicity of God's self-revelation, the complete transcendence of his reality and the continuing imminence of his presence with men.

8

My concern has been with the meaning of the term 'God'; and it should be clear that in the Christian tradition this meaning is more complex than has sometimes been supposed. What must be examined is the function of the term in human life and discourse; and here, it is paradigmatically used in prayer and ritual contexts. I have held that in the liturgy (which provides a rehearsal for and particular paradigm of general attitudes to be adopted to all experience) concepts of 'God' function to preserve a particular tradition of imaginative apprehension, originating in the primary generative experiences of religious visionaries; and to establish a certain conception of man's role, an understanding of one's existence in the light of that apprehension.

Religious concepts are both cognitive and practical, revealing new depths in experienced reality and enjoining a practical re-orientation towards revealed reality. It should not be thought, however, that the cognition precedes, either logically or psychologically, the re-orientation. It is rather in making such a practical re-orientation of one's concerns that one comes to cognise the aspects of reality characterized by the term 'God'. The religious quest is primarily a quest for a new and higher quality of life, freed from the dissatisfactions, inadequacies and deficiencies of secular living. The ritual celebration of 'God' makes this 'liberated' life possible, by re-enacting the primal authoritative event in which a new vision of reality originated and in which a fulfilling relationship to that reality was established. By such ritual repetition, the new relationship is actually effected in the life of the believer, the one who binds himself to the way of life outlined in the rite. The ritual provides a way of coming to achieve a fulfilling relation with God. For the Christian, this way is based on a repetition of the death and resurrection of Christ, which can be construed as a participation in the life of Christ. Thus Jesus was the exemplar of the way of salvation—he defined what salvation was to be and how it was to be attained.

The main and properly religious function of ritual is to establish and sustain a fulfilling relation to the reality disclosed in revelatory situations. There are, naturally enough, many possible perversions of this central function. But to 'believe' is to participate in the central ritual, thus affirming one's role as depicted in the tradition one accepts, as a rehearsal for the general adoption of the same role, in response to the same insights, throughout the whole of one's life and experience. The concern of religion, and especially of Christianity, is with 'salvation', wholeness, fulfilment of life; and this, it is claimed, is to be found in the adoption of the exemplary role which is defined by the community of the Church, in response to the memory of the revelatory experiences centred around the person of Jesus; this will not be merely a self-commitment, maintained by personal effort alone; for in the sacraments and preaching of the Church a charismatic power is realised, construed as the present action of God, transforming human lives. The Christian concept of the Trinitarian God has its function and meaning in the conceptualisation of this distinctive pattern of life. The models of the transcendent moral demand, principle of intelligibility and historical purpose; the suffering, crucified and risen Lord; and the present power of creative love are taken as complementary forms for conceiving the view of reality and way of life which the Christian Church exists to convey and to proclaim as an authoritative paradigm for human existence.

To see what it means to believe in God, in a Christian context, is to see what it means to live as a member of the Christian community, with its distinctive traditions, rites, disciplines of prayer and conceptions of reality. I have tried to expound what is involved in that way of life, though my account is recommendatory and not simply descriptive. That is, I have written as a member of that community, with a specific position and viewpoint within it, and a specific conception of what are its proper and its pathological forms.

In philosophy, the attempt to clarify the meaning of certain important and puzzling concepts around which one's understanding of life is formed, results in a new development of that understanding and a further discovery of the possibilities involved in one's conceptualisation of it. This is certainly true of the concept of God; and so the exploration of what it means to believe in God leads to a progress in one's understanding of one's own life and the possible use of the concept of God within it. What I have written is the record of such a progress, and an invitation to understand and assess the conceptual possibilities it presents.

INDEX